ADD – ON 13/14

Wiener Beiträge zur Internationalen Politik
Viennese Contributions to International Affairs

ADD – ON 13/14
Jahrbuch/Yearbook oiip

Global Shifts
and Europe

Cengiz Günay und Jan Pospisil (Hg./Ed.)

facultas.wuv

Bibliografische Information Der Deutschen Nationalbibliothek

Die Deutsche Nationalbibliothek verzeichnet diese Publikation
in der Deutschen Nationalbibliografie;
detaillierte bibliografische Daten sind im Internet unter
http://d-nb.de abrufbar.

Satz/Typesetting: Jan Pospisil (jan.pospisil@oiip.ac.at)
Englisches Lektorat: Maria Slater MA (Cantab)
Grafikbüro/Graphic Layout: grafikum, Wien
Druck: Facultas AG, Wien
Printed in Austria

ISBN 978-3-7089-1113-7

Gefördert durch die Kulturabteilung der Stadt Wien, Wissenschafts- und Forschungsförderung
Sponsored by Department for Cultural Affairs/City of Vienna

Inhaltsverzeichnis

Einleitung: Global Shifts and Europe

Cengiz Günay, Jan Pospisil

Die mittlerweile dritte Ausgabe der vom Österreichischen Institut für Internationale Politik – oiip im Jahr 2011 gestarteten Jahrbuch-Reihe ADD-ON steht dieses Jahr unter dem Titel „Global Shifts and Europe". Die Europäische Union steht angesichts der massiven Veränderungen innerhalb sowie auch außerhalb der EU vor mannigfaltigen Herausforderungen. Die globalen Verschiebungen (Global Shifts) treffen auf eine Zunahme der Instrumente der EU zur Gestaltung ihrer Außenbeziehungen – im regionalen Zusammenhang der Nachbarschaftspolitik wie auch in einem globalen Kontext. In zunehmendem Maße ist die EU also angehalten, diesen Veränderungen auf unterschiedlichen Ebenen mit einer größer werdenden Zahl von Policy-Instrumenten zu begegnen.

ADD-ON 13/14 liefert eine kritische Analyse einiger dieser Bemühungen und greift zu diesem Zweck wie schon in den vorangegangenen Jahren auf Arbeiten der InstitutsmitarbeiterInnen ebenso zurück wie auf Beiträge von JungwissenschaftlerInnen und institutsnahen WissenschaftlerInnen. Wir sind überzeugt, dass es dieser Mix ist, der – neben der mittlerweile klaren thematischen Fokussierung der Bände – die besondere Qualität von ADD-ON ausmacht. Zugleich dokumentiert er auch das akademische Leben am Institut, das im vergangenen Jahr 2013 mit der Pensionierung zweier langjähriger Mitarbeiter, dem vormaligen Direktor Otmar Höll und Paul Luif, in eine neue Phase getreten ist.

Die Beiträge von „Global Shifts and Europe" setzen sich aus unterschiedlichen Perspektiven mit den Wechselwirkungen tektonischer Veränderungen im Gefüge der internationalen Beziehungen und den daraus folgenden Konsequenzen, Herausforderungen und Aktivitäten für die Europäischen Union auseinander. Die Artikel gliedern sich in vier Aspekte: Einleitend werden die großen außenpolitischen Linien der EU anhand der Frage einer „Grand Strategy" diskutiert. Daran anschließend erfolgt eine Auseinandersetzung mit spezifischen Politikfeldern und für die EU in ihren Außenbeziehungen maßgeblichen Räumen. Abschließend liefern zwei Artikel eine Rückspiegelung der Außenbeziehungen auf innere Problematiken der EU selbst.

In ihren Beiträgen zu einer möglichen Grand Strategy für eine internationale Positionierung der EU beziehen sich der wissenschaftliche Direktor des oiip, Heinz Gärtner, und Kari Möttölä, Mitglied des wissenschaftlichen Beratungsstabes des oiip, auf US-amerikanische Debatten zu dieser Thematik. Sie diskutieren mögliche Konsequenzen und Entwicklungswege, die sich daraus für die EU ergeben könnten. Derzeit findet eine Debatte zu Möglichkeit und Notwendigkeit einer Grand Strategy für die EU statt. Die diesbezüglichen konkreten Bemühungen sind allerdings seit der Erarbeitung der Europäischen Sicherheitsstrategie im Jahr 2003 nicht mehr auf einem derart vergemeinschafteten Niveau erfolgt. Zudem werden solche Positionierungen auf Makroebene angesichts der zunehmenden Komplexität der befassten Politikfelder, der Diversität der relevanten Räume und nicht zuletzt aufgrund einer wachsenden Zahl an außenpolitischen Akteuren ein zusehends schwieriges Unterfangen.

Diese Komplexität der international wichtigen Politikfelder steht denn auch im Mittelpunkt der folgenden beiden Beiträge, die zugleich auch neue, aber zunehmend bedeutsame Arbeitsfelder des oiip repräsentieren. Jan Pospisil setzt sich mit der Resilienzpolitik der EU auf internationaler Ebene auseinander. Auf Basis des im Juni 2013 von der EU-Kommission veröffentlichten Aktionsplans zu Resilienz in von Krisen betroffenen Ländern diskutiert er die Konsequenzen einer solchen Politik insbesondere für die Bereiche der humanitären Hilfe und der Entwicklungspolitik. Pospisil erarbeitet in seinem Text aber auch mögliche weitergehende Auswirkungen des Konzeptes für die EU-Außenpolitik im Allgemeinen. Lisa Sigl und Carmen Heidenwolf setzen sich wiederum mit der Frage auseinander, wie der Entwicklungsprozess einer europäischen Konzept- und Strategieentwicklung im Kontext einer internationalen FTI-Politik verläuft. Der Bereich der Wissenschafts- und Technologieaußenpolitik wird nicht nur auf nationaler, sondern auch auf EU-Ebene als zukunftsträchtig wahrgenommen. Diese Entwicklung führt zum einen zu neuen Interessenskonstellationen und -konflikten auf internationaler Ebene, zum anderen stellt sie neue Herausforderungen an die Wissenschaft. Das oiip hat der wachsenden Bedeutung dieses neuen Forschungsfeldes durch die Einrichtung einer entsprechenden Forschungsgruppe Rechnung getragen.

Die aus Sicht der EU-Sicherheits- und Außenbeziehungenpolitik wichtigen geographischen Räume in der direkten Nachbarschaft Europas gehen zurzeit durch eine Phase der revolutionären Umbrüche. Cengiz Günay diskutiert in seinem Beitrag kritisch die Grundlagen, aber auch die Beschränkungen europäischer Politiken gegenüber dem MENA-Raum. Günay beleuchtet dabei insbesondere die Frage, wie weit normative Ansätze europäische Handlungskapazitäten angesichts der Vielschichtigkeit der laufenden Entwicklungen in den nordafrikanischen Staaten einschränken. In seinem Beitrag plädiert er für eine grundlegende Neuausrichtung. Insbesondere die Öffnung gegenüber bislang ignorierten wichtigen Akteuren wie islamistischen Organisationen steht im Mittelpunkt. John Bunzl zeigt in seinem jüngsten Beitrag zu seinem „Lebensthema" die Dilemmata der europäischen Politik gegenüber dem Nahostkonflikt auf. Der Text analysiert die Probleme der Zweistaaten-Lösung. Bunzl plädiert in diesem Zusammenhang die Hereinnahme bestimmter Prinzipien in den Friedensprozess. Dabei könnte die EU angesichts der von ihr außenpolitisch propagierten Werte einen positiven Beitrag leisten.

Ein dritter wesentlicher Aspekt ist die Orientierung in den weiteren östlichen, respektive südöstlichen Raum, der eng mit der Energiefrage, aber auch mit geopolitischen Herausforderungen in den Verhältnissen zu regionalen Playern wie Russland, der Türkei und China verknüpft ist. Zwei Beiträge setzen sich mit dieser Thematik auseinander: Ufuk Şahin betrachtet auf Basis eines explizit geopolitischen Zuganges die Entwicklungen bezüglich de „Südkorridors", also der zentralen energiepolitischen Versorgungslinie für einige EU-Mitgliedsstaaten. Şahin zeigt dabei auf, dass es der EU immer weniger gelingt, den Beitrittskandidaten Türkei für eine gemeinsame EU-Energiepolitik zu gewinnen – was auch das Eingeständnis mit sich bringen würde, das sich die internationalen Interessen der EU nicht mit den entsprechenden türkischen Interessen decken – solange der Türkei die Beitrittsperspektive verwehrt bleibt.

Bernardo Mariani von Saferworld, mit dem oiip in einer fruchtbaren Bürogemeinschaft verbunden, diskutiert die aktuellen Entwicklungen im ebenfalls energiepolitisch hoch relevanten zentralasiatischen Raum. Mariani erläutert die wachsende Rolle Chinas in der Region und die Fragen, vor die die Gestaltung der EU-Außenbeziehungen gegenüber China und Russland in diesem regionalen Kontext gestellt ist.

Das internationale Profil der EU spiegelt in vielerlei Hinsicht innere Prozesse wider. Einerseits betrifft dies die realpolitische Ebene, auf der nach wie vor der Zypernkonflikt komplexe Implikationen nicht nur auf die Gestaltung der Beziehungen zum Beitrittskandidaten Türkei, sondern auch zur NATO nach sich zieht. Auch die Verfasstheit der Union als Organisation „*sui generis*" ist dabei umfasst und in Frage gestellt. Dies erörtert Hakan Akbulut in seinem Beitrag unter dem Titel „Unreif für die Insel?". Ebenso ist die Frage gesellschaftlicher Beziehungen in den Mitgliedsstaaten notwendigerweise eng mit internationalen Problemlagen vermengt. Sarah Ponesch arbeitet in ihrem Beitrag die repräsentative Gegenüberstellung von „Schwulen" und „Muslimen" in europäischen Gesellschaften heraus und beleuchtet die sich daraus ergebenden Konsequenzen. Der Beitrag steht in einer mittlerweile etablierten Tradition der Auseinandersetzung mit den Wechselwirkungen von Außenpolitik und Identität, die allerdings gerade in Bezug auf die EU oftmals mit einer stark normativen Ausrichtung diskutiert werden. Ponesch liefert dazu einen erfrischenden konstruktivistischen Kontrapunkt.

Die Vielfältigkeit der angebotenen Beiträge zeigt auf, wie weitläufig das Feld des Außenwirkens der EU mittlerweile geworden ist. Die Beiträge zeigen zudem, dass die akademische Auseinandersetzung an Schärfe gewonnen hat, zugleich aber ebenso, dass jenseits der oft primär technokratisch angelegten Analysen über die institutionellen Gestaltungsprozesse nach der GASP-Neuausrichtung durch Lissabon eine Vielzahl zu vertiefender, spannender, vielversprechender Forschungsfragen besteht. Das oiip wird diese Herausforderung weiterhin annehmen und sich in kritischer, aber engagierter Weise mit diesen Entwicklungen auseinandersetzen. In diesem Sinne ist das vorliegende Jahrbuch als weiterer Beitrag in diese Richtung zu verstehen.

Where is Europe?

Heinz Gärtner

The world requires global solutions. What is the right approach? Since the end of the Bush administration in 2009, there has been an international debate on what kind of world will emerge. Where is Europe in this debate? In American academic debates, Europe plays only a marginal role. Their main concerns are the decline of America and the rise of China. Europe is not considered to be a major power factor in the new world. In the best case, Europe is seen as a natural ally because it consists of market economies and liberal democracies. In the worst case, it is seen as irrelevant because it lacks military capacities with global reach. Barack Obama's announced a free trade agreement between the United States and the European Union (EU) in his State of the Union address 2013.

The "Transatlantic Trade and Investment Partnership" (TTIP) has introduced a new element into the debate, however. For liberal internationalists, the TTIP could provide a stable basis for market economies and liberal democracies to strengthen their global influence. Such an agreement could help to enlarge their standards and extend it to the emerging powers, from India to China. On the one hand, it would pull them into the new system. On the other hand, it would push them towards it. The US and Europe would create not only an economically but also an politically unifying force that would integrate the new emerging actors such as China, India, Brazil, Russia and other established economic powers. Geo-strategists and realists would argue that, on a grand strategic level, closer US-European ties – the TIPP together with the "Transpacific Partnership" (TPP) – would enhance the West's leverage with China. Furthermore, it would isolate China's autocratic capitalist model, and the US and Europe would not only consolidate their status as leading economies, but also build a political bloc of liberal democracies.

The American debate

The world requires global solutions. What is the right approach? Since the end of the Bush administration there has been a debate among American academics on what kind of world will emerge. Where is Europe in this debate? Europe plays only a marginal role. The main concerns of American academics are the decline of America and the rise of China. Europe is not considered to be a major power factor in the new world. In the best case, Europe is seen as a natural ally because it consists of market economies and liberal democracies. In the worst case, it is seen as irrelevant because it lacks military capacities with global reach.

The "bipolarity" of the cold war era is gone. George W. Bush's "unipolarity" or Charles Krauthammer's "unipolar moment" are over – if they ever existed. With the absence of a more suitable expression, most observers unimaginatively speak – very generally – of a "multipolar world" with a few world actors or players, among them the US, Europe, China and Russia (as is mentioned in the report of the National Intelligence Council, *Global Trends 2025*). The term "multipolarity" originates from the realist school and implies polarization, balance of power, zero-sum, win and lose. All actors are potential enemies. Richard Haass (2008) rejects the polarization reference. Rather, he sees a "non-polar world" emerging. This highlights the necessity of common, rather than opposing, strategies in solving global problems. One of the emerging measures to address global issues is the G20. It began by dealing with economic, financial and climate-related questions but sooner or later it will also include other security topics, as was the case with the G7/8.

A similar observation with regard to emerging powers has been made by Fareed Zakaria (2012) and Parag Khanna (2008). Zakaria sees the "rise of the rest" in a "post-American world". Khanna observes the "rise of the second world", i.e. almost all others except the US and Europe. Their analyses are not necessarily as declinist as Paul Kennedy's "Rise and Fall of Great Powers" from 1987. For both of them, the US will remain the dominant power (especially in military terms), but their argument is that the US will not be able to act alone.

According to Joseph Nye (2008, 2011), in today's world, the distribution of power varies according to context. It is distributed in a pattern that resembles a three-chess game. On the top chessboard, military power is largely unipolar, and the US is likely to remain the only superpower for some time. However, on the middle chessboard, economic power has already been multipolar for more than a decade, with the US, Europe, Japan and China as the major players, and others gaining in importance. The bottom chessboard is the realm of cross-border transactions that occur outside of government control. It is only the middle chessboard – in the economic realm – where Europe has a role to play. Nye (2013) rejects the notion of a "post-American world"; he recognizes that the "America of the late twentieth century is over". American primacy remains, however. This means that the United States will be the "first" but not the "sole" world power. The US will most likely remain "primus inter pares" among the other great powers. The preferred outcomes will, according to Nye, require "power with others as much as power over others".

Similarly to Joseph Nye, Richard Haass (2013) does not support the thesis of America's decline. Globalization has created a "non-polar world" of American primacy, but not domination. The US has to restore its economic foundations and foreign policy at home. He argues that the US is underperforming at home and overreaching abroad. For Haass, American primacy still means superiority: the US economy is the largest, American higher education the best, American society the most innovative and adaptive in the world. Europe, in contrast, performs far below its collective economic weight in the world. This is the result of Europe's "parochialism, its pronounced antimilitary culture, and the unresolved tensions between nationalism and its commitment to a collective union." Europe will, according to Haass, be less significant in the half-century ahead than it was in the past half-century. For him, "we are living in a post-European world". In the 21st century, for Haass it is rather the Asia-Pacific region that will be the centre of gravity of the world's economy than Europe – if it can be managed peacefully.

According to John Ikenberry (2011), in the new world order the US will find itself in the position to share power and rely in part on others. The contested and unstable US-led hegemonic order will not destroy the American built liberal international order, but rather will make it more inclusive. In this context, Ikenberry does not talk of an American-European built order. The new world would be built around rules, norms of non-discrimination and market openness, creating opportunities for countries – including rising countries on the periphery of this order. Such a liberal international order would create a foundation on which states could engage in reciprocity and institutionalized cooperation. Such an order can be contrasted with closed and non-rule-based relations like geopolitical blocs, exclusive regional spheres, or closed imperial systems.

Charles Kupchan (2012) sees time running out on the West's global dominance. Power will become more widely distributed around the globe. The next world will belong to no one. Rather, the coming world will be both multipolar and politically diverse. The diffusion of global power ultimately means the diffusion of international responsibility from the Atlantic community of democracies to a broad array of states in all quarters of the globe. For Kupchan the goal would be to forge a consensus among major states about the foundational principles of the next world. The rules must be acceptable to all powers.

For Zbigniew Brzezinski (2012), the American system's capacity to compete globally depends increasingly on its ability to confront problems at home. If America falters, the world is unlikely to be dominated by a single preeminent successor, such as China. No single power will be ready to exercise the role that the world expected the United States to play after the end of the cold war. The US must constructively accommodate China's rising global status and engage Russia and Turkey to avert global chaos. Europe remains through its cultural, ideological, and economic connections – and more concretely through NATO – a junior geopolitical partner to the United States.

Liberals versus conservatives

The American debate about the world is very much a domestic one about America's role in the world. The promotion of democracy has always been one central tenet to US foreign policy debate. The export of American values is not limited to liberals but is also the dominant principle of neoconservatives. However, liberal values and democracy are hardly the only driving force (Bouchet 2012). The prevalent elements in US foreign policy have always been national security and economic interests. Representatives of the realist school are the most outspoken advocates of American interests; they can be found in both the Democratic and the Republican Party. The same is true for liberal internationalists (Ikenberry 2011), who also stress the importance of international institutions in managing interdependence and security. Liberals as well as conservatives focus on reforming the domestic political and economic structure to reinforce the basis for a strong foreign policy. Neither liberals nor conservatives are monolithic groups. In each camp, there are those who believe that the US should not engage too much in the world (Posen 2013) and those who think the US should remain a global leader, stay engaged, and influence global and regional developments.

Conservatives claims greater competency when it came to security and defence and accused liberals of being weak on these issues. Liberals have always been caught by the contradiction between their own values and US national security interests. The liberal foreign policy dilemma began with the presidential candidacy of George McGovern in 1972, when a strong anti-war sentiment emerged among liberals. Since then, they have been suspicious of any large military involvement by the US government. For liberals in the Democratic Party, it was almost impossible to reclaim security competency The Democrat Gary Hart, who ran for president in 1984 and 1988, was the last person before President Obama who attempted to do so. Bill Clinton focused on the economy and was reluctant to use force in the Balkans, which he eventually did with a series of airstrikes without deploying ground troops.

With regards to foreign policy, liberals have traditionally preferred economic and diplomatic incentives, rather than resorting to force and military intervention. Barack Obama has been able to strike a balance between those dimensions. Barack Obama has prioritized a policy of multilateralism and engagement; however, the use of force has become a natural part of his foreign policy. In Libya, the Obama administration justified the use of force on humanitarian grounds, drones were used for tactical strikes in Afghanistan and Pakistan, and it was Obama who gave the final go-ahead to kill Osama bin Laden. He referred the decision whether to use force against the Assadregime in Syria to Congress and then negotiated an agreement on Syria's chemical weapons, instead.At the same time, within the framework of his engagement policy, Obama committed himself to political solutions with rival states. During the Inaugural Address in January 2013, Obama rededicated himself to the engagement policy and the peaceful resolution of differences "not because we are naïve about the dangers we face, but because engagement can more durably lift suspicion and fear". Obama was the first president who could reclaim competency on security and defence issues for the Democratic Party. Still, liberals struggle with high defence expenditures, with support for conservative governments in Israel, and with the potential use of force against Iran. "True liberals" or libertarians support deep cuts in defence budgets because they believe US Foreign Policy should be constrained anyway. There is some overlap with isolationists on these issues.

Many liberals do not believe in American moral leadership because they hesitate to claim that America is superior to other cultures and systems. Liberals reject George W. Bush's neo-conservative democracy promotion with the use of force as in Iraq. They do believe, however, that the support of democracies all over the world is a good thing. They stress the pull rather than the push factors. The differences are often blurred when it comes to a neo-conservative league of democracies, that has been promoted by presidential candidate McCain in 2008 and a liberal society of democracies (Kagan 2008). Should such a concept replace the Security Council of the United Nations? Liberals are divided on this issue. More concrete, military intervention for humanitarian reasons might be supported by some liberals (e.g. in Libya and Kosovo) or neo-conservatives (e.g. in Syria). Realist conservatives oppose humanitarian interventions. Liberal institutionalists and international lawyers, in contrast, request that military interventions be consistent with international law, either authorized by the UN-Security Council or justified by self-defence.

More generally, the academic world (Kupchan 2012) discusses a concert of powers, which goes back to the Democrat Franklin Roosevelt and was reinvented by the Republican Henry Kissinger. Such a concert would include both democracies, such as the US and European states, as well as non- or semi-democratic powers, such as Russia and China, as well, but could lead to a safer peace and more security among world powers.

Liberal internationalists (Ikenberry 2011, Brooks et al. 2013) argue that a liberal international order emerged under US leadership after the Second World War. The order is rule-based, organized around international institutions and market economies. The order would survive even without US hegemony. Liberal internationalists who believe in international cooperation are not limited to Democrats; they can also be found in the Republican Party.

On the one hand, the strategic relationships that Americans formed in Europe and Asia became pillars of the liberal world order during the cold war, Europe is now supposedly passé and the world is entering the "Asian century". On the other hand, Robert Kagan (2012) believes that Americans also have an interest in whether the global trend is toward more democracies. Consequently, Kagan (2013) criticized the ousting of Egypt's president Mohamed Morsi in summer 2013 as a "coup against a democratically elected government", and requested the end of US assistance to Egypt's military. For Kagan it would make a huge difference to the future world order if the United States eventually had to share global power with a richer and more powerful but also autocratic China. "The United States and Europe must not give up on each other." It is not without irony that Kagan advised the presidential candidates John McCain and Mitt Romney, both of whom have been very critical about the European social model. Kagan himself once categorized the Americans as coming from Mars and ridiculed the Europeans as being from Venus. With this position, he stood in contrast not only to the Obama administration but also to the majority of the Republican Party. He took the same position as the isolationist minority in the GOP which is represented by Senator Rand Paul, and a liberal minority in the Democratic Party.

However, while democracy may help political cooperation, it is not sufficient. The commitment to democracy is good for citizens, but it is no guarantee for improved international problem solving (Kupchan 2010a, 2010b). When it comes to nuclear weapons, terrorism, war and peace, crisis management, the economic crisis and carbon dioxide emissions, pragmatic co-operations are required, rather than ideological finger-pointing and intransigencies.

Heinz Gärtner

Europe's economic power: an American asset?

Are traditional "transatlantic relations" that are based on a common threat, economic interdependence and common values better suited to address global questions, or is Europe's role in the world, and specifically in relation to the US, contingent on its contribution to world affairs? Is Obama's approach of "engaging" partners, competitors, and potential rivals the right approach?

It goes without saying that economic ties can stabilize relations between the US und the EU and prevent bloc building between them and with other parts of the world. Mutual investments of European and American companies in the US and in Europe generate approximately ten million jobs. The US and Europe account for 50 percent of global production and 40 percent of global trade (Neuss 2009). Mutual direct investment (almost 60 percent of overall investment) did not suffer during Bush's unilateral foreign policy. The Euro-zone accounts for 16 percent of world exports, well above eight percent for the US and five percent for Japan. Europe is also economically engaged in Asia: it is China's first and India's second largest trading partner. China has also become the biggest investor in Germany. For the Association of Southeast Asian Nations (ASEAN), Europe is also the most important commercial address. The EU is beginning to negotiate free trade areas with various Asian countries (Leonard/Kundnani 2013).

US president Barack Obama formally endorsed a free trade partnership between the United States and the European Union in his State of the Union Address in February 2013. Such an agreement is not only about stimulating trade and investment, creating jobs and eliminating tariffs, but also about the future of the world. Liberal internationalists see a chance to support a rule-based liberal world order. This agreement, known as the "Transatlantic Trade and Investment Partnership" (TTIP), could provide a further stable basis for market economies and liberal democracies to strengthen their global influence. Such a transatlantic partnership could help to enlarge their standards to the emerging powers. It could complement and reinforce the multilateral system, and contribute to the development of global rules (Hormats 2013). Liberal internationalists argue that, in the long term, the TIPP has the potential to create new international standards, common bonds and shared values. On the one hand, it would pull the non-participating powers into the new system, because they would want to benefit from access to the new market; on the other hand, it would push them towards it, because they would become dependent on it. Any country might join if it accepts the norms and principles of the TTIP. The US and Europe would create an economically and politically unifying force that would integrate the new emerging actors such as China, India, Brazil, Russia and other established economic powers (Hormats 2013). Turkey has expressed its interest in participating in the TIPP, and Brazil wants to revive an old trade pact with Europe.[1] The agreement would support efforts for similar deals with Asia and the Pacific such as the multilateral "Trans-Pacific Partnership" (TPP) or the bilateral free trade agreement with Korea (KORUS) and Vietnam. The US is also working with Canada, Mexico, Peru and Chile on the eastern shore of the Pacific to negotiate the Trans-Pacific Partnership with trading partners in East Asia.[2]

The more detailed rules and standards might be very different, however. There are profound differences in agricultural policies, such as disputes on genetically modified products, in labour laws, with regard to minimum wages and economic policies on deficit spending. Additionally, critics would say that such a US-EU accord would exclude poorer nations and a global trade agreement involving more countries would be more desirable. Also, it would undermine the regulatory work of the "World Trade Organization" (WTO).

Geo-strategists and realists would argue that on a grand strategic level, closer US-European ties (via the TIPP) and improved cooperation of the US with Asia-Pacific states (via the TPP) would enhance the West's leverage with China (Barker 2013). It would isolate China's autocratic capitalist model that could dominate the world order, as Kagan and others fear it will. The deal would enable the US, together with Europe, to set global rules to maintain their control over global economic governance. The US and Europe would

[1] The Economist (2013): A transatlantic tipping-point: An historic trade pact between America and Europe needs saving. 27 April.

[2] Kurata, Phillip (2013): Biden Calls for Stronger Ties in Western Hemisphere. US Department of State, Vice President Biden, IIP Digital, 9 May.

not only consolidate their status as leading economies, but also build a political bloc of liberal democracies.

Economic interdependence neither necessarily hinders nor helps to improve political relations, however. It is no guarantee for solving political problems. Achieving political rapprochement is by no means sufficient to solve common problems. Both sides of the Atlantic remain extremely vulnerable to the economic and financial crisis, to climate change, nuclear proliferation, and terrorism. Realists even argue that interdependence can be a cause of conflict because it increases vulnerability. Before the First World War, mutual trade relations among what were later to become enemies were stronger than trade relations between the US and Europe are today. On the other hand, Anglo-American economic relations declined before this war, while critical rapprochement occurred (Kupchan 2010a, 2010b).[3]

Europe's political and military power: sufficient?

The "European Union Institute for Security Studies" is not sure whether it prefers "multipolarity" with the EU as a confident global actor, or "interdependence." Therefore, one author (Grevi 2009) has come up with a combination of the two: the "inter-polar world".

The "European Council on Foreign Relations" (Shapiro/Witney 2009) argues that Europe's role in the world –specifically in relation to the US – is contingent on its contribution to world affairs. This is because the world requires global solutions to global challenges, such as the economic and financial crisis, climate change, nuclear proliferation and disarmament, terrorism, organized crime, pandemics. Additionally, regional conflicts like those in Afghanistan, the Balkans, the Middle East, and those relating to Iran and North Korea's nuclear programmes require common global involvement.

---

[3] Crises among the highly interdependent European powers in the decades leading up to the war were generally resolved without bloodshed, however. Among the less interdependent powers in Eastern Europe, crises regularly escalated to militarized violence (Gratzke 2012).

In many ways, the analyses of Europe's global role are based on a realist scenario of powers, a "balance of power system" or a "global network of political and military alliances" (Kagan 2009), although they are not sufficient means to solve global problems. Global solutions are not based solely on military contributions. In this context, Europe should not be undervalued or ignored.

After all, about 60,000 European troops are deployed in various missions abroad and Europeans spend about half of what the US spends on defence. In that respect, the EU looks like a real "military heavyweight" (Hellmann 2010). The austerity policies on both sides of the Atlantic caused cuts in military spending. This in turn led to accusations from the former Secretary of Defense Robert Gates that European countries are failing "to pull their weight" in military affairs. NATO responded with concepts like "smart defense" and "pooling and sharing" as a way to reduce costs and set priorities. But why should Europe compete with the US regarding defence expenditures? They are neither enemies nor rivals.

EU military expenditure accounts for more than one fifth of total military spending worldwide, compared to comparable US expenditure at about 45 percent. The Europeans spend as much on defence as Russia, China, India and Brazil combined. Russia spends a little more than the UK or France; China about twice as much as Russia (SIPRI 2012, de Wijk 2012). In 2000, Britain sent troops to Sierra Leone; in 2002, France to the Ivory Coast to suppress unrest. In Afghanistan, Europeans lost about 1,000 troops. In Bosnia and in Kosovo Europeans provide most of the troops. In the missions to Libya the UK and France took the lead even though they still lack sufficient capabilities. In Mali, and Central Africa France intervened with little international support. It is doubtful if the US would have conducted these operations without there being European initiative, however.

Nevertheless, the real question is what the focus of security is: "national security" to protect your domestic territory; "human security" to protect individuals all over the world under conditions of regional destabilization, dysfunctional states, poverty, demographic changes and refugee flows, pandemics; or "global security" to meet challenges like global warming, nuclear proliferation, international terrorism? It seems that the US still concentrates more on "national security", whereas the EU focuses more on "human and global security". The latter, of course, can only be addressed cooperatively and multilaterally.

NATO is transforming. It no longer faces an outright territorial assault by Soviet and Warsaw Pact forces. Today, it deploys its forces in support of peace and stabilization operations mandated by the UN "out-of-area" and "out-of-continent". At the Chicago summit in May 2012, NATO has recognized that the most direct threats to the security of its member states will be neither military nor territorial in character, but rather encompass problems like climate change, nuclear proliferation, terrorism and demographic transformation. At the same time, NATO has the huge legacy of the armed forces left over from the cold war. It still has to decide how to deal with territorial defence, as defined in Article 5 of its treaty, because it does not expect a major onslaught on Alliance territory. Rather, its forces have to operate hundreds or even thousands of kilometres away from home. Because of the global requirements NATO and the EU will have to agree to some division of labour regarding capacities and geographical fields of operation. The EU appears to be focusing on the west Balkans and Africa, while the US is concentrating on the Gulf region, the Middle East, the Pacific and East Asia.

The examples of Libya and Mali

The EU and its individual member states are able to act when problems arise and common interests are at stake, as the examples of Libya and Mali demonstrate.

NATO's Libyan operation was a successful US-European (military) cooperation in which the US provided most of the intelligence, the fuelling and targeting capabilities, the surveillance, and reconnaissance. The coalition of the willing, consisting of the US and European countries with support of the Arab League, decided to use force to protect Libyan civilians against armed attacks by the Libyan regime. UN Security Council Resolution 1973 of March 2011 emphasizes the responsibility of the Libyan authorities to protect the Libyan population and of the parties in armed conflicts "to take all feasible steps to ensure the protection of civilians." The intervention met the criteria of the concept of human security because its primary purpose was the protection of civilians from grave and systematic violations of human rights. For the US State Department, humanitarian reasons were the decisive factor, not potential military hazards, and it overruled the Pentagon, which had doubts about military feasibility. There was a Security Council mandate that was implemented by a coalition of mainly NATO states. In addition, the resolution was endorsed by the Arab League. The United States in particular signalled that – this time – it renounced a unilateral approach. France und the UK officially took the lead.

Based on the principles of "Responsibility to Protect" (R2P), the Libyan intervention is an expression of change in the norms of state sovereignty. They have given way to the human rights revolution and new ideas about a more complex array of norms concerning legitimacy and authority. Opposition to the 2003 Iraq war was not about the use of force as such, but rather about the principles and procedures for using military power (Ikenberry 2012: 270-277). If there were no legitimate, international, competent and enduring authority, liberals in both governments and NGOs might want to decide for themselves if and when human rights are violated, and neoconservative nationalists might want to determine whether and where to promote democracy (with or without the use of force). Instead, both camps feel constrained by multilateral institutions, and may even benefit from unipolar structures. There is no viable alternative to an international order based on rules, principles and institutions.

France's military intervention in Mali in February 2013 demonstrated that France still has the capability to deploy a large military force in Sub-Saharan Africa. As the Libyan example from 2011 showed, the EU's security and defence policy is highly dependent on Britain and France's military capabilities. France and Britain are the only EU members that are both able and willing to project hard power. Still, the Europeans are dependent on US support at least indirectly, without the involvement of US troops. In Libya and Mali, the United States supplied intelligence, drones, fighter jets, and the refuelling and transport of aircraft, ammunition stocks and missiles to destroy air defences.

The US seems to accept this division of labour, since the US is determined to devote more resources to the Pacific. However, it wants the Europeans to provide more capabilities. It is not only a question of military spending, but rather of a new philosophy. The European armies still appear to be preparing for a massive land invasion, a scenario that more or less disappeared together with the Warsaw Pact. Only 30 percent of European forces are capable of being deployed in an expeditionary context.[4] The Mali intervention once more raises the question: under which criteria and conditions will European states use force with the approval of the EU? The legitimacy of the Libya intervention was based on the principle of R2P. In Mali, France claimed that it was not trying to promote democracy but to bring stability, that it was not securing resources but supporting the Mali government, that it was not extending Françafrique but defending European interests. The fact that France was acting militarily on behalf of the EU highlights the weakness of its "comprehensive approach" for security and development that it has pursued in the Sahel zone since 2011.

According to the United Nations Security Council Resolution 2100 of 25 April 2013, the "Multidimensional Integrated Stabilization Mission in Mali" (MINUSMA)[5] replaces the "African-led International Support Mission in Mali" (AFISMA). To support political processes in Mali, it covers a broad security-related mandate: support the transitional authorities of Mali in the stabilization of the country and in the implementation of the transitional roadmap, focusing on major population centres and lines of communication, protecting civilians, human rights monitoring, the creation of conditions for the provision of humanitarian assistance and the return of displaced persons, the extension of state authority and the preparation of free, inclusive and peaceful elections. The broad mandate would enable the EU or some of its member states to participate on various levels of the mission.

---

[4] Among others Daniel Korski, *Deutsche Welle*, March 3, 2010. John Dowdy, Gundbert Scherf, and Wolff van Sintern, Enlisting productivity to reinforce European defense, *McKinsey & Company*, August 2013.

[5] Resolution 2100 was adopted by the Security Council at its 6952nd meeting, on 25th April 2013.

Conclusions

In the American academic debate, Europe's role in the future world is largely ignored. The debates mainly revolve around the US and China. The challenges for the US and Europe alike are almost all on the global level. They include regional conflicts that involve state and non-state actors, climate change and resource shortages, the danger of nuclear weapons, massive human rights violations, criminal and terrorist organizations who also use cyberspace.

Traditional "transatlantic relations" that were based on a common threat are not sufficient to address global questions. President Barack Obama's approach of "engaging" partners, competitors, and potential rivals goes beyond these relations. It is about strength rather than weakness and is a strategy for problem solving rather than a goal in itself. In the long term, "engagement" can also contribute to democratization and regime change.[6]

The best concept for global problem solving could be Hillary Clinton's "multi-partner world", in place of the "multipolar world" concept. This does not mean that competition, polarity, and ideological differences would disappear, but it would create a level of global cooperation. Such attempts have emerged after every major crisis: after 1815 with the "Concert of Vienna", after 1918 with the "League of Nations", after 1945 with the "United Nations", after 1989/90 globalization took place (disrupted by George W. Bush's unilateralism).

We are moving towards a new world but we do not yet know for sure what it will look like. Of course, the US and Europe will be important actors in it, but it is equally clear that traditional concepts will no longer be desirable. The new focus now is on what the US and Europe can achieve in the world, rather than on the relationship as an end in itself.

---

[6] Examples are: the improving relations between US-Chile, US-Brazil, US-Argentina, and Brazil-Argentina in the 1980s; also US-Philippine relations under Ferdinand Marcos.

The EU and its member states are able to act once the need for action becomes obvious and once a problem arises, as the examples of Libya and Mali demonstrate. It need not always be NATO or the EU, but in many ways coalitions of the able and willing are more flexible and can act on a case-by-case basis. They can use the infrastructure provided by NATO, the EU and the respective member states. The cases of Libya and Mali made it clear that the US will increasingly expect contributions from allies and rely on partners when it comes to international military missions (see also Gross 2013). NATO and Europe must accept that they need to build not only a European but a global security architecture.

References

Barker, Tyson (2013), "For Transatlantic Trade, This Time Is Different: Why the Latest US-EU Trade Talks Are Likely to Succeed." *Foreign Affairs*, Snapshot, February 26.

Bouchet, Nicolas (2013), "The democracy tradition in US foreign policy and the Obama presidency." *International Affairs*, 89:1, 31-51.

Brooks, Stephen G., J.G. Ikenberry, and William C.Wohlforth, (2013), "Don't Come Home, America: The Case against Retrenchment." *International Security*, 37:3, 7-51.

Brzezinski, Zbigniew (2012), *Strategic Vision: America and the Crisis of Global Power*. New York, NY: Basic Books.

de Wijk, Rob (2012), "The geopolitical consequences of the €-crisis." *Europe's World*, Summer 2012.

Gartzke, Erik (2012), "Trading on Preconceptions: Why World War I Was Not a Failure of Economic Interdependence." *International Security*, 36:4, 115-150.

Grevi, Giovanni (2009), *The Interpolar World: A New Scenario*. Occasional paper 79. Brussels: European Union Institute for Security Studies.

Gross, Eva (2013), "The American sequester – and us." Brief 19. Brussels: European Institute for Security Studies.

Haass, Richard. N. (2008), "The Age of Nonpolarity: What Will Follow US Dominance." *Foreign Affairs,* 87:3, 44-56.

Haass, Richard N. (2013), *Foreign Policy Begins at Home: The Case for Putting Amerika's House on Order.* New York, NY: Basic Books.

Hellmann, Gunther (2010), *Demilitarization of Europe? If the Atlantic Alliance has a Problem it is that is that Europe is Transnationalizing Security while the US is Remilitarizing along National Security Lines.* Washington, DC: American Institute for Contemporary German Studies.

Hormats, Robert D. (2013), *The Transatlantic Trade and Investment Partnership: America's New Opportunity to Benefit from, and Revitalize its Leadership of, the Global Economy*. Remarks at the Center for Transatlantic Relations. Washington, DC: John Hopkins University SAIS.

Ikenberry, G. John (2011), *Liberal Leviathan: The Origins, Crisis, and Transformation of the American World Order*. Princeton, MA, Oxford: Princeton University Press.

Kagan, Robert (2008), *The Return of History and the End of Dreams*. New York, NY: Vintage.

Kagan, Robert (2012), *The World America Made*. New York, NY: Alfred A. Knopf.

Kagan, Robert (2013), "American aid makes the U.S. complicit in the Egyptian army's acts." *Washington Post*, 08-01-13.

Kennedy, Paul (1987), *The Rise and Fall of the Great Powers: Economic Change and Military Conflict from 1500 to 2000*. New York, NY: Random House.

Khanna, Parag (2008), *The Second World: Empires and Influence in the New Global Order*. New York, NY: Random House.

Kupchan, Charles A. (2012), *No One's World, the West, The Rising Rest, And The Coming Global Turn*. New York, NY: Oxford University Press.

Kupchan, Charles A. (2010a), "Enemies Into Friends: How the United States Can Court Its Adversaries." *Foreign Affairs*, 89:2, 120-134.

Kupchan, Charles A. (2010b), *How Enemies Become Friends: The Sources of Stable Peace*. Princeton, MA: Princeton University Press.

Kupchan, Charles A. (2012), *No One's World, the West, The Rising Rest, And The Coming Global Turn*. New York, NY: Oxford University Press.

Leonard, Mark, and Kundnani Hans (2013), "Think Again; European Decline." *Foreign Policy*, May/June.

Moravcsik, Andrew (2010), "Europe, the Second Superpower." *Current History*, 109:725, 91-98.

National Intelligence Council (2008), *Global Trends 2025: A Transformed World*. November 2008. Washington, DC: NIC.

Neuss, Beate, (2009), "Asymmetric Interdependence: Do America and Europe Need Each Other?" *Strategic Studies Quarterly*, 3:4, 110-124.

Nye, Joseph S., Jr. (2008), *The Powers to Lead*. Oxford: Oxford University Press.

Nye, Joseph S., Jr. (2011), *The Future of Power*. New York, NY: Public Affairs.

Nye, Joseph S., Jr. (2013), *Presidential Leadership and the Creation of the American Era*. Princeton, MA: Princeton University Press.

Posen, Barry R. (2013), "Pull Back: The Case for a Less Activist Foreign Policy." *Foreign Affairs*, 92:1, 116-130.

Shapiro, Jeremy, and Nick Witney (2009), *Towards a post-American Europe: A Power Audit of EU-US Relations*. London: ECFR.

SIPRI Yearbook (2012), *Armaments, Disarmament and International Security*. Stockholm: SIPRI.

United Nations Security Council (2011), Resolution 1973, adopted on 17 March.

Heinz Gärtner

Zakaria, Fareed (2012), *The Post-American World: Release.* New York, NY: W. W. Norton & Company.

Grand Strategy as a Syndrome: The United States' Review of Liberal Institutionalism[1]

Kari Möttölä

Introduction: the conundrum of liberalism in US foreign policy

With his second term underway, President Barack Obama can prudently be considered to be leading a moderately successful foreign policy for the United States, considering the ongoing transformation of the international order affecting power, governance and values, and notwithstanding that his record neither entails what he set out to accomplish nor what the world at large expected him to represent in terms of domestic and international change. Grand visions and systemic openings made at the outset – such as engaging with adversaries and rogue states, reaching towards a nuclear zero, launching an inter-cultural dialogue with Islamic countries, consolidating great-power relations or reforming international institutions – have largely stalled or remained incomplete.

At the same time, Obama is appropriately credited with "bending history" in a direction commensurate with the liberal values underpinning his ambitious goals and his presumed worldview, resulting in a remarkable initial improvement of the image of the US in global public opinion. Obama has moved forward not by means of a distinct grand strategy but by using, reactively and proactively, the wide choice of instruments at his disposal, consequently emerging as a "progressive pragmatist" or "reluctant realist", blending liberalism with realist methods (Indyk et al. 2012, Lynch 2012).

---

[1] This article is drawn from Kari Möttölä (2013), "Liberal internationalism – a sustainable US strategy for world order?" Paper presented at the ISA Annual Conference, San Francisco, CA, 3rd-6th April 2013

With all its arbitrary characteristics, Obama's foreign policy will be explicable and judged as a juxtaposition of structural constraints and human agency. That the expectation-performance gap in Obama's record is met with understanding is largely due to the extraordinarily demanding environment he faced, not made easier by the political legacy inherited from his predecessor.

Among the immediate tasks to be addressed were two of the longest wars in American history, the global threat of transnational terrorism, the spectre of internal and regional conflicts from North Africa/the Middle East to Southern Asia and the Far East, and the threat of proliferation spearheaded by the nuclear ambitions of Iran and North Korea.

Among the structural issues, the global financial and economic crisis has proved to be of historic proportions, with deep political and societal consequences for established market democracies. The shift of economic and, consequently, political power from the West to the East and the South seems undisputable for the longer term, while the institutions of global governance have proved inadequate to manage the pressure of globalization.

In addition, while connected to the uncertain fiscal and economic recovery and the ideological dispute over the role of the federal government, the political gridlock, which has extended beyond his re-election, has highlighted the organic linkage between domestic politics and foreign policies.

Grand strategy: concept and policy

Critically for the Obama administration's foreign policy, these global changes are not only forcing the United States into making choices in its promotion of values and interests but also into defending and protecting its position as a singular leading power in world politics. At stake is the current international order, associated with the American Century and linked to US primacy. In view of the precarious position of the United States, it is understandable that the policy and scholarly discourse on foreign policy is reaching beyond normalcy to strategic heights.

As a concept, grand strategy generates a picture of how the world is, develops a perception of how it should be, and sets guidelines on how such a goal could be realized and ensured. As an effort to manage the future, grand strategy is a visionary and aspirational projection rather than a pragmatic and immediate plan of action. Grand strategy, as an art of creating power in the international system, is about a calculated relationship between large (political) ends and (military, economic, political, cultural) means (Heuser 2010: 26-28).

Although the dilution of the exclusive position of states and governments as actors and the complexity of drivers of globalization have made it indispensable for every strategy to have a broad-ranging combination of military and non-military variables – hard and soft power – military doctrines and capabilities tend to emerge as vital indicators of American strategic narratives, particularly in times of transformation or crisis (Strachan 2011: 1281).

With all indications pointing towards a historical turn, it is not surprising that pundits have called for is a wide-ranging and deep discussion about defining, reconfirming, updating or revising a workable grand strategy for the United States (Slaughter 2013).

It is assumed in this article that the overarching grand strategy for the United States since the end of the Second World War, reconfirmed at the end of the cold war, has been one variation or another of *liberal internationalism*, as theory and policy. American global liberalism has aimed at pursuing favourable global change: creating and maintaining an expansive multilateral order based on common norms, principles and institutions, as value-based factors, and entrenching security-defence alliances as well as promoting free trade, security cooperation and democracy promotion as well as crisis management, as policy elements (Dunne/McDonald 2013).

As a system of open and loosely rule-based relations among states, liberal order can be hegemonic – and has been since the post-second world war emergence of US primacy. In liberal hegemony, the leading state operates at the service of the order, albeit using its rules and institutions to preserve its power. Hegemony is not democratic in the sense that it is hierarchical, but it is liberal in the sense that even the leading state operates within the common rules and institutions where its power is embedded (Ikenberry 2011).

In this article, the sustainability of liberal internationalism as the US grand strategy is analysed as it is reflected and presented in the American policy-oriented and academic scholarly debates and narratives. For a global leader, liberal internationalism has been generated and pursued as much by political doctrine as by material power. The dominant discourse reflects a continued belief in the freedom of choice, including voices in favour of constancy, but there is growing recognition that the room for manoeuvre has been constrained even for the United States. With the world having changed to the extent that the very survival of the liberal international order has been called into question, the foundation of US grand strategy has now been forced under reappraisal.

Global trends: think tank responses

The *Global Trends 2030* report, issued in the series of foresight assessments by the National Intelligence Council (NIC) prior to the inauguration of a new American president, depicts a world order without a supreme power but predicts a unique position for the United States as the first among equals because of its multi-dimensional power. The shift of economic power to rising markets and regions is inevitable. At the same time, the global order is shaped by transnational social drivers such as the growing middle class and the empowered individual, which have the potential of underpinning further democratic enlargement through soft power (NIC 2012).

In a collection of American think tank reports pertaining to advice for the second Obama administration, policy analysts address the question whether domestic and external pressures are transforming foreign policy into a continued exercise in responses to risks and surprises, or whether a distinct new grand strategy is being or should be adopted (Allin/Jones 2012, Fontaine/Lord 2012, Goldgeier/Volker 2013, Indyk et al. 2013, Mathews 2012, Manning 2012).

Despite identifying and recognizing the exceptional challenge to the United States posed by global change, the policy-oriented reports are broadly united in calling for proactive US global leadership to maintain the liberal democratic order and in refuting proposals for American strategic retreat.

At the same time, the reports admit the existence of new limits to what the United States can do, and assert an increased necessity for prioritization. As the US cannot dictate global developments or solve all problems, qualitatively better and wider cooperation is needed with allies and partners and also with comparable great powers as well as within international institutions. The task of (de-) prioritization will be an extraordinarily demanding aspect of policy and strategy formation.

The immediate and longer-term tasks listed foresee a continued involvement in the spectre of local and regional conflicts, disputes and problems extending from North Africa, the wider Middle East and South Asia to East Asia/the Pacific. Structural issues include managing the rise of China, engaging other emerging powers, rebuilding transatlantic and Asia-Pacific trading and economic communities, promoting democracy and addressing such new security tasks as proliferation, cyberspace, energy, climate and resources, while maintaining responsibility for addressing state fragility and assisting development.

While a minority does call for a scaled-down or a less interventionist strategy, most analysts consider continued active and forward-leaning US presence and influence the best strategy for promoting American values and interests. Most are ready to accept moderate defence cuts, to be compensated by better institutional efficiency, less costly and more precise technologies and refocused strategies.

The credibility of a continued role for US leadership is based on the conviction that the United States will remain the singularly most powerful actor politically, militarily and economically – not to mention culturally – for an indefinite time into the future. The US has the preconditions for adapting its strategy as needed to changes in the global environment to ensure continued leadership. Despite recent indications of relative decline, the United States has a historically rare second chance for global leadership.

On the other hand, in his effort to restore a balance between the nation's international commitments and its capabilities, Obama is seen by some as undertaking a degree of strategic retrenchment, with the changing milieu modifying liberal activity by default if not by design. Difficult to categorize as a leader, Obama is mindful of dangers of strategic over-extension and acts flexibly, moving at times back and forth, within the constraints of the diffusion of power, while maintaining a leading global position for the US.

A pinnacle: academic alternatives

The consensual picture changes when attention is directed away from the Washington circles and towards the debate that is underway in American academia. The starkness of alternatives presented has provoked the leading proponents of liberal internationalism to claim that advocates for strategic *retrenchment* form the majority among university-based scholars. For proponents of *deep engagement*, such adversaries are ready to put an end to 65 years of globally engaged US grand strategy (Brooks et al. 2012/2013: 7-10, Brooks et al. 2013).

Retrenchment

A leading advocate of retrenchment, Layne derives his arguments from the decline of US power, which, as a culmination of a decades-long process, has led to the end of unipolarity and the demise of *Pax Americana*. He rebuts the liberal argument that a declining US could conserve the essential features of the liberal order by strengthening and reforming the legacy of international institutions. As a result of the financial crisis, the American economy has crumbled, ideational and institutional pillars of the liberal order have weakened and US military dominance is being challenged. In accordance with hegemonic stability theory, as the US is no longer able to discharge the tasks required, the liberal order has come to an end. Hegemonic decline has consequences as rules and institutions reflect the distribution of power. With the rise of China, the balance of power realists have won over the unipolar stability realists who trust in US predominance (Layne 2012: 212).

As a response to Layne, Nye notes that power has come to be distributed in a complex way: military power continues to be largely unipolar, economic power has been multipolar for some time and transnational power is diffused among non-state actors. Absolute and relative decline should not be confused when making policy conclusions (Nye 2012).

From a realist viewpoint, Wohlforth sees no sign of a balancing coalition generating systemic pressure towards multipolarity. Realism predicts responses to a rising power among competing great powers, but it does not give guidance on responses to a state – such as the US – whose preponderance has already been established (Wohlforth 2012).

From a military-security angle, Posen wants to put an end to what he calls unnecessary, undisciplined, expensive, inefficient and bloody hegemonic strategy, which has become unsustainable, and replace it with a grand strategy of restraint. As a consequence of a faulty post-cold war policy, the US has generated soft balancing by comparable great powers; and harder balancing can be expected as the emerging powers convert their economies into military power. Moreover, involvement in identity politics by confronting nationalism has led to futile conflicts. A nimbler strategy would refocus US efforts on three security challenges: preventing a rival power from upending the global balance of power, in particular in Eurasia; fighting terrorists; and countering nuclear proliferation. The new strategy would call for recasting alliances, making partners share real responsibility for their security, and scaling down the US military by half to a third, while leaving global problem solving to diplomats. A strategy of restraint would not only save lives and resources but also prevent systemic pushback (Posen 2013).

Scepticism about the expansive policy of using military force drives the urge for greater caution and restraint as advocated by Betts. Liberal post-cold war foreign policy, which was pursued universally from the left to the right of the American polity, linked an aggressive use of force with the habit of empire without proper consideration or control of its political, societal and strategic price. As a result, national security policy was driven not by threats but by opportunities; it was aimed at tackling indirect and local threats not vital to US material interests. Betts argues for a prioritized agenda of threats to national security. A sensible strategy would embrace soft primacy, fielding the superior American military but using it sparingly, and burden-shifting, leading to a primacy of reaping passive benefits instead of trying to forcefully control world order (Betts 2012).

Deep engagement

The proponents of liberal internationalism reject the core claim that in the current grand strategy – which they call "deep engagement" – high and rising costs would dwarf its benefits. Accordingly, they decline assertions that US security and other commitments would be overextended and unrelated to US interests, generating systemic pushback as a consequence of resentment and balancing by others, allowing free riding by subsidized allies and resulting in the risk of entrapment. According to their counterargument, a strategy of retrenchment means in essence that the US would minimize or eschew efforts to foster and lead the liberal institutional order, while leadership is essential to promoting cooperation, driving collective action and avoiding security dilemmas and is most effectively exercised by creating multilateral institutions (Keohane 2012).

For liberals, the advocates of retrenchment overestimate the costs of the current strategy and underestimate its benefit to security and wider interests, without explaining the risks and costs involved in a world without an engaged leading liberal power. For them, sustaining the core commitments of the current strategy is a reasonable choice even though full certainty can never be guaranteed.

According to the advocates of continued global engagement, the United States has advanced its core interests in security, prosperity and domestic liberty by pursuing three overlapping core objectives: (1) to reduce near- and long-term threats to US national security by managing the external environment; (2) promoting a liberal economic order to expand the global economy and domestic prosperity; and (3) creating, sustaining and revising the global institutional order to advance international cooperation on terms favourable to US interests. Maintaining security commitments to allies and partners in Europe, East Asia and the Middle East is the most consequential choice of the strategy, as they are a necessary condition of US leadership, which again is necessary to pursue the three core objectives. Embedding US leadership in international institutions offers functional, political and legitimacy benefits; because the US is not strongly constrained by such institutional commitments, the benefits outweigh any costs to sovereignty (Brooks et al. 2012/2013: 9-12).

For proponents of deep engagement, the dividing line between the two approaches concerns the judgement whether the three core objectives are necessary for US values and interests and whether the security commitments are necessary in order to pursue them. On other aspects of foreign policy such as democracy promotion, humanitarian intervention or human rights, there are no uniform opinions in either camp, and such issues are not constant or defining elements of US grand strategy. In addition, US commitments to them have varied from one administration to another – indeed, even within a single administration. Deep engagement does not imply an aggressive use of military force, which remains an instrument of choice (Brooks et al. 2012/2013: 13-14).

Democratic internationalism

As a move to a new phase of strategic development, refocusing liberal internationalism as *democratic internationalism* is advocated by Deudney and Ikenberry for a world where an increasing amount of countries beyond the core Western world is liberal, capitalist and democratic. Despite its potential, they admit that the community consisting of established Western and rising non-Western and postcolonial democracies is a challenge to US policies because it is politically weak and strategically diverse (Deudney/Ikenberry 2012).

In the strategy of democratic internationalism, the United States would focus on renewing and deepening democracy globally, preventing democratic backsliding and consolidating bonds among democratic states. The policy would aim to ensure that a community of democracies be a prevailing force, leading efforts to solve global problems and manage global governance by burden-sharing and societal innovation, preventing the global order from sliding to weak institutions and great power rivalry (Deudney/Ikenberry 2012: 1-2).

The new strategy would return liberal internationalism to its roots of social democratic ideals, redressing imbalances between fundamental capitalism (neoliberalism) and socioeconomic equity. A policy akin to that from the immediate post-second world war era to the mid-1950s, when the United States was a model for Europe in promoting and equalizing development and prosperity, would combine a strong federal government engaged in infrastructure reconstruction at home with an active foreign policy of being a global liberal pivot. Reference is made to the Truman era and the Marshall Plan as well as to the policies of societal renewal of the New Deal and the Great Society.

A new liberal drive is needed because the domestic foundations of liberal internationalism have eroded, casting doubts over the US leadership, as public support for international engagement has become more selective, and the grand strategy is under attack by neoconservatives, sovereigntists and neonationalists. At the same time, established and new democracies elsewhere are struggling under the economic and social crisis. The crisis of democracy creates opportunities for nondemocratic and revisionist powers such as China to build their own coalitions.

The diversity among democracies is reflected in obstacles to convergence and cooperation in human rights and democracy promotion. Such swing states as India, Brazil, South Africa, Turkey and Indonesia are committed to universal standards and prefer constructive engagement in multilateral bodies, averting condemnations and sanctions pursued by established democracies. Driven by the legacy of colonialism, and stressing sovereignty and non-interference, the swing states resist regime change by outside interventions. As for geopolitical and structural considerations, non-Western rising states are wary of joining US-led joint actions and are apt to pursue South-South solidarity as well as focus their power and influence on regional contexts (Piccone 2012: 9-11).

The Deudney-Ikenberry report would solve the composite domestic and international crisis by means of a strategy of reinforced and refocused liberal internationalism based on progressive domestic renewal. The authors admit that their proposal would require a winning domestic political coalition, along populist, progressive and liberal lines, to counter laissez-faire fundamentalists and nationalists, which they view as threats to the success of American democracy both at home and abroad. Established Western and postcolonial non-Western states would advance the aspiration of societal equity and the responsibility for solving global problems by coalitional leadership and community building. As a response to the threat of rising systemic illiberalism, the liberal pivot would overwhelm China and Russia and pull them to further mutual engagement with the democracies, provided the democratic front avoids the risk of appearing to pursue a strategy of confrontation and containment.

Conclusion: bending, recasting and replacing liberal internationalism

Think tank findings and academic debates indicate that liberal internationalism is a useful, albeit variable framework for evaluating and prescribing American strategic thinking. The think tank discourse perceives a "muddling-through" mode with a wide agenda for the United States, while the academic narrative generates distinct alternatives to the prevailing and struggling grand strategy. Both groups of analysts can be seen as policy-oriented advocates even though they act in different institutional settings.

Liberal internationalism can be seen as a baseline for the pursuit of values and goals drawn from the American historical, constitutional and political legacy in world politics. The mutual fertilization of ideas and practices witnessed in the Obama administration's grand strategy displays the complexity and suppleness of the concept of liberal internationalism when taken onto the practical level of policy making. A standard for pure liberalism is not easy to establish, as even those who identify the current policy with liberal internationalism call for modifications to ensure its sustainability.

In an effort to compile a concluding synthesis for this article, the various voices heard in the public debates are grouped according to the nature of the change to US policy they advocate: bending, recasting or replacing liberal internationalism. Such strategic variations correspond, respectively and broadly, to democratic internationalism, deep engagement and retrenchment as outlined the above review of debates.

The substantive contents of policy in the three strategic profiles are illustrated by indicating the urgency or significance, as an order of priority, they place on the key components of grand strategy formation: international order; large ends; and means (see Table 1).

GRAND STRATEGY OF LIBERAL INTERNATIONALISM			
Profile of strategy Priority of drivers	*BENDING*	*RECASTING*	*REPLACING*
1	ENDS	ORDER	MEANS
2	ORDER	MEANS	ENDS
3	MEANS	ENDS	ORDER

Table 1. The United States under strategic review. Protagonists of bending, recasting and replacing liberal internationalism as profiled by the order of urgency and significance placed on reappraising drivers of grand strategy.

Bending is an ends-driven strategy with a focus on enlarging and strengthening liberal ascendancy in the international order. Recasting is an order-driven strategy, which calls for structural and institutional adaptations in global governance by sharing burdens. Replacing is a means-driven strategy necessitating an overhaul of the means and resources invested in – and used for – promoting selective or prioritized interests and values.

Furthermore, for protagonists of bending, global change and power shift are manageable by a modified leadership of global governance, supported by a steady investment in resources and capabilities, primarily in domestic infrastructure. For proponents of recasting, a moderate recalibration of the usage of resources is called for to maintain a stable environment. For advocates of replacement, some reduction of liberal features in the global order is inevitable and tolerable in a policy with a narrower but prioritized agenda towards a less governable environment.

Within the above analytical framework, President Obama seems to pursue a crossover strategy of bending and recasting liberal internationalism, while at the same time blending engagement with tactical retrenchment, with the ideas of bending history through liberal and democratic ascendancy remaining largely in the domain of rhetoric. The agility of his composite strategic profile, driven by ideational and structural factors, helps to ensure the sustainability of liberal internationalism when defined in a sufficiently broad and flexible manner.

Postscript: what is in it for Europe?

Transatlantic partnership is an ideational and structural core of the strategy of liberal internationalism for the United States. Historically, the relationship has been in constant search for balanced reciprocity.

On one hand, Europe – whether coalesced within the European Union or NATO – has benefitted from the global goods provided by the US leadership for the liberal order. On the other hand, the EU has been charting its course as an institutional actor in regional and global developments, while the European members of NATO have been involved in the politics of burden-sharing.

Consequently, using the above analytical framework, the EU seems to entertain similar syndromes to the US in its strategic reappraisal under the pressures of the transformation of the world order.

In the context of a comprehensive discussion on a new security strategy (Fägersten et al. 2013), while strongly identified with the goals of democratic enlargement (i.e. bending), the European Union is struggling to establish and pursue an effective institutional position in global governance (i.e. recasting). Moreover, an aspect of the critical public opinion rising within the EU advocates an inward-looking response to external pressures (i.e. replacing).

As for the transatlantic partnership, it has become progressively more complex in the post-cold war decades. The acrimony surrounding the debate on the end of the West, which seemed to create a cleavage between the partners on the value of multilateralism and global engagement, has been followed by a new wave of demands for greater European responsibility for regional if not global security. As a consequence of Obama's signature strategy of rebalancing towards Asia, Europe seems to have ended up being driven in its strategic formation by an element of US retrenchment.

Most recently, the prospect of transatlantic renaissance has emerged in the form of a transatlantic trade and investment partnership (TTIP) project. Viewed strategically, if concluded successfully and comprehensively, the transatlantic manifestation of economic power would have the appearance and effect of a joint Western effort at bending history through liberal democratic rise in global governance.

In conclusion, all of the orientations identified in the American debates will have significant strategic consequences for Europe, which is engaged in strategic reappraisals of its own. While the United States and the European Union face similar challenges to – and enjoy common interests in – liberal international order, how their strategic turns are conflated will remain a central question for both partners in the future.

References

Allin, Dana H., and Erik Jones (2012), *Weary policeman: American power in an age of austerity*. London: The International Institute for Strategic Studies.

Betts, Richard K. (2012), *American Force: Dangers, Delusions, and Dilemmas in National Security*. New York, NY: Columbia University Press.

Brooks, Stephen G., G. John Ikenberry, and William C. Wohlworth (2012/2013), "Don't Come Home, America: The Case against Retrenchment." *International Security*, 37:3, 7-51.

Brooks, Stephen G., G. John Ikenberry, and William C. Wohlworth (2013), "Lean Forward." *Foreign Affairs*, 92:1, 130-142.

Deudney, Daniel, and G. John Ikenberry (2012), "Democratic Internationalism: An American Grand Strategy for a Post-exceptionalist Era." Working Paper, November 2012. New York, NY: Council on Foreign Relations.

Dunne, Tim, and Matt McDonald (2013), "The politics of liberal internationalism." *International Politics*, 50:1, 1-17.

Fontaine, Richard, and Kristin M. Lord, eds. (2012), *America's Path: Grand Strategy for the New Administration*. May 2012. Washington, DC: Center for a New American Security.

Fägersten, Björn, Allessandro Marrone, Martin Ortega, and Roderick Parkes (2013), *Towards a European Global Strategy. Securing European Influence in a Changing World*. May 2013. IAI, PISM, RIE, UI.

Goldgeier, James, and Kurt Volker, co-chairs (2013), *Setting Priorities for American Leadership: A New National Security Strategy for the United States*. March 2013. Project for a United and Strong America.

Ikenberry, G. John (2011), *Liberal Leviathan: The Origins, Crisis, and Transformation of the American World Order*. Princeton, MA, Oxford: Princeton University Press.

Indyk, Martin S., Kenneth G. Lieberthal, and Michael E. O'Hanlon (2012), *Bending History: Barack Obama's Foreign Policy*. Washington, DC: Brookings Institution Press.

Indyk, Martin, Tanvi Madan, and Thomas Wright, eds. (2013), *Big Bets Black Swans: A Presidential Briefing Book*. January 2013. Washington, DC: Foreign Policy at Brookings.

Keohane, Robert O. (2012), "Hegemony and After." *Foreign Affairs*, 91:4, 114-118.

Layne, Christopher (2012), "This Time It's Real: The End of Unipolarity and the Pax Americana." *International Studies Quarterly*, 56:1, 203-213.

Manning, Robert, principal drafter (2012), *Envisioning 2030: US Strategy for a Post-Western World*. A report of the Strategic Foresight Initiative at the Brent Scowcroft Center on International Security. Washington, DC: Atlantic Council.

Mathews, Jessica T., ed. (2012), *Global Ten: Challenges and Opportunities for the President in 2013*. Washington, DC: Carnegie Endowment for International Peace.

NIC – National Intelligence Council (2012), *Global Trends 2030: Alternative Worlds*. December 2012. Washington, DC: NIC.

Nye, Joseph S., Jr. (2012), "The Twenty-First Century Will not Be a 'Post-American' World." *International Studies Quarterly*, 56:1, 215-217.

Piccone, Ted (2012), *Global Swing States and the Human Rights and Democracy Order*. Global Swing States Working Paper, November 2012. Washington, D.C.: The German Marshall Fund of the United States/Center for a New American Security.

Posen, Barry R. (2013), "Pull Back." *Foreign Affairs*, 92:1, 116-128.

Slaughter, Anne-Marie (2013), "Does Obama have a grand strategy for his second term? If not, he could try one of these." *The Washington Post*, 01-18-13.

Strachan, Hew (2011), "Strategy and contingency." *International Affairs*, 87:6, 1281-1296.

Wohlforth, William C. (2012), "How Not to Evaluate Theories." *International Studies Quarterly*, 56:1, 219-222.

At the End of Relief and Development? Assessing the EU Approach of Resilience in Crisis Prone Countries

Jan Pospisil

On 19th June 2013, the European Commission presented the European Union's "Action Plan for Resilience in Crisis Prone Countries", which is intended to cover the extensive time period from 2013 to 2020. This action plan is a remarkable step. It focuses a relevant part of the international engagement of the EU by utilizing a concept – "resilience" – which is not only new, but also controversial. Obviously, resilience – at least for the European institutions – must offer some particular advantages for international engagement that were significant enough for them to risk taking up a concept that was unheard of among most of the officials responsible for EU's external policies just a few years ago.

What has resilience to offer for the EU, particularly when utilized as the main approach in crisis prone countries? What are the primary intended – and also potentially unintended – consequences of this EU resilience policy? This article will discuss these questions, but, due to the recentness of the events, has to do so mainly by drawing on the policy documents and public statements provided by the European Union. After an analysis of the Action Plan itself, its main statements will be put in the context of some accounts of critical resilience research, which has developed in parallel to the increasing popularity of the concept both in the policy realm and in politics. Therefore, conclusions will be elaborated which not only concern the EU Action Plan as such, but also deal with the wider aspects and potentially far-reaching consequences of a resilience-based approach in international humanitarian, development and security policy.

Resilience frontrunners

The Action Plan on resilience represents the final step in the take-up of the resilience concept on the EU policy level. The EU is thus following in the footsteps of the United States, which has been implementing the resilience agenda for several years (cf. USAID 2012), and the United Nations Development Program (UNDP), which had decided to "[put] resilience at the heart of the development agenda" (Clark 2012). Even if it is taken into account that other important international development actors like the World Bank (WDR 2011) also rely on the resilience concept to a certain extent, the EU still is considered to be a frontrunner in the international application of the concept.

Therefore, the resilience initiative now set is without doubt a courageous move. It has to be considered that in other international development forums the concept is approached much more hesitantly, if not reluctantly. At the discussions on statebuilding in the International Network on Conflict and Fragility (INCAF), located within the Development Policy Committee (DAC) of the OECD, the main forum of bilateral donor exchange and coordination, resilience is currently discussed rather in the sense of an indistinct vision. For a stronger impetus in the DAC policy discourse, there obviously is not enough common ground within the DAC member states at present.

Some sceptics are also to be found in the European Union itself: while some member states – like the UK – orient their whole foreign and security policy towards resilience, others – in particular France – hesitate to take up the concept at all. Legal and practical concerns, but not least also matters of principal, inform this position. Resilience is seen as a concept that could undermine non-negotiable principles of statehood and the particular legitimacy of state institutions. Nevertheless, the advocates of the concept in the relevant European institutions (in particular in the European Commission) have proved to be strong enough to successfully push for the implementation of the concept.

What does resilience mean for the European Union?

The Action Plan defines resilience as "the ability of an individual, a household, a community, a country or a region to withstand, to adapt, and to quickly recover from stress and shocks" (EC 2013: 3). While the main orientation of the definition – withstanding, adapting and recovering from two particular kinds of systemic disturbances, stresses and shocks – equals many of the other definitions that are debated internationally, the approach still differs in one important aspect: it defines five specific levels in the context of resilience policy, from the single individual to entire states or regions. Such a differentiation addresses one of the most significant critiques faced by the resilience approach: that the concept in many of its incarnations does not answer the question about its stakeholders, or put more directly: who or what should be (or has to be) made resilient?

While the visibility of potential addressees is certainly welcome and necessary, such visibility at the same time poses severe challenges. Although the levels at which a resilience policy should create impact have now been made explicit, the levels are nevertheless inconsistent and it remains an open question in which way they could be incorporated into a policy programme for the development or inducement of resilience. The main challenge is the merging of these widespread levels: how is it possible to practically deal with individuals and regions under the same conceptual heading? This problem is even intensified by the – without doubt correct – understanding of resilience as a certain "ability". The convergence between a top-down oriented action plan, a bottom-up process like the improvement (of an already existing) or the inducement (of a lacking) ability would be a viable governance challenge in itself. Thus, while it is certainly valuable to name the different levels of policy addressees, the shortcoming of indeterminacy regarding whom to approach and how is by no means solved in the definitions of the action plan.

It is worth noting as well from which policy fields the EU resilience approach stems. In stark contrast to pioneers in resilience policy like Britain, the US or Israel, where resilience has mainly been developed in the field of internal or national security (cf. Canetti et al. 2013), the EU intends to utilize the concept primarily as a design for various aspects of its international policy. Resilience emerged initially in reflections on a potential realignment of statebuilding, as they were discussed in the European Report on Development 2009 (ERD 2009). Later on, the concept was also debated as a response to food crisis, in particular in the context of the Global Food Crisis in 2011.

In the following, resilience became the central link between the domains of humanitarian aid and development policy.

In the latter context, resilience can be seen as a prolongation, but also a renewed orientation of the longer standing approach of LRRD ("Linking Relief, Rehabilitation and Development"). LRRD has roughly 15 years' history within EU institutions; EC communications regarding LRRD were already issued in 1996 and 2001 (EC 2012b: 7).[1] However, there are significant differences between both concepts. LRRD is understood by the EC as a process "of smoothly coordinating rapid humanitarian intervention and sustainable development [...] when addressing violent conflicts, natural disasters and other catastrophes" (ibid: 10). Initially, resilience was seen as a distinct and much looser concept than LLRD, and was examined quite critically. In 2012, the Directorate-General for External Policies, for example, named resilience (put in quotation marks) as an important goal of LRRD, but with a different focus (ibid: 16). It was seen as a potentially confusing factor: "The explicit commitments to LRRD should not be diluted by loose provisions on alleged synonyms such as transition and flexibility. It has to be ensured that enough flexibility is provided but that flexibility does not lead to arbitrariness" (ibid: 16-17).

Meanwhile, the interpretation obviously has changed to a considerable amount. Resilience seems to be implemented as the main angle of bridging relief and development, and as including the third dimension of foreign policy too: "It [the Action Plan on resilience] lays the foundations for more effective EU collaborative action on building resilience, bringing together humanitarian action, long-term development cooperation and on-going political engagement" (EC 2013: 1). Resilience thus is endorsed as the overarching policy goal of all the various strands of international policy. While LRRD was just applying for cooperation and coordinating the fields for the sake of effectiveness and necessity, resilience is now seen – in contrast to the concerns from 2012 – as the main vision of such a joint undertaking.

---

[1] COM(96) 153,COM(2001) 153

But what are the challenges for which resilience is designed to provide visionary orientation? In addition to natural disasters (addressed via humanitarian relief) and fragility (addressed via state-building), the Action Plan introduces climate change as a third constitutive content element of the EU resilience approach. These three challenges have to be faced with an approach that connects the demands of "prevention" and "preparedness" in contexts defined as particularly "vulnerable" (ibid: 4). Security policy concerns (regarding national security threats) astonishingly seem to be considered of little relevance in this approach, which is remarkable given the strong historical interconnectedness of the security-development-nexus with domestic security issues (like terrorism, illegal migration and drug trafficking). Furthermore, there is also no specific reference to potential applications or lessons learnt from the field of internal security, where, at least in some countries, for example the UK, the resilience approach is already widely used and implemented. Remarkably, such references are completely absent from the Action Plan.

History of the resilience concept within the EU framework

One explanation for this absence might be in the history of the concept within the EU policy agenda. The Action Plan for resilience is the final step in a meanwhile long list of relevant documents and in the practical steps that the EU has set as part of their resilience agenda. Depending on the perspective, humanitarian aid and development policy either played a role as drivers or as the main targets of this approach. The history of resilience in the EU's international policies started in remarkable prominence: in 2009, the first ever European Report on Development, designed to represent a significant step in the evolving collective European development policy, used the resilience concept in order to build a rationale for a "common European approach" to state fragility, in particular in Sub-Saharan Africa (ERD 2009).

Hence, the concept quickly gained prominence due to the trigger function played by the publishing of the first ever ERD. This prominence, aggravated by the debates held about resilience and statebuilding at the DAC OECD level at the same time (cf. OECD-DAC 2008), proved to be short-lived, however. Soon, reality proved that the actual political impact of the ERD would be severely limited. There were no follow-up activities on policy level, and the ERD remained a mainly academic document. This changed over the course of the next two to three years, mostly due to debates in the areas of humanitarian aid and social security (and not in the realm of statebuilding). While relief policies very much showed an awareness of the resilience concept and had already endorsed it at the UN level (UNISDR 2005), the impetus regarding development issues was again provided by another European Report on Development. The 2010 report dealt with the issue of social security and prominently referred to the resilience concept. In contrast to the ERD 2009, however, resilience was not discussed regarding concepts like state-society relations, but rather it was put in the context of three global crises: the food crisis, the fuel crisis and the financial crisis, and their particular impact in and on Sub-Saharan Africa (ERD 2010). Resilience thus came to be the name of a renewed approach to security policy in the context of risk (cf. Pospisil 2013) and can be termed as one of the particular labels of what Olaf Corry (2012) has called "riskification".

At this time, practical steps were taken, mainly along an extended LRRD agenda. In the aftermath of the extended drought in the Horn of Africa in 2011 and the food crisis in the Sahel region, which became virulent in 2012, the EC initiated specific programme lines based on a resilience approach. These so-called "flagship resilience initiatives" (EC 2013) addressed both regions by the financially well-equipped programmes SHARE (*"Support Horn of African Resilience"*, funded with €270 million for 2012/13) and AGIR Sahel (*"l'Alliance Global pour l'Initiative Résilience Sahel"*, funded with €1.5 billion for the years 2014 to 2020, mainly from the budget of the European Development Fund, EDF). Both initiatives were designed along the LRRD approach (linking activities of the EU programme for humanitarian relief, ECHO, with EDF funding and development policy activities), but they were categorised under the explicit aim of building resilience.

This was made public for the first time in an EC communication in October 2012, where SHARE and AGIR were both put in the context of an "EU Approach to Resilience" (EC 2012a). The communication also laid out the particularities of a resilience-based approach, therefore providing the foundations to qualitatively offset the concept from actor-focused approaches like LRRD. Besides defining resilience for the first time in an official EU context (with the exact same wording as in the later Action Plan), the communication highlights three specific elements:

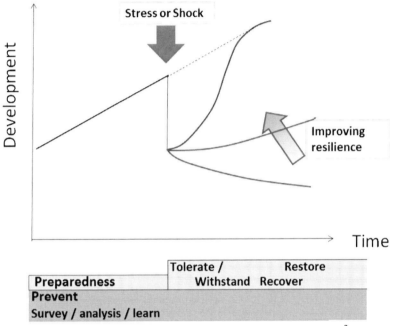

Figure 1: Resilience scheme of the European Commission[2]

(1) Resilience demands a multi-dimensional strategy based on two central aspects of its conceptual meaning – the reduction of the multiplicity of risks on the one hand, and the improvement of adaptation and recovery mechanisms on the other. Figure 1 graphically demonstrates the underlying scheme and provides, at the same time, a remarkable ontology. While resilience in

---

[2] "'Adapted from Montpellier Panel – Growth with Resilience: Opportunities in African Agriculture', March 2012" (EC 2013: 4).

the current state of the art is understood as characteristic of complex adaptive systems (e.g. cf. Gunderson/Pritchard 2002: 8-15), this framework understands shocks and stresses not as necessary conditions of such a system, but rather as disruptions in a linear development path. Such a rendering of resilience, which has been coined "engineering resilience" (de Bruijne et al. 2010: 19), is now presumed to be antiquated and is seen as an expression of stability-oriented thinking in resilience research. This points to a superficial dealing with the theoretical aspects of the concept at the responsible policy level, which was hence obviously more taken with serving immediate practical purposes than giving new, perhaps qualitatively different policy orientations.

(2) The strength of resilience is seen as its being at the interface of humanitarian aid and development cooperation in the context of complex emergencies; (3) the improvement of resilience requires a long-term approach, which addresses the structural causes of crisis and focuses on capacity development in the context of crisis management. While the first aspect, even with its severe shortcomings, indeed represents a distinct feature of a resilience-based approach, the latter two elements just reflect already existing patterns from established concepts like LRRD and DRR (Disaster Risk Reduction). From an analytical standpoint, it is therefore necessary to suppose resilience to be indeed a more visionary concept, designed to answer risk-oriented approaches to security policy on the one hand, and at the same time to incorporate already existing forms and methods of implementations on the other.

However, this communication not only initiated the work on the following Action Plan, but also consolidated the resilience agenda on a high policy level. Consequently, other steps followed shortly after the communication was released. In May 2013, the Council of Foreign Ministers adopted its conclusions on an "EU approach to resilience" and explicitly mandated the Commission to draft the Action Plan (Council of the European Union 2013). Crisis-ridden and fragile states were designated as the main targets for implementation. There, an integrated, resilience-based approach based on inclusive, shared, multi-sector and flexible policies should be realized. Additionally, the international dialogue on resilience should be promoted on all relevant multilateral forums (from the UN to the G8).

The Council therefore relies on a very ambitious application of a concept that in fact has no track record in terms of implementation, neither on the EU level nor in the wider international context. It seems that the EC, instead of looking to improve policies on the practical level, has identified resilience as an anchor to bridge institutional gaps in its own organization, but also as a unique feature of a distinct European approach, as it was once suggested by the ERD 2009. Hence, resilience could provide the visionary narrative necessary to overcome the long-standing prejudice regarding EU development policy as a technocratic giant that has a lot of means at its disposal, but few ideas on how to use them.

Where are we heading? Aspects of implementation

What are the concrete steps the Action Plan now intends to initiate to bring this ambitious agenda to life? Overall, the potential actions fall under three defined priorities. The first priority focuses on the implementation of national and regional resilience approaches, as well as respective capacities and partnerships. Essentially, this priority incorporates the two ongoing initiatives, AGIR and SHARE. Drawing on these experiences, the EU intends to develop more "flagship" initiatives, which should be built on joint EU and member states' country (or probably also regional) strategies. Additionally, cross-policy field approaches are envisioned as being integrated into programming in the context of Disaster Risk Management, in particular regarding the two main perceived challenges of climate change and food security.

Regarding strategy development, the agenda will presumably follow up the experience of the country programming process on South Sudan from 2011. This process resulted in the first ever joint country strategy of the European Commission and all concerned member states (EU 2011). Current research, however, suggests – with explicit reference to the case study of South Sudan – that besides the two flagship initiatives, the resilience agenda is not even at the stage of being reflected at the level of EU donors' country programmes (Pospisil/Besancenot 2013).

The second, broadly designed priority is summarized under the heading "innovation, learning and advocacy". It offers very different components. It encompasses traditional fields of development policy interventions in areas such as social security, private sector development or fiscal policy, which are all to be linked up to the resilience concept. Essentially, this is done via appropriate consultation mechanisms with the partner countries. Joint pilot projects should be identified and implemented, particularly in areas such as innovative insurance mechanisms. Another highlighted priority is the sector of "urban resilience" – presently one of the main topics of the international resilience debate – and more traditional relief and development challenges like refugee assistance and capacity development on the local level.

The crucial weakness in these – at first glance very promising – initiatives is revealed in the "learning and advocacy" component. This component consists of the two elements of an extension of a so-called "resilience knowledge base" and the promotion of the approach on various international and regional levels. Of course, it is a necessary symbol of self-reflexivity and, at the same time, an acknowledgement of the necessity to learn to admit that the current knowledge base on resilience is inadequate. Furthermore, it makes perfect sense to design a strong resilience component in the upcoming calls for the pan-European research programme "Horizon 2020", as it is now published as part of the "secure societies" challenge.

However, it remains questionable why the EC is obviously highlighting and promoting a concept of which there is no common understanding, no experience whatever in the (potential) particularities of its implementation nor in the governance challenges surrounding it. Despite all efforts of fill resilience with concrete measures and initiatives, from the outset it has not been possible to identify what is now being done on a concrete level in a different manner than before. The full array of planned tools, mechanisms and instruments provided in the third priority of the Action Plan ("Methodologies and Tools to support resilience") is not able to prove the contrary. The task of developing specific instruments for measuring resilience (provided in measure 17) could be seen as something specific in that regard, but, given the fact that the EC definition of resilience has remained unchanged for two years, also as a step coming rather late. Despite the self-confident promotion of resilience, which demands some respect for its innovativeness, the persistence of bureaucracy seems to be still very much intact.

Aims and implications of the resilience agenda

Despite the problems in implementation, there are important consequences resilience will have, even in the short term. Moreover, there will be mid- to long-term implications, some of them not intentional. This is due to the high probability that resilience, like sustainability, will become a key concept in the realm of relief and development for years to come, and therefore will develop a conceptual life of its own. Based on the understanding of resilience offered by the EC communication and the subsequent Action Plan, three main implications the EU's resilience approach will have are highlighted in the following, one on the level of policy and policy development, one regarding governance, and one on a more fundamental level.

(1) As already shown, the importance of resilience in the context of the EU's external policy is placed on its linkage between relief, humanitarian aid and development policy. It acts as a "LRRD plus" approach, very much drawing on the actor-specific demands of LRRD, but connecting it structurally with a certain vision. Obviously, resilience acts as a bridging concept in two distinct respects: first, it offers the opportunity to renew the almost forgotten Whole-of-the-Union approach (cf. EC 2009). Resilience offers a much livelier agenda setting for inter-agency cooperation than a technocratic, merely actor-focused approach can give. Second, resilience simultaneously comes to play an instrumental role in the harmonization of international policies, i.e. non other than the traditional agenda of Policy Coherence for Development (PCD). In particular for highly bureaucratic entities like the EU institutions, it proves true that cooperation cannot take place just for cooperation's sake: it needs enhanced theoretical underpinning. Resilience obviously is expected to deliver such an underpinning.

Currently, the main focus is on bridging humanitarian aid and development policy. Resilience becomes the catalyst for putting into practice the long-standing demands for closer ties between these two policy fields (with all the problems such a composition could imply for the particular mandates for humanitarian relief, which are based not least on impartiality). Foreign policy and international security policy could follow, while the then logical connection to internal security – which seems obvious due to the comparable challenges humanitarian relief and civil protection policies sometimes face – seems to lie further afield. This is mainly caused by the different ways of dealing with the concept of resilience at the nation state level, where some EU member countries, like the UK, are, as mentioned above, frontrunners; others are very sceptical of applying the concept in the field of internal security, which states tend to perceive as highly crucial.

(2) On the level of governance, most likely, the application of the resilience concept will have a severe impact not only on the selection of the addressed beneficiaries, but also on the way they are approached by the resilience intervention. David Chandler (2013) has envisioned a swing away from the "civil society" focus, emphasized in particular in development policy for decades, towards "community". In spite of the five levels the EC highlights in its resilience definition, "community" has the strongest connection to resilience research, and the resilience agenda in crisis management in particular (e.g. Tobin 1999, Coaffee/Wood 2006). Other levels, like society, the individual itself, but also the state obtain a new meaning in the resilience context, as they are defined primarily via their relation to the community level.

This process implies a serious governance challenge. As Ostrom and Janssen (2004: 240-243) highlight, the long-standing "belief in the efficacy of top-down solutions" cannot be held up in the context of resilience policies. Resilience can be neither developed nor imposed – resilience cannot be implemented with traditional development measures like capacity building. On the contrary, resilience is a genuine bottom-up process, and the highly complex governance challenge of any resilience policy is to induce such a bottom-up process via, at least in the context of relief and development policy, predominantly top-down policies. While the EC's approach still is far away from working with such demanding concepts as the multi-scale adaptive processes suggested by Ostrom and Janssen (ibid: 251-254), the EU's agencies will have to confront the governance challenge resilience implies sooner rather than later.

(3) Finally, in catalysing the policy bridging of most policies of international engagement and in fundamentally changing not only the addressees of these policies, but also the ways in which they are addressed, resilience has at least the potential of transforming the whole concept of relief and development on a fundamental level. Mark Duffield has already identified such a potential in the concept of sustainable development, which he frames as the ultimate shift of responsibility from the developed world – initially bound by their promises of modernization and catch-up development – to the perceived underdeveloped world. They themselves now have the responsibility to act sustainably. "Rather than reducing the life-chance gap between the developed and underdeveloped worlds, sustainable development is better understood as a means of containing the latter" (Duffield 2007: 68).

Resilience has the potential ability to follow these footsteps and to radicalize the sustainability agenda. The whole emphasis now is put on "developing" the self-reliance of those subject to malfunctions like underdevelopment or disaster. They are now assigned the responsibility of becoming resilient towards these malfunctions. While such a responsibility of course can be rendered as international and shared, a responsibility that at the same time builds on the self-efficacy of those concerned, it nevertheless provides for the eventuality of development and relief becoming the "art of being tough".

Conclusions

Any current assessment of the resilience agenda of the European Union has to deal with its ambivalence. Resilience is a concept with potentially huge implications and a substantial political character. At present, it is understood in a primarily technocratic way, and is not matched by appropriate measures in implementation. The major weakness of the EU's resilience approach, however, remains on the conceptual level. This affects less the definition – the definition given by the EC represents the main aspects of the current international state of the debate – but rather the substantive understanding of the concept. Still, resilience seems to be interpreted as the ability to follow a linear development path despite all possible disturbances, rather than as a complex systemic approach. As shown, content-wise resilience, in its present conception in the EU Action Plan, builds on the concept of sustainable development and radicalizes it in laying the foundations for an ultimate end of relief and development policy and their transformation into a fully-integrated resilience agenda based on the self-reliance of those whose resilience is emphasized.

Resilience, however, is a very political concept and it offers serious opportunities for engagement. Precisely by questioning the ideal-type linearity of the development path by emphasizing the complexity and adaptability of a non-linear system, resilience provides the opportunity for a critical self-reflexivity of long-standing relief and development policy practice. Of course, this is not mentioned in the Action Plan and also not reflected in the measures and steps envisioned therein. It is a welcome step in this context that the EC is putting a strong research focus on this agenda in its "Horizon 2020" programme. "Horizon 2020" indeed could be a good vehicle for elaborating a self-reflective approach for a resilience agenda in international intervention policies, if – and, unfortunately, this is a big "if" – innovative thinking about the concept is promoted and looked for. If the EC interprets resilience research in the security realm just as an issue of swiftly designing an implementation agenda[3], then prospects are doubtful.

In general, it will nevertheless be crucial how successful the anchoring of the concept in the different policy areas will be, and if a permanent critical reflection is integrated and called for. Such anchoring of resilience is the necessary prerequisite to allow findings from fundamental research and from first best-practice examples to be integrated in a framework for resilience action. Experience shows that such processes of policy implementation take a long time and are rarely straightforward. Therefore, much will depend on what the EU policy level "makes" out of resilience. The Action Plan offers significant and potentially promising opportunities in that respect; still, experience

---

[3] In the course of an official presentation of the "Secure Societies" challenge of "Horizon 2020" at the FFG in Vienna (18-11-13), the representative of the EC made a very unfortunate statement in this regard: "security research just can be applied research, and not research for the research sake."

shows that efforts towards concept development and alignment in EU development policy are far from flawless. Taking into consideration the strongly political character of resilience and the opportunities for engagement given at the moment, however, such an engagement is an important responsibility.

References

Canetti, Daphne, Israel Waismel-Manor, Naor Cohen, and Carmit Rapaport (2013), "What Does National Resilience Mean in a Democracy? Evidence from the United States and Israel." *Armed Forces & Society*, Online First, DOI: 10.1177/0095327X12466828, Mar 26, 2013.

Chandler, David (2013), "International State Building and the Ideology of Resilience." *Politics*, 33:4, 276-286.

Clark, Helen (2012), "Putting Resilience at the Heart of the Development Agenda." Humanitas Visiting Professorship Lecture, 16 February 2012. Cambridge: UNDP.

Coaffee, Jon, and David Murakami Wood (2006), "Security is Coming Home: Rethinking Scale and Constructing Resilience in the Global Urban Response to Terrorist Risk." *International Relations*, 20:4, 503-517.

Corry, Olaf (2012) "Securitisation and 'Riskification': Second-order Security and the Politics of Climate Change." *Millennium – Journal of International Studies*, 40:2, 235-258.

Council of the European Union (2013), *Council Conclusions on EU approach to resilience*. Foreign Affairs Council meeting N°3241/2013, Brussels: Council of the European Union.

de Bruijne, Mark, Arjen Boin, and Michel van Eeten (2010), "Resilience: Exploring the Concept and Its Meanings." In *Designing Resilience: Preparing for Extreme Events*, edited by Louise K. Comfort, Arjen Boin and Chris C. Demchak, Pittsburgh, PA: University of Pittsburgh Press, 13-32.

Duffield, Mark (2007), *Development, Security and Unending War: Governing the World of Peoples*. Cambridge, UK: Polity Press.

EC – European Commission (2009), *Policy Coherence for Development – Establishing the policy framework for a whole-of-the-Union approach*. Communication from the Commission to the Council, the European Parliament, the European Economic and Social Committee and the Committee of the Regions, COM (2009) 458 final, Brussels: EC.

EC – European Commission (2012a), *The EU Approach to Resilience: Learning from Food Security Crises*. Communication from the Commission to the European Parliament and the Council, COM (2012) 586 final, Brussels: EC.

EC – European Commission (2012b), *Strengthening LRRD in the EU's Financing Instruments*. Policy Study, DEVE, Directorate B, Brussels: EC.

EC – European Commission (2013), *Action Plan for Resilience in Crisis Prone Countries, 2013-2020*. SWD (2013) 227 final, Brussels: EC.

ERD – European Report on Development (2009), *Overcoming Fragility in Africa – Forging a New European Approach*. San Dominico di Fiesole: Robert Schuman Centre for Advanced Studies.

ERD – European Report on Development (2010), *Social Protection for Inclusive Development: A New Perspective in EU Co-operation with Africa*. San Dominico di Fiesole: Robert Schuman Centre for Advanced Studies.

EU – European Union (2011), *South Sudan joint EU / MS Programming Document 2011-2013*. Brussels: EU.

Gunderson, Lance H., and Lowell Pritchard Jr., eds. (2002), *Resilience and the Behavior of Large-Scale Systems*. Washington, DC: Island Press.

OECD-DAC (2008), *Concepts and Dilemmas of State Building in Fragile Situations: From Fragility to Resilience*. Paris: OECD.

Ostrom, Elinor, and Marco A. Janssen (2004), "Multi-Level Governance and Resilience of Social-Ecological Systems." In *Globalisation, Poverty and Conflict. A Critical 'Development' Reader*, edited by Max Spoor, Dordrecht: Kluwer Academic Publishers, 239-259.

Pospisil, Jan (2013), "Resilienz: Die Neukonfiguration von Sicherheitspolitik im Zeitalter von Risiko." *Österreichische Zeitschrift für Politikwissenschaft*, 42:1, 25-42.

Pospisil, Jan and Sophie Besancenot (2013), "EU Donor Policies in Situations of Fragility: Promoting Resilience?" *European Journal for Development Research*, OnlineFirst, doi: 10.1057/ejdr.2013.51.

Tobin, Graham A. (1999), "Sustainability and community resilience: the holy grail of hazards planning?" *Environmental Hazards*, 1:1, 13-25.

UNISDR (2005), *Hyogo Framework for Action 2005-2015: Building the Resilience of Nations and Communities to Disaster*. Geneva and Kobe: International Strategy for Disaster Reduction.

USAID (2012), *Building Resilience to Recurrent Crisis*, USAID Policy and Program Guidance. Washington, DC: USAID.

WDR – World Development Report (2011), *Conflict, Security, and Development*. Washington, DC: The World Bank.

Scientists as Diplomats?! On the Challenges of Researching International Science, Technology and Innovation Policies

Lisa Sigl, Carmen Heidenwolf

The EU's internationalization of Science, Technology and Innovation (STI)

STI cooperation is not a new arena in which international relations are shaped. Probably the most cited example is the establishment of CERN, the European Organisation for Nuclear Research. Only the sharing of costs between 12 European countries made it possible to cover the high costs of nuclear physics research in Geneva. As one of the most respected research centres worldwide, CERN is often celebrated as a paragon for what can be made possible via international collaboration. Its establishment in 1954 was the result of the initiative of individual scientists who were later also backed by UNESCO. However, in the past decade international STI collaboration has been pursued much more strategically on a policy level in the European context. The "International Strategy for Research and Innovation" (EC 2012) is a visible demonstration of the efforts towards internationalization. For some time before the formal strategy, these efforts encompassed the identification of target countries for international cooperation, the establishment of new institutions and the development of more coherent policies.

The broader context for this shift is the aim of transforming Europe into "the most dynamic and competitive knowledge-based economy in the world" that was first explicated in the Lisbon Strategy 2000. It builds on the idea that the European Union (EU) "is confronted with a quantum shift resulting from globalisation and the challenges of a new knowledge-driven economy" (EC 2004: 5). In the past years, the international spectrum of European policies has started to reach beyond Europe: the first six Framework Programmes (FP) of the EU mainly aimed at establishing what later came to be called the European Research Area (ERA). In contrast, FP7 and "Horizon 2020" (the follow-up framework programme for research and innovation supporting the new growth strategy "Europe 2020") have opened up the international dimension by putting more emphasis on collaboration with third countries. The participation of third countries is now mainstreamed, i.e. an integral option in all funding schemes (EC 2013).[1]

This internationalization of STI is propelled by quite different objectives. The most prominently mentioned driving factor in the policy discourse is to deal with global challenges such as climate change, food security, infectious diseases and others on a global scale. The increasingly international approach is not only the consequence of the sheer magnitude of these problems, but also because different perspectives are needed to understand and to cope with the complexity of "global challenges". Further objectives of the international approach are to increase the scientific quality, to open new markets for innovative products, to acquire well-educated human resources and – last but not least – to improve international relations.

Alongside the efforts of the European Commission, member states are individually developing their own approaches towards STI internationalization. This becomes visible for example in national internationalization strategies, such as those of the UK or Germany (BIS 2011, BMBF 2008). They reflect the double aim of member states in maximizing their participation in EU funding opportunities while also strategically positioning themselves internationally with their particular scientific and technological specializations. To do so, many member states are setting up their own infrastructures to support international science and technology cooperation: the UK has established a "Science and Innovation Network" (SIN), Germany has "German Science and Innovation Houses" and Finland promotes internationalization via international FinNode Innovation Centres. Until now, Austria has been relatively

---

[1] The following text refers to cooperation with third countries when it uses the terms "international" or "internationalization".

modest in that regard, setting up only two Offices of Science and Technology Austria (OSTA) in the past 13 years (2001 in Washington, 2012 in Peking).

It should be mentioned at this point that STI internationalization is of course not only a European or Western phenomenon. The STI policies of China and India, for example, are characterized by a move towards internationalization as well – even if the driving factors for this move are context-specific. China consciously builds on international collaboration in order to enhance capacities for "indigenous innovation" (Heidenwolf et al. 2012, cf. Bound et al. 2013). India too is increasingly open with regard to scientific exchange, investment, intellectual property and research – at the latest, this has been the case since the market-based economic reforms in 1991 (cf. Bound/Thornton 2012: 58-59).

In this paper, we discuss some pressing questions that these developments raise for researching international relations: as we have briefly outlined, international STI policies seem to increasingly shape the ways in which the EU and its member states forge and maintain international relations. However, what remains unclear is how (far) scientific and technological collaboration will contribute to global power shifts. We thus reflect on how diplomatic responsibility is – at least discursively – assigned to scientists and stakeholders in STI along the idea of "science diplomacy". We do so by first elaborating on the analytical perspectives that are needed to understand the on-going internationalization of STI policies. Further, by drawing attention to the EU's policies towards China, we illustrate that international STI policies yield a dynamically changing institutional landscape. Analysing these institutional transformations will be a precondition for understanding how (soft) power dynamics are unfolding in the context of STI internationalization as well as for understanding how innovation and diplomatic activities have started to mutually shape each other.

Lisa Sigl, Carmen Heidenwolf

Analytical perspectives for understanding global innovation systems

The increasingly international approach in STI not only challenges a fundamental basic assumption of STI policies; it also changes the analytical perspectives needed to research STI policies. From the 1960s onwards, both have followed a national system approach. Even though the term "National Innovation System (NIS)" was only coined in the 1980s (Freeman 1987), the early works of the OECD on STI – as well as the publications of science policy researchers – focused on national (and regional) systems of innovation (Godin 2009). While it was clear from the beginning "that not all innovative activity is national in scope", this analytical frame was nevertheless considered appropriate, since most research activities indeed seemed to be framed by national funding opportunities. However, the nation-oriented analytical framework is losing its legitimacy because its empirical basis is diminishing: STI (policies) are developing an increasingly international dimension and multi-national corporations have become key players "not just with regard to manufacturing but more recently with regard to innovation and R&D as well" (Martin 2012: 4-5, cf. Waltman et al. 2011). In this context, Ben Martin concludes that the challenge for future innovation studies is to "identify, map and analyse these global systems of innovation" and to "understand their interactions with national (and regional) systems" (Martin 2012: 10).

We argue, however, that in order to reflect on how strategic policies in STI internationalization shape global innovation systems and to trace the effects of diplomatic considerations on them, we need to go one step further and address the involved power dynamics by asking: how do international relations policies shape international STI policies? And conversely: how (far) will international STI policies change global power relations?

"Soft Power", "Power Diffusion" and "Science Diplomacy" – Understanding STI collaborations in international power relations

To discuss the interrelations between international STI cooperation and power dynamics in international relations more generally, the conceptual framework of "soft power" by Joseph Nye is often applied. It addresses a form of power that is realised by the "ability to affect others through the co-optive means of framing the agenda, persuading, and eliciting positive attraction in order to obtain preferred outcomes" (Nye 2011: 21). Nye was primarily addressing military science and technology when he reflected that in the "twentieth century, science and technology have added dramatic new dimensions for power resources" (Nye 2004: 18). In the past years, the term "soft power" has been used to address the role of STI in international relations in a broader sense. The Royal Society of London (for Improving Natural Knowledge) in the UK and the American Association for the Advancement of Science (AAAS) apply the term when arguing that the scientific community "often works beyond national boundaries on problems of common interest" and thus contributes to "emerging forms of diplomacy that require non-traditional alliances of nations, sectors and non-governmental organisations" (The Royal Society/AAAS 2010: 15).

Within Nye's framework, new actors, new institutions and new national and international coordination and cooperation structures count as an example for "power diffusion": the shift of power from governments to nongovernmental actors (Nye 2011: xv). The broader subject under which these power shifts are often discussed is "science diplomacy". It captures the idea that scientific and technological collaboration will gain more relevance in shaping the character of international relations in different ways (science in diplomacy, diplomacy for science and science for diplomacy; The Royal Society/AAAS 2010: 5-6). The terminology of "soft power" and "science diplomacy" has recently gained more relevance in policy debates, as it has been taken up in the internationalization strategy of the EU for research and innovation. In this context, it reflects the expectation that, in the future, international cooperation in STI and the international relations of the EU in general will mutually support each other:

"Science diplomacy" will use international cooperation in research and innovation as an instrument of soft power and a mechanism for improving relations with key countries and regions. Good international relations may, in turn, facilitate effective cooperation in research and innovation... The Union will continue to engage with countries and regions across the globe. This will allow the Union's researchers and innovators to engage on a stakeholder-driven basis with their counterparts worldwide" (EC 2012: 4).

This hope that new actors ("researchers", "innovators" and "stakeholders") will enter the arena of international relations in the EU and worldwide was, however, institutionalized long before 2012 in infrastructures like the Strategic Forum for International Science and Technology Cooperation (SFIC) that was set up in 2008. It aims, amongst other things, at coordinating internationalization efforts and shaping the agenda of EU policies. Such institutional developments suggest that science, technology and international affairs do indeed affect one another (cf. Weiss 2005). However, how they do so and which actors and institutions will succeed in the struggle over the soft power involved is still under heavy negotiation and is strongly entangled with the historical development of international relations between countries. In the following, we will use the relations between the EU and China to depict how the political rapprochement process is being accompanied and supported by internationalization efforts in STI.

China and the EU

Diplomatic relations between the European Economic Community (EEC) and China were established in 1975 and were formalized in 1985 with a trade and cooperation agreement between the EEC and China. After a short break because of the violent suppression of the Tiananmen Square protests of 1989, diplomatic relations reached a normal level again in 1992. In 1995, the EC issued its first communication on EC-China cooperation ("A long-term policy for China-Europe relations"). From the beginning, cooperation in environmental challenges as well as in science and technology (mobility, education and the development of a shared research culture) was seen as a precursor to follow-up relations (EC 1995: 15). The rapprochement process between the EU and China was shaped by efforts from both sides to develop further knowledge-based societies and economies. While the EU has set the goal to become an innovation union (Europe 2020), China is heading toward becoming an innovation society by 2020 (The State Council of China 2006). A further step for strategic and longer-term cooperation in STI was made in 1998 with the "Agreement for scientific and technological cooperation between the European Community and the Government of the People's Republic of China" (ChinaAccess4EU 2012: 11). China's participation as a third country in the 7th framework programme was remarkable, with there having been almost 400 successful applications. Only the USA and Russia were more successful (EC 2011: 30-31).

Currently, the SFIC is developing initiatives for STI internationalization for four countries: China, India, the USA and Brazil (EC 2012). The coordination of strategic approaches, however, seems to be most advanced with regard to China. Generally, STI topics are increasingly discussed in the context of diplomatic relations in different working groups and steering committees. The most recent example in this context is the "EU-China Innovation Cooperation Dialogue" that was established in 2012. The group met for the first time in November 2013. Overall, new forms of collaboration are continually being developed in the STI area between the EU/EU member states and China: they range from regular meetings of different actors (policy makers, stakeholders, scientists, innovative industry) and massive investment in export for innovative products to student exchange programmes, joint calls and joint institutions.

Newly developed funding schemes like the Joint Programming Initiative (JPI) aim at, amongst others, making a common approach of member states towards third countries possible. The JPI "Urban Europe", for example, facilitates a collaboration of member states to provide a strategic international framework for questions of urbanization (e.g. on sustainable urbanization in China). In such projects, new relations are forged not only between scientists but also between the European counterparts of ministries and stakeholders (in this JPI: Belgium, Cyprus, Denmark, Finland, France, Ireland, Italy, Malta, the Netherlands, Norway, Sweden and Turkey) and the respective counterparts in third countries (BMeiA 2013, cf. Heidenwolf et al. 2012). This is but one example of how new dynamics in international relations – revolving around a common research agenda – are introduced.

Conclusion & outlook

In this paper, we have reflected on how international policy research can respond to the increasing internationalization of STI cooperation. We have shown that to understand the increasing entanglement of innovation with diplomatic activities we need to raise the question of what kind of power is performed in the context of international scientific and technological collaboration. A continuing analysis of the transforming institutional landscapes will be necessary in order to understand which actors or institutional structures will be ascribed decision-making power in this regard. Is it for example really scientists who will take over diplomatic tasks or are they merely used as an instrument to re-position member states in the global power structures of the evolving global knowledge economy? It will require further in-depth analyses of internationalization strategies as well as of the actual collaboration projects in order to understand how the entanglements of international relations policies with economic collaboration and STI collaboration are changing right now. The trend to formulate internationalization strategies along market opportunities in and technological needs of third countries supports the latter hypothesis.

Another question that deserves attention in this context is whether we are in fact observing a globalization of innovation systems or a re-framing of national innovation systems: when member states, for example, focus their internationalization efforts on the establishment of nationally framed infrastructures, it might be the case that behind the curtain of "internationalization policies", STI policies will largely remain nation-centric. In this case, the epistemic advantages of an international science system might be seriously compromised. On the other hand, the development and support of global governance structures might help prevent such re-nationalization dynamics. In this respect, it will be important to observe what role newly emerging or long-existing EU and international institutions (like the OECD or UNESCO) will gain (cf. Nichols 2003). Whether the cooperative or competitive dynamics between member states will gain the upper hand in their approach towards third countries will thus inherently depend on the character of the institutions that are being created to govern the internationalization of STI (cf. Sigl/ Witjes forthcoming).

The changing institutional landscape that contemporary STI policies yield will certainly continue to be a site for observing how both international relations and the character of knowledge production mutually shape each other. The analytical challenge of gaining a comprehensive understanding of their interrelation is an inherently interdisciplinary one: it lies in managing to combine approaches from different disciplines and schools of thought, such as political science, international relations, innovation studies, science policy research, science and technology studies, post-colonial studies, and maybe many more. The perspectives they have to offer can be used for a critical reflection on how concepts like "soft power" and "science diplomacy" have come to be used in the policy debate today. Moreover, we have to explore the potential of other conceptual approaches, like that of "co-production" by Sheila Jasanoff (2004, cf. Müller 2012, Müller/Witjes 2014), which explicitly addresses the mutual shaping processes between science, technology and society to gain a differentiated perspective on the shifts in global power dynamics that the internationalization of STI collaboration might yield.

These dynamics also harbour the challenge of going beyond methodological "isms" (Dale/Robertson 2007); we suggest meeting this challenge by adopting a symmetrical and a comparative perspective when researching international STI activities. The symmetrical perspective is necessary, first, because a focus on European initiatives often prevents a perception of third countries as active pursuers of STI policies themselves. Second, it helps to start appreciating the different developments of STI systems and the existence of different notions of "innovation" around the globe. A perspective that is inspired by comparative approaches in political and social sciences (George/Bennett 2005, Drozdova/Gaubatz 2013) should provide the epistemic advantage in seeing these differences and utilizing them to formulate internationalization policies that are worth their name.

Lisa Sigl, Carmen Heidenwolf

References

BIS – Department for Business Innovation & Skills (2011), *Innovation and Research Strategy for Growth*. BIS Economics paper N° 15. London: BIS.

BMeiA – Bundesministerium für europäische und internationale Angelegenheiten (2013), *Wissenschaft und Bildung Office of Science and Technology an der Österreichischen Botschaft in Peking.* Available at: http://www.bmeia.gv.at/botschaft/peking/bilaterale-beziehungen/bilaterale-beziehungen-oesterreich-und-china/wissenschaft-und-bildung.html (27-11-13).

Bound, Kirsten, Tom Saunders, James Wilsdon, and Jonathan Adams (2013), *China's absorptive state.* London: Nesta, Available at: http://www.nesta.org.uk/publications (21-11-13).

Bound, Kristen, and Ian Thornton (2012), *Our frugal future: lessons from India's innovation system.* London: Nesta, Available at: http://www.nesta.org.uk/publications/our-frugal-future-lessons-india%C2%92s-innovation-system (28-11-13).

BMBF – Bundesministerium für Bildung und Forschung (2008), *Deutschlands Rolle in der globalen Wissensgesellschaft stärken.* Strategie der Bundesregierung zur Internationalisierung von Wissenschaft und Forschung, Berlin: BMBF.

China Access4EU (2012), *Supporting the EU access to Chinese research&innovation programmes.* Strategy Paper for enhancing reciprocity in EU-China S&T Cooperation. Project deliverable available at: http://www.access4.eu/_media/D12_-_Strategy_Paper_for_enhancing_reciprocity_in_EU-China_ST_Cooperatio....pdf (26-11-13).

Dale, Roger, and Susan L. Robertson (2007), "Beyond Methodological 'Isms' in Comparative Education in an Era of Globalisation." In *International Handbook of Comparative Education*, edited by A. Kazamias and R. Cowan, Dordrecht: Springer, 1113-1127.

Drozdova, Katya, and Kurt T. Gaubatz, Kurt (2013), "Reducing Uncertainty: Information Analysis for Comparative Case Studies." *International Studies Quarterly,* OnlineFirst, DOI: 10.1111/isqu. 12101.

EC – European Commission (1995), A long term policy for China-Europe relations. Brüssel: EC, 15. Available at: http://eeas.europa.eu/china/docs/com95_279_en.pdf (27-11-13).

EC – European Commission (2004), Extracts from Presidency Conclusions on the Lisbon Strategy by Theme, European Councils: Lisbon (March 2000) to Brussels (June 2004).

EC – European Commission (2011), Fourth 7FP Monitoring Report. August 2011, Brussels: EC. Available at:http://ec.europa.eu/research/evaluations/pdf/archive/fp7_monitoring_reports/fourth_fp7_monitoring_report.pdf (26-11-13).

EC – European Commission (2012), "Enhancing and focusing EU international cooperation in research and innovation: A strategic approach Communication from the Commission to the European Parliament, the Council, the European Economic and Social Committee and the Committee of the Regions." COM(2012) 497 final. Brussels: EC.

EC – European Commission (2013), Horizon 2020 – the EU's new research and innovation programme. MEMO. From 21.11.2013, Brussels: EC. Available at: http://europa.eu/rapid/press-release_MEMO-13-1034_en.pdf (26-11-13).

Freeman, Chris (1987), *Technology policy and economic performance. Lessons from Japan.* London: Pinter.

George, Alexander L., and Andrew Bennett (2005), *Case Studies and Theory Development in the Social Sciences.* Cambridge/MA [u.a.]: MIT Press.

Godin, Benoit (2009), "National Innovation System. The System Approach in Historical Perspective." *Science, Technology & Human Values*, 34:4, 476-501.

Heidenwolf, Carmen, Ruth Müller, Babette Rampke, and Lisa Sigl (2012), Wissenschafts- und Technologiekooperationen mit China. Hoffnungen, Möglichkeiten, Herausforderungen. Wien: oiip (on behalf of the bmvit, unpublished).

Jasanoff, Sheila, ed. (2004), *States of Knowledge: The Co-production of Science and the Social Order.* London: Routledge.

Martin, Ben (2012), "The evolution of science policy and innovation studies." *Research Policy*, 41:7, 1219-1239.

Müller, Ruth (2012), *Wissen und Forschen in einer globalisierten Welt.* Vorstellung des neuen Forschungsschwerpunkts „Internationale Wissenschafts- und Technologiepolitik" am oiip. Oiip Policy Paper, September 2012. Wien: oiip.

Müller, Ruth, and Nina Witjes (2014), "Of Red Threads and Green Dragons: Austrian Sociotechnical Imaginaries about STI cooperation with China." In *International Relations and the Global Politics of Science and Technology, Vol. II: Perspectives and Cases*, edited by Maximilian Mayer, Mariana Carpes, and Ruth Knoblich, Berlin, Heidelberg: Springer.

Nichols, Rodney W. (2003), "UNESCO, US goals, and international institutions in science and technology: what works?" *Technology in Society*, 25:3, 275–298.

Nye, Joseph S., Jr. (2004), *Soft Power. The Means to Success in World Politics.* Cambridge, MA: Perseus Book Group.

Nye, Joseph S., Jr. (2011), *The Future of Power.* New York, NY: Public Affairs.

Sigl, Lisa, and Nina Witjes (forthcoming), "Internationalisation of National Science, Technology and Innovation Policies: De- or Re-enactment of the Nation State?" Paper to be presented at the conference *Science in the Nation-State: Historic and Current Configurations in Global Perspective, 1800-2010*, Universität Tübingen, 11th-13th September 2014.

The Royal Society/AAAS – American Association for the Advancement of Science (2010), *New frontiers in Science Diplomacy. Navigating the changing balance of power.* London: AAAS.

The State Council of China (2006), *Medium- and Long-term National Plan for Science and Technology Development 2006-2020.* Available at: http://erawatch.jrc.ec.europa.eu/erawatch/opencms/information/country_pages/cn/policydocument/policydoc_mig_0004 (27-11-13).

Waltman, Ludo, Robert J.W. Tijssen, and Ness Jan van Eck (2011, unpublished), *Globalisation of science in kilometres.* Leiden: Centre for Science and Technology Studies. http://arxiv.org/abs/1103.3648.

Weiss, Charles (2005), "Science, Technology and International Relations." *Technology in Society*, 27:3, 295-313.

Troubled Neighbourhood: The EU and the Transformations in the Arab World

Cengiz Günay

Europe's perceptions of its southern neighbourhood have mainly been informed by security issues such as Islamist terrorism, migration and energy disruptions. Consequently, the EU's policies towards the region have traditionally been shaped by these concerns. For the last two decades, the EU has sought to stabilize and pacify its troubled neighbourhood through economic integration and the export of legal norms, processes, procedures and common rules into its periphery. In the case of the Arab world this has meant collaboration with authoritarian regimes. Indeed, authoritarian regimes in the Arab world have also become indispensable partners in the West's fight against Islamist terrorism and irregular migration. Political turmoil and the partial collapse of state structures in the Arab world has led to Europe being confronted with new challenges.

Europeans have not only lost their allies within Arab elites, but they also have to question the foundations of their relations with the region as such. As long as Europe regards itself as the only point of reference and European strategies suggest the universality of the cultural premises that infuse European and Western institutions and practices, it will fail to understand the dynamics in the region and to play a role in the political transitions. The discrepancy between its self-perception as a normative power that has placed at the centre of its relations with the world universal norms and principles, such as the consolidation of democracy, human rights, the rule of law and fundamental freedoms, has strongly damaged Europe's moral authority in the region. This article aims at pointing out fundamental deficiencies in the EU's strategies towards the region by highlighting the failures of economic liberalization and integration policies and by emphasizing the EU's failure to reach out to Islamist parties and Islamic organizations as important agents of change in the region.

Cengiz Günay

The EU's reading of the uprisings

Despite several indicators (such as increased individual activism, the formation of social movements, a growing number of spontaneous social protests and self-emulations), to most parts of the European and Western policy communities, the Arab uprisings came as a surprise. In order to understand but also to predict the trajectory of developments, some members of the policy community made analogies with the liberal European revolutions in 1848, with the fall of communist regimes in Central and Eastern Europe in 1989 or with the so-called coloured revolutions in Serbia, Ukraine and Georgia in the mid-2000s (Cheterian 2011, Sasnal 2012, Segura 2012).

Such comparisons, even though they highlight possible challenges during transitions, are deeply rooted in European contexts, discourses and experiences. These debates are mainly theory based and policy oriented. In order to provide foresight, they focus on the phenomenon of radical political change and often ignore particularities regarding the structure and the conditions under which these changes have been taking place, such as the nature of the respective regimes, the social and societal conditions – fractured or not fractured societies – the economic situation, socio-political cohesion and external factors such as the neighbourhood and the role external actors play.

Economic liberalization:
The erosion of state authority and the rise of new agents

The fall of the Berlin Wall in November 1989 had implied the defeat of communism and the moral triumph of capitalism and Western democracy. While the West celebrated this victory as a moral victory of its own values, this also entailed a certain moral responsibility for the peoples who had been freed from tyranny. The US and Western European states quickly set out to develop strategies to support democratic transitions and the establishment of liberal market economies. From a Western perspective, the overthrow of authoritarian leaders in the Arab world did not symbolize the victory of one ideology over the other. Instead, economically and politically crisis-ridden policy makers in the West lacked enthusiasm for the developments in their southern neighbourhood.

Neoliberal economic policies had found their way into the Arab world from the 1970s on. A state-centric economic model was gradually replaced by a neo-liberal model. Economic liberalization diversified neither political nor economic power centres. Contrary to expectations that political liberalism would follow economic liberalism with seeming inevitability (Fukuyama 1989), neoliberal restructuring programmes strengthened the authoritarian systems even further. Political liberalizations remained limited and led in many countries to controlled multi-party systems, dominated by the ruling parties. As the regimes held all ultimate powers in their hands, their highest representatives, including the ruling families, directed privatization and regulated access to the national market through the granting of licences. Hence, economic liberalization under authoritarianism fostered cronyism and helped supply clientalistic networks with financial benefits and buttressed neo-patrimonialistic, monarchic presidential systems.

Economic restructuring did not help reduce poverty, but instead widened the social gap. The Tunisian experience displayed that there is no positive linear correlation between economic growth, the reduction of poverty and the improvement of human development indicators (Hurt et al. 2009: 307). From a macroeconomic perspective, the Tunisian economy was doing remarkably well before the outbreak of the Arab Spring. Economic growth had averaged five percent per annum since the 1990s. Tunisia was hailed as a success story, not only in the MENA region, but in Africa as a whole. This was mainly due to perceptions of business-friendly government policies and a favourable macroeconomic environment. According to the World Bank's *Doing Business Report 2010*, Tunisia was among the top ten most improved economies in terms of business regulation. The country was praised as a model for private sector competitiveness (IILS 2011: 40). However, in reality, a steady decline in capital accumulation in the public sector could not be compensated by a rise in private investments, and whilst there were annual growth rates of between 4-5%, the country could not create new jobs or reduce unemployment (Hurt et al. 2009: 307). Economic liberalization policies did not support the increase in developed industries, but they did support the region's global function as a location for labour intensive production (AFDB 2012: 28). Moreover, those who benefited from economic growth were members of a small circle of businessmen with strong affiliations with the presidential family.

Economic restructuring in line with the (pre-)conditions of the IMF (International Monetary Fund) induced the state's slow and covert withdrawal from public services. This process was accompanied by the substitution of formalized means of engagement between state and society and of enforceable citizen rights with a new "social pact of informality". Informal networks based on kinship, neighbourhood, origin or religious affiliations replaced or merged with formal controlled channels such as the ruling parties, the trade unions or syndicates (Harders 2008). Ideologically vacated, political institutions such as the ruling party dwindled to mere patronage networks, increasingly dominated by business elites, loyal to the regime. More than political parties in the classical sense, the ruling parties were a conglomeration of individuals who sought proximity to the regime. The parties were welded together through the "presidential majority", which guaranteed that legislation worked to the benefit of the regime. Elections were a farce. Gerrymandering, manipulations and fraud guaranteed that the ruling parties had strong majorities within parliament and that the opposition was tamed (Günay 2008: 300).

The state's almost total withdrawal from welfare and social policies led to the rise of un-institutionalized and hybrid social activities, particularly among the disenfranchised. Silent encroachments such as the land-take over, illegal constructions or street vendors selling their products illegally on the streets have challenged the authority of the state (Bayat 1997: 55).

At the same time, Islamic welfare and charity organizations emerged as one of the few well-organized alternatives. They gradually compensated the state's eroding welfare services. Particularly in remote and neglected areas, Islamic organisations replaced the state's role (Günay 2012). Thus, economic restructuring not only limited the government's scope of action in directing and influencing social policy, but also its authority and hegemony.

Different Islamic actors on the stage

Having a relatively long history of service provision, being deeply entrenched in the grassroots of society and having widespread networks, NGOs with Islamic affiliation are a major force for change (Allam 2012). One can distinguish between more traditional Islamic NGOs (such as *vakf,* Islamic endowments) based on traditional teachings, active in social work and mainly funded by *zakat* (alms), and modern Islamic NGOs which operate in fields such as human rights, education, social justice and empowerment and which are funded through donations (Allam 2012).

Besides these more institutionalized Islamic NGOs, religious networks around independent mosques and street sheikhs developed into important informal non-governmental agents. These, for instance Salafists, mainly gained a foothold in rural-urban areas, which were neglected by the state authorities. Rural-urban areas are impoverished, previously rural areas at the periphery of growing cities, inhabited by poor people with mainly poor education backgrounds. In the absence of the state, mosques have been the centres of authority, information exchange and personal encounter. Mosque related organisations such as charity and welfare networks or education institutes have played an important role in the socialization of young people.

In the wake of the Arab uprisings, Islamists of various shades came to the political arena. Even Salafists, who had been considered to be an apolitical movement, decided to form parties and to participate in elections. While Islamists have gained a dominant role in post-revolutionary Tunisia and Egypt, they have been careful to act within the framework of the constitutional orders. Despite their growing adaptation to the system, Islamist parties and organizations have tried to distinguish themselves as being the only real alternatives to the old regimes and as being the defenders of change, social justice and integrity.

European Neighbourhood Policy towards the region

European and American policies towards the region have traditionally been informed by security considerations. From a European perspective, due to geographic proximity and a number of historical and economic linkages, Europe has been highly vulnerable to spill over effects of terrorism, migration, trade or energy disruptions from the region. Security concerns also played a role in the Euro-Mediterranean Partnership (EMP), initiated in 1995 by the Barcelona Declaration. Following European enlargement in 2004, the EU sought to re-define relations with neighbouring countries that will not become members of the European Union, at least in the foreseeable future. According to the European Commission, the European Neighbourhood Policy (ENP) is "designed to prevent the emergence of new dividing lines between the enlarged EU and its neighbours", while offering them the "chance to participate in various EU activities, through greater political, security, economic and cultural cooperation" (Del Sarto/Schumacher 2005: 20).

The ENP has sought to approximate legal and administrative standards in neighbouring countries to those of the Union as a means of managing interdependence and fostering integration below membership at the level of sectors (Freyburg 2011). This entails the export of legal norms, processes, procedures and common rules into its periphery. Schimmelfennig (2010: 5) labels the EU as a power that is: "civilizing the international system by transforming it into a system of rule-based governance according to its own model". In that regard, the ENP is about creating a geographical space broader than its borders that is governed by common rules. Or as the former President of the Commission Romano Prodi called it: "Everything but the institutions" (Balfour 2012: 17). Thus, what the EU had to offer its neighbours was more engagement and integration into parts of its single market; however, it did this only by leaving the important areas of agriculture and migration aside.

The EU's strategy towards the region was not designed to promote democracy, but to maintain peace and create security through economic cooperation and migration management. The Arab regimes were important partners in controlling irregular migration, securing peace and stability in the region (Pax Americana) and in regard to energy issues. In the post-9/11 environment, Arab dictators became indispensable allies in the "War on Terror". Although these policies towards the region also included a call for reform, democratization and respect for human rights and were accompanied by increased financial support for civil society, this felt like double-talk as sensitivities with regard to human rights abuses were rather low, particularly when Islamists were concerned (Mullin/Shahshabani 2001, Tocci 2011). On the other hand, the authoritarian regimes used the new security paradigm to eliminate their oppositions.

Generally, the EU's already weak efforts to promote democratization and political reform faced a setback around 2005 and 2006 when Islamist parties such as Hamas and the Muslim Brotherhood made substantial gains in elections. In the eyes of many Arabs who saw the European Union as the paramount example of a benign democracy promoter and as a welcomed counterweight to American security driven policies in the region, the EU lost credibility when it decided together with the US to punish Palestinians for the electoral victory of Hamas. Instead, the EU increasingly decided to concentrate on economic integration and to leave out controversial political issues. The Union for the Mediterranean founded in 2008 under the aegis of French President Nicolas Sarkozy in order to re-launch the Euro-Mediterranean Partnership mainly focused on economic development, environmental issues, education and infrastructure projects. Thus, one can conclude that the EU and its members' strategies towards the region entailed political and economic partnership with the authoritarian elites, who had become important allies in the fight against irregular migration and terrorism. Focusing on economic cooperation, the EU had also increasingly abandoned its rhetoric on human rights and political reform. The rationalization of this strategy was that economic reform would eventually spill over to political reforms.

More economic integration for more reforms?

The revolts in the Arab world demonstrated the weakness of EU policies towards the region. Despite self-criticism that the EU and its member states had fallen prey to the assumption that authoritarian regimes were a guarantee for stability in the region (Füle in Tocci 2011), the EU has not been able to radically change its strategies. Instead, the EU adjusted and revised its established policies. The EU offered further economic integration and promised financial support for emergent Arab civil society.

In order to award political reform with economic integration, the EU introduced the so-called "more for more" approach as a tool in relations with the countries in the region. Based on EU conditionality in relations with candidate countries, the "more for more" approach aims at rewarding those countries that have embarked on the reform path with more economic integration and increased financial support (ENPI – European Neighbourhood Instrument, the SPRING – Support for Partnerships, Reforms and Inclusive Growth and CSF – Civil Society Facility). While conditionality has proved to be an important tool in the "Europeanization" process of candidate countries, the "more for more" approach as a weakened form of conditionality has various shortcomings. On the one hand, it further propagates inequality and hierarchy in relations between Europe and its south, which are already charged with a common colonial past. On the other hand, the tool does not entail any real incentives for the countries in the south. Whereas the conditionality principle has been based on membership perspective, the "more for more" tool does not offer anything comparable to it. Moreover, the process is dictated more by the EU's needs and conditions rather than oriented to the needs of its partners.[1] Another deficiency in the strategy is that the "more for more" approach does not provide any mechanisms in case of setbacks in the reform and democratization process, as was the case in the Egyptian example of 2013.

The promotion of European models of democratization

In reaction to the uprisings, the EU announced to substantially increase financial support for Arab civil society and acknowledged that there is a need to extend engagement with civil society actors. In this regard, the EU launched several initiatives and policy tools, for instance the new Neighbourhood Civil Society Facility that aims to strengthen civil society and to enable

---

[1] The EU has promoted the creation of a Free Trade Area with MENA – it was first proposed at the beginning of the Barcelona Process in 1995 and was provisioned to be realised in 2010 – however, it is also rather clear that the terms of such a Free Trade Area would be set by the EU.

it to promote reform and increase accountability (Behr/Siitonen 2012). However, the EU's strategies do not address the question of how to reach out to civil society organizations beyond Western-style NGOs, new platforms and social movements that are, however, playing a crucial role in the ongoing changes (ibid).

The EU's focus on European experiences as a point of reference suggests a universal linear line of development which puts democracy, as a genuinely Western value, at the top of an evolutionary civilizational process (Sadiki 2004). In the post-cold war era it has been the model of liberal democracy which has become universally dominant. "[…] Especially in the UN, the core of what is understood to be democracy conforms to a fairly standard view of liberal democracy as entailing free and fair elections and constitutional guarantees of individual political civil and associational rights" (Kurki 2010: 365). It is not only the concept, but also the meaning of democracy which has been universalized. The model of liberal democracy has become hegemonic in the democratization discourse.

After the third global wave of democratization which swept through Latin America, moved on to Asia and decimated dictatorship in the Soviet bloc (Huntington 1991), the question why the Arab/Muslim world was not seized by the wave of democratization emerged. Neo-orientalists defended a new universalism to which the Arab/Muslim world was seemingly an exception. According to these ideas, obstacles to democratization were deeply rooted in cultural factors. The oft-repeated orientalist cliché was that Islam is not just a religion but a total way of life. These scholars ascribe any political or social particularity to the Islamic religion. They portray Islam as a social entity whose "essential" core is immune to change (Sadowski 1993: 16). Thus, Islam was considered incompatible with the Western ideals of liberal democracy entailing individual liberties, women's rights, human rights and the rule of law. Orientalists and neo-orientalists have mistakenly overemphasized cultural and religious aspects and have ignored other variables that have shaped the history and societal development of the Middle East, such as colonialism, rapid urbanization, socio-economic dislocations and others. Besides the fact that Islam has undeniably influenced local culture, most of the Middle Eastern societies face the same problems as people in other developing countries.

An orientalist perspective – one which puts European/Western experiences at the centre of considerations – risks ignoring important regional and domestic dynamics.

Although the EU claims not to promote a single model of democracy, there is a broad consensus on the belief that democracy promotion entails liberal democracy promotion, that is the promotion of certain key liberal democratic procedures – encompassing electoral processes and the institutionalization of rule of law, freedoms of expression, press and association (Kurki 2010: 2012).

Vivid and pluralist civil society has often been seen as a sine qua non of democratization. Some, mainly secular, Arab intellectuals believed that the resurgence of civil society, connected with economic liberalization from the 1970s on, would be evidence for democratic transformation in the Arab World. The renowned Egyptian scholar Saad Eddin Ibrahim argued, for instance, that civil society constitutes an optimum channel of popular participation in governance. Ibrahim also highlighted that the reinforcement of civil society also implies values and behavioural codes of tolerating and accepting others and a tacit or explicit commitment to the peaceful management of differences among individuals and collectivities, sharing the same public space or state (Ibrahim 1995: 28-29).

However, civil society in the form of voluntary associations is essentially dependent on a state under the rule of law, a condition which was hardly met by Arab autocracies, where the government controlled any possibility of altering the legal framework and where the constitution was limited by the state of emergency laws. In Egypt, the Mubarak regime applied, in most cases of civil organizations' applications for licence, the same formula: licences were refused on security grounds, but the organizations were allowed to be formed and to function with a high public profile. This practice illustrated the contradictions in the regime; on the one hand, the regime was characterized by authoritarian rigidity when it came to preventing potential political opposition, and yet on the other hand it was informed by a high sensitivity to international public opinion, before which Mubarak's Egypt had to appear moderate and liberal (Zubaida 1992). In Tunisia, the regime promoted secular women's rights organizations. Their female activism was seen as part of the regime's secular modernization paradigm, as a weapon against Islamism and as an important flagship for Tunisia's international image. Since civil society's existence and scope of operation were dependent on the state's goodwill, emerging civil society could not contribute to the democratization of the system.

EU policies towards the region in the framework of the Barcelona Process also entailed the promotion of an active role for civil society in the Arab world. However, Arab governments were eager to tightly control the process and only a small number of government-approved organizations were eligible for EU funding and cooperation (Behr/Siitonen 2013: 20).

Many of the EU's additional initiatives aim at strengthening emergent civil society in the Arab world by offering financial support and assisting in the interconnection with European NGOs. The new emphasis on civil society reflects a long-term trend in Western development assistance that has highlighted civil society's role in promoting good governance, democracy and economic development (ibid: 6).

However, while the EU has highlighted the importance of active civil society engagement, it has been rather normative in its definition of civil society. Despite the fact that even within Europe civil society does not represent a uniform concept, but has rather been shaped by different traditions, in particular with regard to relations with the state, there have been serious doubts whether the European perspective, which builds on specific experiences from 18th century Europe, does have explanatory power for the complexities of associational life beyond European societies, such as in Africa (Behr/Siitonen 2012: 8). The rigid Western/European conceptualization of civil society ignores a variety of Islamic organizations and networks which have built upon the notion of brotherhood, and it has certainly belittled vast arrays of often un-institutionalized and hybrid social activities such as informal networks (Bayat 1997: 55).

Despite its crucial role in the region, Europe has, so far, failed to reach out effectively to Islamist actors and organizations. Islamists, often without any distinctions, are considered to be enemies of democracy. Instead, government and EU programmes, but also peers from within European civil society, have almost exclusively established contacts with secular civil society organizations. Most of these organizations have advocated the importance of a specific principle such as women's rights or human rights. They are often interlinked with Western partners through international networks and projects, but most importantly they are almost entirely dependent on foreign funding. They often have strong support abroad but shallow roots at home, allowing them to be easily discredited by hostile governments (Langohr 2004: 182).

Secular civil society organizations (CSOs) have mainly been dominated by representatives of the elites. Their fields of interest, campaigns and social activities have reflected the worldview and the approaches of the secular, often western educated, elites. After the uprisings, many of these secular CSOs have been blamed for their affiliations with the old regimes. The fact that women's rights had been a subject taken up and promoted by two former Egyptian first ladies certainly complicated the situation of CSOs operating in this field after the uprisings.

Conclusion

The developments in the Middle East have rekindled debates contesting the universality of the cultural premises that infuse European and Western institutions and practices (Schaffer 1998: 14). The blurring of religion and politics is common place in politics in the Middle East, even under self-professed secular elites (Sadiki 2004: 9). Whereas minimum standards with regard to human rights, women's rights and minority rights have gained ground and have become a part of the political discourse of all political parties, liberalism has a different connotation in the Arab context. Liberalism with regard to societal questions does not usually entail liberal positions with regard to such controversial issues as gay rights or extra-martial sex. The number of those who support greater liberalism in these areas are marginal or even nonexistent. Conservative moral values, closely connected with religious values, have prevailed. "Since the 'death of God' in the West, liberal democracy has, more or less, assumed the role of a new religion, and the nation-state has become quasi transcendental. This death has no analogue in the Middle East" (Sadiki 2004: 8). Although the normative claims of Western democracy have been challenged in the Middle East, the democratic ideal has not (Sadiki 2004: 9).

The fact that Islamist parties and Islamic organizations are important agents of change and that they are playing a pivotal role in the countries' political transitions makes them important counterparts for European partnership programmes.

Although Islamists claim authenticity and are trying to bridge globalized modernity with local culture, their discourses have been strongly influenced by global discourses. Faced with the despotism of illiberal authoritarian regimes, Islamists increasingly adopted notions of democracy, human rights, political freedoms and accountability in their conceptions. What Asef Bayat and others have termed as "post-Islamism" represents an endeavour to fuse religiosity and rights, faith and freedom, Islam and liberty (Bayat 2007).[2] Instead of trying to promote its own understanding of liberal democracy that is deeply rooted in the enlightenment's critique of Christianity and based on secularization, Europe should consider that there are different paths to democracy.

While Islamists are not flawless democrats, neither are secularists. On the contrary, since the Arab uprisings, secularist opposition parties have often relied on the support of non-elected institutions such as the army or the higher courts, rather than embracing democratic means such as persuading the electorate, while Islamists were able to promote themselves as the champions of democracy.

Eurocentric normative approaches blur the West's view of reality and create false categories of good and evil, which do nothing but reflect European fears. A dogmatic universalist understanding of liberal democracy prevents the development of new strategies and approaches. A critical approach entails

---

[2] Bayat defines post-Islamism first in reference to post-Khomeini Iran. The term describes the departure from ideological Islamist concepts and constructions in favour of pragmatism and policy approaches. However, this did not mean that Islamists lost their belief in Islamic politics, rather it entails the analysis that the focus shifted from legal and purely political issues to moral and behavioural ones. Bayat mentions in this context that post-Islamism is not anti-Islamic, but rather reflects the tendency to re-secularize religion, as it is marked by a call to limit the ideological role of religion.

a closer look at developments within Europe – such as the unresolved question of how to integrate migrant communities into liberal democracy and open to them channels of participation – but also a critical engagement with populist, nationalist and xenophobic tendencies within Europe. The developments in the south could serve as a trigger for questioning foundationalist approaches with regard to liberal democracy.

References

Allam, Rabha (2012), "Engaging with traditional and modern Islamic NGOs in Egypt." IRP Cairo Policy Brief 3, May 2012. Cairo: Flemish Institute.

Balfour, Rosa (2012), "EU Conditionality after the Arab Spring." Papers IEMed 16, June 2012.

Bayat, Asef (1997), "Un-Civil Society: The Politics of the informal people." *Third World Quarterly*, 18:1, 53-72.

Bayat, Asef (2007), *Making Islam Democratic. Social Movements and the Post-Islamist Turn, Stanford Studies in Middle Eastern and Islamic Studies and Cultures.* Stanford, CA: Stanford University Press.

Behr, Timo, and Aaretti Siitonen (2013), "Building Bridges or Digging Trenches? Civil Society Engagement after the Arab Spring." Working Paper 77, January 2013. Helsinki: FIIA.

Del Sarto, Raffaella, and Tobias Schumacher (2005), "From EMP to ENP: What's at Stake with the European Neighbourhood Policy towards the Southern Mediterranean?" *European Foreign Affairs Review*, 10:1, 17-38.

Durac, Vincent, and Francesco Cavatorta (2009), "Strengthening Authoritarian Rule Through Democracy Promotion? Examining the Paradox of the US and EU Security Strategies: The Case of Bin Ali's Tunisia." *British Journal of Middle Eastern Studies*, 36:1, 3-19.

Freyburg, Tina (2011), "Transgovernmental networks as catasts for democratic change? EU functional cooperation with Arab authoritarian regimes and socialization of involved state officials into democratic governance." *Democratization*, 18:4, 1001-1025.

Fukuyama, Francis (1989), "The End of History." *The National Interest*, Summer 1989.

Günay, Cengiz (2008), *From Islamists to Muslim Democrats? The trajectory of Islamism in Egypt and Turkey against the background of historical, political and economic developments.* Saarbrücken: VDM.

Günay, Cengiz (2012), *The marriage of Islamism and the system.* Policy Brief No.32/2012. Istanbul. Global Political Trends Center.

Günay, Cengiz (2013), *Tunisia at the Crossroads. A Study on Transition and Democracy Consolidation.* Unpublished study, Vienna, March 2013.

Harders, Cilja (2008), "Autoritarismus von unten: Lokale Politik in Ägypten." *GIGA Fokus Nahost*, No. 12/2008.

Harders, Cilja (2002), *Staatsanalyse von Unten: urbane Armut und politische Partizipation in Ägypten. Mikro- und mesopolitische Analysen unterschiedlicher Kaioer Stadtteile.* Hamburg: Deutsches Orientinstitut.

Hurt, Stephen, Karim Knio, and J. Magnus Ryner (2009), "Social Forces and the Effects of (Post)-Washington Consensus Policy in Africa: Comparing Tunisia and South Africa." *The Round Table: The Commonwealth Journal of International Affairs*, 98:402, 301-317.

Ibrahim, Saad Eddin (1995), "Civil Society and Prospects of Democratization in the Arab World." In *Civil Society in the Middle East*, Volume 1, edited by Augustus Richard Norton, Leiden: E.J. Brill Publishers, 27-55.

IILS – The International Institute for Labour Studies (2011), *Studies on growth with equity.* Tunisia: A new Contract for Fair and Equitable Growth.

Kurki, Milja (2010), "Democracy and Conceptual Contestability: Reconsidering Conceptions of Democracy in Democracy Promotion." *International Studies Review*, 12:3, 362-386.

Kurki, Milja (2012), "How the EU can adopt a new type of democracy support." Fride-Working Paper No 12, Madrid: FRIDE.

Langohr, Vickie (2004), "Too much Civil Society, Too Little Politics: Egypt and Liberalizing Arab Regimes." *Comparative Politics*, 36:2, 181-204.

Lavenex, Sandra, and Frank Schimmelfennig (2011), "EU democracy promotion in the neighbourhood: from leverage to governance?" *Democratization*, 18:4, 885-909.

Mullin, Corinna, and Azadeh Shahshahani (2011), "Western Complicity in the crimes of the Ben Ali regime." *Open Democracy*, 24-06-11.

Norton, Augustus Richard, ed. (1995), *Civil Society in the Middle East*. Leiden: E.J. Brill Publishers.

Sadiki, Larbi (2004), *The Search for Arab democracy. Discourses and Counter-Discourses.* New York, NY: Columbia University Press.

Sadowski, Yahya (1993), "The New Orientalism and the Democracy Debate." *Middle East Report*, 183, Political Islam, 14-21+40.

Schaffer, Frederic C. (1998), *Democracy in Translation. Understanding politics in an unfamiliar culture.* New York, NY: Cornell University Press.

Schimmelfennig, Frank (2010), Europeanization beyond member states, unpublished manuscript, available from: http://www.eup.ethz.ch/people/schimmelfennig/publications/10_ZSE_Europeanization_manuscript_.pdf [20-08-13].

Schraeder, Peter J., and Hamadi Redissi (2011), "Ben Ali's Fall." *Journal of Democracy*, 22:3, 5-19.

Tocci, Nathalie (2011), "Rethinking EuroMed policies in the light of the Arab Spring." *Open Democracy*, 03-25-11.

Zubaida, Sami (1992), "Islam, The State & Democracy. Contrasting Conceptions of Society in Egypt." *Middle East Report*, 179:22, 2-10.

Dilemmata europäischer Palästinapolitik

John Bunzl

„Israel and Palestine are not two different places that can be imagined to coexist side by side, but are in effect different readings of the same place... Against the endless search for the form and mechanisms of "perfect" separation comes the realization that a viable solution does not exist within the realm of territorial design. Instead, a non-territorial approach based on cooperation, mutuality, and equality must be taken to bring about a new politics of space sharing." Eyal Weizman

Am 19. Juli 2013 veröffentlichte das „Amtsblatt der Europäischen Union" neue Leitlinien für die Vergabe von Forschungsförderungen an israelische Institutionen. Die EU stellt darin eine Bedingung: keine finanzielle Unterstützung für israelische Projekte, die in Siedlungen jenseits der Grenze von 1967 („Grüne Linie"), also in den besetzten Gebieten, durchgeführt werden. Als entsprechende Territorien werden ausdrücklich genannt: die Westbank, die Golan-Höhen und Ost-Jerusalem. Die Richtlinien sind für das 2014 startende EU-Programm „Horizon 2020" relevant. In allen Verträgen, die ab 2014 mit der EU geschlossen werden, sollen Siedlungen aus dem künftigen Forschungsprogramm ausgeschlossen sein. Zuvor waren schon Maßnahmen zur Kennzeichnung von Produkten aus den Siedlungen in den besetzten Gebieten beschlossen worden. Bisher etikettierten allerdings nur Großbritannien, Niederlande und Dänemark Siedlungsprodukte explizit als solche. Bis Ende 2013 sollen, laut Außenkommissarin Catherine Ashton, alle EU Mitglieder erklären, wie sie die Vorschrift umsetzen (TAZ 08-08-13).

Die darauf folgende Kontroverse war paradigmatisch: Arabische Stimmen begrüßten – nicht überraschend – die vorgesehenen Vorgangsweisen. Die EU habe viel zu lange gewartet, hätte zugesehen wie von ihr finanzierte Projekte durch israelische Repression zerstört wurden, und anderes mehr. (Shabi 2013) Die jeweils wichtigsten wirtschaftlichen Beziehungen zu Israel und zur PA (Palestinian Authority) machen die EU tatsächlich zum bedeutendsten

Sponsor des israelisch-palästinensischen Status Quo – und damit auch der Okkupation (Cronin 2010).

Siedler wiederum organisierten eine von Juristen ausgearbeitete Petition an Ashton, in der sie die „Grüne Linie" als völkerrechtlich inexistent bezeichnen und die Anwendbarkeit der Genfer Konvention (1949), wonach der Transfer von eigener Bevölkerung in besetzte Gebiete unzulässig sei, als nicht gegeben ansehen. In Gesprächen mit dem EU Foreign Affairs Committee beklagte das Knesset-Mitglied Ayelet Shaked von der Siedler-Partei Habayit Hayehudi (Das jüdische Haus) die „Delegitimierung von Teilen Israels", die sie als den „neuen Antisemitismus" bezeichnete (Forsher 2013). Der „alte Antisemitismus führte zur Zerstörung unseres Volkes in den Gaskammern" (ebd.). Der (voreilige und taktische) Antisemitismus-Vorwurf durchzieht die Argumentation der Siedler-Vertreter. So meinte Shaked etwa (ebd.): „Wenn Europa denkt, Juden würden zu den Tagen zurückkehren, wo ihre Produkte gekennzeichnet waren – dann können Sie das vergessen". So die – häufig ins Treffen geführte – Anspielung auf den Nazi Boykott-Aufruf: "Kauft nicht bei Juden" (Bunzl 2012a). Eine ähnliche bewusste Argumentationslinie findet sich in der Behauptung, Europa sei von den Kräften des radikalen Islam besetzt und eine fortschreitende „Islamisierung" des Kontinents sei der Schlüssel zum Verständnis von negativen Haltungen gegenüber Juden und/oder Israel (vgl. Bunzl 2012b).

In Israel wurde nicht nach den eventuell legitimen Gründen der EU-Richtlinien gefragt, sondern die Schwachstelle im eigenen Außenministerium gesucht, das sich hätte „überraschen" lassen und „unvorbereitet" gewesen sei. Man müsse die „Schuldigen" ausfindig machen (Somfalvi 2013). Bei EU-Israel Verhandlungen in Brüssel (Rettman 2013) drängte Israel auf eine Verschiebung der Maßnahmen; auch die USA wurden ersucht in diesem Sinn auf die EU einzuwirken. Israelische Delegierte argumentierten gegen die Festlegung von Grenzen, wie sie im europäischen Dokument explizit vorgenommen wird. Die Grenzen von 1967 („Grüne Linie") seien irrelevant und/oder inakzeptabel geworden. Sie seien höchstens ein Verhandlungsgegenstand aber keine Vorbedingung. Das gelte besonders für Ost-Jerusalem, das im israelischen Diskurs als Teil der ewigen und ungeteilten Hauptstadt des Landes gefeiert wird.

Die europäischen Maßnahmen lösten in Israel heftige Debatten aus. In einem Editorial begrüßte etwa die Zeitung Haaretz (27-11-13) die „Leitlinien" als wichtigen Beitrag zur Zukunft Israels. Prominente WissenschaftlerInnen meldeten sich zu Wort und forderten die Regierung auf, einen „Kompromiss" mit der EU anzustreben (Haaretz 26-11-13). Israel würde sonst die lukrative Beteiligung am höchstentwickelten Forschungsprogramm (Horizon 2020) verlieren (ebd.). Die EU zeigte sich jedoch nur in unwesentlichen Details „kompromissbereit".

Darüber hinaus richteten 600 israelische Intellektuelle einen Brief an Ashton (ECCP 2013), sich von den Protesten nicht beeinflussen zu lassen. Stellvertretend argumentierte Avraham Burg (2013), ehemals Vorsitzender der Knesset und Präsident der Zionistischen Weltorganisation, Europa wäre ein unentbehrlicher politischer Player im Nahen Osten. Ohne Europa seien keine substantiellen Änderungen möglich. Die neuen Richtlinien der EU seien weise und gerecht. Es müsse zwischen Israel „proper"[1] und der Okkupation unterschieden werden. Kritik an der Okkupation und den Siedlungen sei weder anti-israelisch noch gar anti-semitisch. „Israel ja, Siedlungen nein".

In ähnlichem Sinn sprachen sich zahlreiche ehemalige europäische Führungspersönlichkeiten aus (Ravid 2013). Unter der Führung des früheren französischen Außenministers Hubert Vedrine unterzeichneten u.a. Javier Solana, Miguel Moratinos und Benita Ferrero-Waldner einen Text, der besonders in Hinblick auf die laufenden Verhandlungen zur israelischen Beteiligung am Forschungs-Programm „Horizon 2020" von Bedeutung ist. Dem Argument, die Richtlinien würden dem „Friedensprozess" schaden, halten sie entgegen, dass die fortgesetzte Siedlungstätigkeit das eigentliche Hindernis sei. Demgegenüber seien die Leitlinien das „Minimum", das die EU tun könne, um Steuergelder nicht in die Kolonisierung der besetzten Gebiete fließen zu lassen. Zukünftige Vereinbarungen müssten klarmachen, dass diese Gebiete nicht Teil Israels sind und daher nicht in den Genuss europäischer Investitionen geraten könnten. Erläuternd wird an anderer Stelle hinzugefügt, dass die europäische Haltung zu den Siedlungen mit jener gegenüber Nord-

---

[1] Der Begriff bezieht sich auf die Grenzen Israels vor 1967.

Zypern vergleichbar wäre und zwar im Sinn einer Nicht-Anerkennung von vollendeten Tatsachen (Haaretz 22-09-13).

Zwei Staaten als Problem

Als Konsensus der internationalen (vor allem auch europäischen) Diplomatie gilt die so genannte Zweistaatenlösung: Israel in den Grenzen von 1967 neben einem palästinensischen Staat in der Westbank, Ost-Jerusalem und Gaza. Als Haupthindernis für dieses Projekt gelten die israelischen Siedlungen und in zweiter Linie die politische Spaltung zwischen Westbank (Fatah) und Gaza (Hamas). Da der Kolonisierungsprozess schon sehr weit fortgeschritten ist und weiter zügig voranschreitet, gibt es ernsthafte Zweifel an der realistischen Umsetzbarkeit einer Zweistaatenlösung. Dennoch hält die europäische Politik weiterhin an einer Zweistaatenlösung mit einem israelischen und einem zukünftigen palästinensischen Staat – ähnlich wie auf Zypern – fest, auch wenn diese Lösung in der Wirklichkeit immer unwahrscheinlicher wird. Es drängt sich daher die Frage auf, ob nicht schon jetzt auch mit der Suche nach alternativen Szenarien begonnen werden sollte. Bisher hat die Europäische Kommission im Rahmen der Nachbarschaftspolitik versucht, über ökonomische Entwicklung Staaten mit in ihr Wertesystem einzubinden („Conditionality").

Im Falle Israels haben die Differenzen zwischen der EU und der israelischen Siedlungspolitik allerdings zu keinem Rückgang in den wirtschaftlichen Beziehungen geführt. Im Gegenteil: Israel genießt nach wie vor einen privilegierten Zugang (seit 1996) etwa zu europäischen Forschungsprogrammen, die einen nicht unwesentlichen Beitrag zur israelischen High-Tech Ökonomie darstellen. Im Jahr 2004 betrug das bilaterale Handelsvolumen (Diamanten ausgenommen) mehr als 15 Milliarden Euro. 33% der israelischen Exporte gingen in die EU und fast 40% der Importe stammten von dort. Dennoch hat der Umfang der wirtschaftlichen Beziehungen bisher keine „politischen Früchte" im Sinne besonders eines Entgegenkommens in der Siedlungspolitik getragen. Europaweite Umfragen zeigen Präferenzen für eine „ausgewogenere" Politik in Nahost. Mehrheiten befürworteten etwa den palästinensischen

Antrag um Anerkennung bei den Vereinten Nationen (Herbst 2011, Witney 2013: 21); auch in Deutschland.

Diese Stimmung wird nicht immer von europäischen Regierungspolitiken widergespiegelt. Viele Faktoren wie wirtschaftliche Interessen, Sicherheitsinteressen (hauptsächlich im High-Tech und im militärischen Bereich), sowie diesbezüglicher Druck von Seiten der USA (der entsprechend den amerikanisch-israelischen Beziehungen variieren kann), bzw. die historische Verantwortung Europas, aber auch die Angst vor dem Antisemitismusvorwurf beeinflussen europäische– und insbesondere deutsche – Eliten. Signifikant ist in diesem Zusammenhang die Frage der Aufwertung des Staates Palästina zum Beobachter bei den Vereinten Nationen, wo sich sogar Deutschland der Stimme enthielt. Dies gilt als ein Abrücken von der bedingungslos pro-israelischen Position dieser europäischen Schlüsselmacht. Insgesamt hat also eine kritische Distanzierung von bestimmten israelischen Politiken stattgefunden, allerdings vorwiegend und vorläufig auf einer symbolischen Ebene.

Ein Ansatz zur Umsetzung in konkrete Maßnahmen kann in den eingangs besprochenen „Leitlinien" gesehen werden. Diese resultierten letztendlich aus der Perzeption von drohender Irreversibilität der Kolonisierungsprozesse in der Westbank und damit der Undurchführbarkeit eines Zweistaaten-Projekts, wenn darunter ein unabhängiger, lebensfähiger, territorial verbundener Staat neben Israel gemeint sein sollte. Das Wort „Apartheid" für die Verhältnisse in der Westbank und Ost-Jerusalem wurde enttabuisiert; selbst der ehemalige US Präsident Jimmy Carter verwendete den Begriff, das so genannte „A-word", im Titel seines Buches über den Konflikt (Carter 2006).

Welche Zukunft erwartet die PalästinenserInnen unter solchen Voraussetzungen?

Indirekt wird die Antwort in israelischen Diskussionen über die so genannte demografische Frage gesucht. Eine Seite sieht in einer stabilen jüdischen Mehrheit die Voraussetzung für das Selbstverständnis Israels als jüdischer und demokratischer Staat – die andere Seite kann sich die Herrschaft einer jüdisch-israelischen Minderheit vorstellen, welche durch Abschiebung von

PalästinenserInnen und/oder eine jüdische Masseneinwanderung in die Herrschaft einer Mehrheit umgewandelt würde. Das Primat liegt in beiden Fällen beim jüdischen und nicht beim demokratischen Element. Mehrheitsherrschaft wird ethnokratisch definiert, wie die Lage der palästinensischen Minderheit in Israel „proper" beweist. Rund 20% der israelischen BürgerInnen sind PalästinenserInnen. Sie werden allerdings nicht als nationale Minderheit anerkannt und werden meist als AraberInnen bezeichnet (dazu v.a. Yiftachel 2006).

In Europa scheint allerdings der Punkt erreicht worden zu sein, wo einer immer kritischeren Rhetorik nun auch vorsichtige Maßnahmen folgen. Die neuen Leitlinien der EU sind ein erster Schritt in dieser Hinsicht. Sie sollen Israel „überreden", den Kolonisationsprozess zu beenden und eine De-Kolonisierung der besetzten Gebiete einzuleiten, und sie sollen den PalästinenserInnen helfen, eine lebensfähige Ökonomie und Staatlichkeit aufzubauen. Deshalb sollten europäische Aktivitäten gegenüber den Siedlungen und Israel „proper" strikt unterschieden werden. Es müsse Israel klargemacht werden, dass die Intensivierung der Beziehungen zu Europa nicht ohne eine Berücksichtigung europäischer Interessen weitergehen könne (vgl. Witney 2013).

Alternativen?

Die EU hält an der Zweistaaten-Formel fest und unterstützt den „Friedensprozess". Seit Jahrzehnten liegt jedoch der Schwerpunkt mehr auf dem „Prozess" als am Ziel, dem „Frieden". In den letzten 20 Jahren hat sich die Zahl der Siedler in der Westbank mehr als verdoppelt. Sie liegt – inklusive Ost-Jerusalem – bei mehr als 500.000. Trotz der Existenz der Palestinian Authority (PA) hat Israel die Gebiete mit einer „Matrix der Kontrolle" (Halper 2009) zugunsten der Siedler überzogen. Laut Halper sind damit alle israelischen Maßnahmen auf politischem, rechtlichem und wirtschaftlichen Gebiet gemeint, welche die Okkupation aufrechterhalten und den Kolonisierungsprozess absichern, beziehungsweise irreversibel machen. Das Konzept von zwei Staaten konnte diesem Prozess nichts entgegensetzen. Selbst Barack Obama war es nicht gelungen, Benjamin Netanjahu zu einem (temporären) Stopp im

Siedlungsbau zu bewegen. Die israelische Führung nimmt zwar periodisch den Begriff „zwei Staaten" in den Mund, macht jedoch klar, dass ihre praktische Politik und ihre Verhandlungspositionen einen unabhängigen, lebensfähigen palästinensischen Staat nicht zulassen würden.

Außerdem stellt sie Bedingungen, von denen bekannt ist, dass sie für die palästinensische Seite kaum akzeptabel sind. Als ein Beispiel dafür gilt die Forderung die Palästinenser müssten zunächst Israel als Staat des jüdischen Volkes anerkennen. Dies ginge praktisch weit über die Anerkennung des Staates hinaus und würde auch die Anerkennung der Ideologie beziehungsweise die Legitimierung des Entstehungsprozesses auf Kosten der PalästinenserInnen bedeuten, ganz zu schweigen vom Leugnen nationaler Rechte der palästinensischen BürgerInnen Israels. Diese Forderungen zeigen im Übrigen, dass es den israelischen Führungen (und letztlich auch den PalästinenserInnen) nicht nur um 1967, sondern auch um 1948 geht; d.h. um Themen, die mit einer „unbewältigten Vergangenheit" zu tun haben. Das betrifft nicht nur die Frage der Flüchtlinge, sondern auch die Anerkennung, Legitimität, Unabhängigkeit und eine Reihe von Werten, die über eine territoriale Dimension des Konflikts hinausgehen. Palästinensische Unabhängigkeit in einem Teil des Landes zieht in zionistischer Sicht die Gefahr eines Anspruch auf den Rest des Landes nach sich; daher muss das eventuell entstehende Gebilde, wenn überhaupt, dann so konstruiert werden, dass es zu weitergehenden Ansprüchen nicht in der Lage ist. Die internationale Zweistaaten-Diplomatie berücksichtigt diese existenziellen, elementaren Aspekte zu wenig und hält sich mehr bei den Folgen als den Ursachen des Konflikts auf. Folglich wäre das Schwergewicht weniger auf territoriale Grenzziehungen und mehr um die Verwirklichung von individuellen und kollektiven Grundrechten zu orientieren (vgl. Lustick 2013). Hier könnte der Wertekatalog der EU relevant werden.

Im Vertrag über die Europäische Union (Lissabon) heißt es in Artikel 2: „Die Werte, auf die sich die Union gründet, sind die Achtung der Menschenwürde, Freiheit, Demokratie, Gleichheit, Rechtstaatlichkeit und die Wahrung der Menschenrechte einschließlich der Rechte der Personen, die Minderheiten angehören… Nichtdiskriminierung, Toleranz, Gerechtigkeit, Solidarität und Gleichheit". In Artikel 3 werden als Ziele der Frieden und das Wohlergehen der Völker genannt. In der Grundrechtscharta heißt es ebenso unmissverständlich: „Im Bewusstsein ihres geistig-religiösen und sittlichen Erbes gründet sich die Union auf die unteilbaren und universellen Werte der Würde des Menschen, der Freiheit, der Gleichheit und der Solidarität. Sie beruht auf den Grundsätzen der Demokratie und der Rechtstaatlichkeit"(Charta 2000).

Obwohl Israel bisher nicht um die Mitgliedschaft in der EU angesucht hat (einige Stimmen im Lande sprechen sich dafür aus), beinhalten auch die bisherigen Abkommen Verpflichtungen, vor allem im Bereich der Menschenrecht, die von Israel allerdings nicht eingehalten wurden.

Chronik der Beziehungen zwischen Israel und der EU

Ein erstes Freihandelsabkommen zwischen der EG und Israel wurde im Jahre 1975 abgeschlossen. Fünf Jahre später kam es zur historischen Erklärung von Venedig (1980), in der das Selbstbestimmungsrecht beziehungsweise das Recht auf einen Staat für die Palästinenser anerkannt wurde. Dieser Schritt stand auch im Zeichen der besonderen Bemühungen des österreichischen Bundeskanzlers Bruno Kreisky, der den Führer der PLO, Jasser Arafat, 1979 nach Wien einlud und als erster west-europäischer Staatschef die PLO anerkannte. 1981 errichtete die Europäische Kommission eine diplomatische Vertretung in Israel. Im Jahre 1995 erfolgten dann zwei wesentliche Schritte in den europäisch-israelischen Beziehungen: Einerseits unterzeichnete Israel die Barcelona-Erklärung zur Teilnahme am euro-mediterranen Partnerschaftsprogramm, andererseits wurde ein Assoziationsabkommen unterschrieben, das ab 2000 einen privilegierten Zugang zum europäischen Markt garantiert, Israel aber auch zu Einhaltung europäischer Werte verpflichtet. Die Teilnahme an europäischen wissenschaftlichen und technischen Forschungsprogrammen stellte sich als besonders wichtig heraus. 1996 wurde Israel das erste Nicht-EU Mitglied, das in den Genuss dieser Begünstigungen kam. 2004 folgte die Teilnahme am Weltraum-Programm Galileo. Die kontinuierliche Aufwertung der wirtschaftlichen und technologischen Beziehungen zwischen Israel und der EU wurde durch politisch-militärische Ereignisse im Nahen Osten unterbrochen. Nach dem Gaza-Krieg 2008/09 etwa erreichten sie einen Tiefpunkt. Die europäische Unzufriedenheit mit dem mangelnden Fortschritt im Friedensprozess und die israelische Haltung dabei mündeten vorläufig (2013) in den erwähnten Leitlinien.

Zwei Staaten und Bi-Nationalität

Der Widerstand gegen die Siedlungspolitik oder die Befürwortung von zwei Staaten entlang der 1967er Grenze müssen nicht im Gegensatz zu diesen Perspektiven stehen. Für sich genommen reichen sie jedoch heute nicht (mehr?) aus. Es muss neu nachgedacht werden, um eine Verbindung zu finden zwischen (unrealistischen) Gegenwartsforderungen und der Perspektive eines grundsätzlichen Wandels der Beziehungen zwischen Israelis und PalästinenserInnen. Ich habe in einem Kommentar im Jahre 2003 versucht eine solche Brücke zu schlagen:

„Two States and Bi-Nationalism:

Confronted with the worsening external and internal situation of Palestine thinkers on both sides of the Green Line have questioned the feasibility of a Two-States 'Solution'. Bi-Nationalism has been perceived as an alternative approach. The following comments are intended to demonstrate that there is no inevitable contradiction between both perspectives. Much depends on the intentions behind various proposals. In this respect we can be sure that those talking about a 'Palestinian State with provisional borders' now, do not have a future in mind that is acceptable for both peoples.

- Bi-nationalism as I see it, does not exclude two states, it is only less dogmatic about them.
- While a fair bi-national option (as a 'solution') seems less likely than even the 'two states', bi-national policies should be considered.
- Such policies would be more fitting to the realities of both peoples than the focus on the post-1967 occupation only. They would be more comprehensive giving issues such as refugees, the Palestinian minority in Israel and even the settlers' equal attention.

- Even the talk about 'democratisation' of Greater Israel/Palestine need not exclude the right to political-territorial separation, however only as the result of a free and fair deal.

- It is more likely that what is being created now is a bi-national monster, whereby 'bi-national' only signifies the ethnic composition of the populations and not the political superstructure.

- This fact suggests that less emphasis should be given to borders, resolutions and roadmaps – and much more to principles like equality, dignity, mutual recognition and respect, fairness.

- Seeing two states in a bi-national perspective would mean to pay attention to the character of each state, i.e. to promote equality and multiculturalism on both sides of the Green Line.

- However, an eventual Palestinian state would have other priorities such as: redress past and present wrongs protect against the ongoing process of dispossession start transforming the relationship between the two peoples.

- This relationship is characterized by a colonial origin and development, leading to an enormous asymmetry of power and status. No talk about a 'clash of two rights' can beautify or rationalize this monstrous outcome.

- The 'Wall' is an ugly manifestation of the inability to face the Other; it signifies the readiness to destroy the country for the sake of ruling, controlling and negating the Palestinian people.

- Finally, a bi-national perspective should not exclude the presence of Jews beyond the Green Line. Within the framework advocated here they would have to give up their privileges and apocalyptic dreams. Those who are not ready to do so would have to move to Jewish majority area, while the abandoned settlements could be used to rehabilitate Palestinian refugees.

- Bi-national policies focus on the settler-colonial relationship between Israeli Jews and Palestinian Arabs in the country as a whole. 'Only those who want to continue the Zionist process, are forced to justify its past' (Eli Lobel)."

Zusammenfassung

Die vorangehenden Überlegungen ergeben sich zunächst aus der sinkenden Wahrscheinlichkeit der Erreichung eines lebensfähigen palästinensischen Staates mit seiner Hauptstadt in (Ost-)Jerusalem.

Aus der sinkenden Wahrscheinlichkeit ergibt sich eine größere Notwendigkeit von alternativen Modellen. Um mit Nathalie Tocci (2012) zu sprechen, geht es nicht darum die „zwei Staaten" durch „einen Staat" zu ersetzen, sondern den Prozess überhaupt von einer vorgegebenen programmatischen Zwangsjacke zu befreien. Statt diese oder jene Staatsform anzustreben, sollte mehr Gewicht auf individuelle und kollektive Rechte aller Beteiligten gelegt werden; und zwar sowohl von den internen, als auch von den äußeren Mächten (wie z.B. die EU). Solche Politiken würden erst die Voraussetzungen für faire Verhandlungen schaffen, da sie nicht mehr von einem extrem ungleichen Kräfteverhältnis abhängen müssten. Die EU kann dazu beitragen die Asymmetrie zu mildern und die Zusammenarbeit mit Israel stärker von ihrem Wertekodex abhängig zu machen. Indem sie ein klares Signal gegen den weiteren Siedlungsbau beinhalten, könnten die „Leitlinien" der EU zu einer Eingrenzung des Siedlungsbaus führen und ein Zeichen in Richtung einer Zweistaatenlösung und damit der Errichtung eines unabhängigen palästinensischen Staaten setzen.

Hier wird also nicht für die Aufgabe der zwei Staaten durch einen Staat argumentiert. Die Forderung nach zwei Staaten sollte aufrechterhalten bleiben, auch wenn sie nicht realisierbar erscheint; denn sie enthält trotz allem ein Element von Gleichheit und Gegenseitigkeit. Aber der bisherige „Friedensprozess" führte in eine Sackgasse und wurde selbst zu einem Hindernis für einen „gerechten Frieden". Es scheint besser ergebnisoffen zu verhandeln, dafür aber Prinzipien der Vorgangsweise zu vereinbaren. Das Ergebnis von israelisch-palästinensischen Verhandlungen unter solchen Voraussetzungen müssten allseits akzeptiert werden.

John Bunzl

Literatur

Bunzl, John (2012a), „Traumapolitik. Zum Holocaust im israelischen Diskurs." In *add-on 12*, herausgegeben von Cengiz Günay und Jan Pospisil, Wien: facultas.wuv, 109-130.

Bunzl, John (2012b), „Der Feind meines Feindes ist mein Freund? Islamophober Populismus und Israel." In *Jahrbuch für Islamophobieforschung*, herausgegeben von Farid Hafez, Wien: new academic press, 17-34.

Burg, Avraham (2013), „Europe must lead the Way on Arab-Israeli Conflict." *EU Observer*, 09-13-13.

Carter, Jimmy (2006), *Palestine: Peace not Apartheid*. New York, NY: Simon and Schuster.

Cronin, David (2010), *Europe's Alliance with Israel: Aiding the Occupation*. London: Pluto Press.

Forsher, Efrat (2013), „Settlers convene EU lawmakers for special debate on funding ban." *Israel Hayom*, 09-18-13.

Halper, Jeff (2009), „Dismantling the Matrix of Control." *Merip*, 09-11-09.

Lustick, Ian (2013), „Two- State Illusion." *New York Times*, 09-14-13.

Ravid, Barak (2013), „Former EU leaders to Ashton: Stand firm on settlement guidelines." *Haaretz*, 09-16-13.

Rettman, Andrew (2013), „EU-Israel talks fail to agree on funding." *EU Observer*, 09-13-13.

Shabi, Rachel (2013), „EU overtakes US as peace broker with significant clout." *The National*, 07-31-13.

Somfalvi, Atilla (2013), „Deputy Foreign Minister blasts ministery's report on EU boycott", *Jedioth Acharonot*, 10-09-13.

Tocci, Nathalie (2012), „Israel Palestine and the end of the two-state road." *Open Democracy*, 12-06-12.

Witney, Nick (2013), *Europe and the vanishing two-state solution*. London: European Council on Foreign Relations.

Yiftachel, Oren (2006), *Ethnocracy. Land and Identity Politics in Israel/Palestine*. Pennsylvania: University of Pennsylvania Press.

Website:

ECCP, European Co-Ordination Committee for Palestine, http://www.eccpalestine.org/

EU, Türkei und Russland: Eine Neubetrachtung des Südkorridors

Ufuk Şahin

Einleitung

Die Nabucco-Pipeline war der Gegenstand des Südkorridors, über den Energieressourcen unter Umgehung Russlands an die Endverbraucher nach Europa transportiert werden sollten. Obwohl die Aussichten für die Realisierung des Projekts durchaus gut waren, gilt die Nabucco Pipeline inzwischen als gescheitert. Es schien zunächst so, als ob sich die Energieziele der Europäischen Union (EU) mit denen der Türkei decken würden (Winrow 2009: 2). Ankara war tendenziell bestrebt, zur EU-Energiediversifizierung beizutragen (Triantaphyllou/Fotiou 2010a: 103f., Tekin/Williams 2009: 349). Das Projekt deckte sich zum einen mit den Interessen der Türkei, die dadurch eine wachsende Bedeutung als Energiekorridor zu erlangen hoffte und zum anderen wurde es so verstanden, dass der Beitrittskandidat die Pläne zur Diversifizierung der Energieversorgung der EU auch aufgrund des Kandidatenstatus mittragen würde. Die Türkei unterzeichnete im Laufe der Zeit zwar das zwischenstaatliche Nabucco-Abkommen (Nabucco Intergovernmental Agreement, IGA), erklärte allerdings gleichzeitig auch der South-Stream Pipeline, die von der russischen Gazprom initiiert wurde und die im Schwarzen Meer durch die Territorialgewässer der Türkei verlaufen soll, ihre Zusage. Bemerkenswert ist diese Entwicklung, da die South-Stream Pipeline offenbar dazu dient, die Nabucco-Pipeline zu untergraben bzw. die Diversifizierungsbemühungen der EU zu sabotieren. Die South-Stream-Pipeline gilt als Versuch Moskaus den Südkorridor zu kontrollieren. Die Nabucco-Pipeline wiederum sollte die Abhängigkeit von Energielieferungen aus Russland mindern, indem sie Erdgas aus der kaspischen Region oder wahlweise aus dem Mittleren Osten nach Europa liefert.

In Anbetracht der dargestellten Entwicklungen stellt sich die Frage, inwiefern die Türkei die EU-Diversifizierungsvorhaben bzw. die Realisierung der Nabucco-Pipeline gefördert oder nicht gefördert hat. Der vorliegende Artikel beabsichtigt das Verhalten der Türkei bezüglich des Südkorridors zu beleuchten und soll zu einem besseren Verständnis der Zusammenhänge im energiepolitischen Dreieck EU, Türkei und Russische Föderation beitragen. Der Beitrag argumentiert, dass vor dem Hintergrund der problematischen Beitrittsverhandlungen die Anreize der EU nicht ausreichend waren, um die zunehmend selbstbewusster agierende Türkei zu einer Kooperation gemäß den Bestimmungen der EU-Energiediversifizierung zu veranlassen.

Stattdessen stellte die Türkei ihre nationalen Interessen, die sich in Bezug auf die Energiepolitik und die Außenpolitik nicht notwendigerweise mit den Interessen der EU- Kommission decken, in den Vordergrund. Um das Verhalten der Türkei theoretisch zu erklären, wird die Politische Geographie nach David Calleo (1978) herangezogen. Dieser liegt die geopolitische Positionierung Deutschlands von der Kaiserzeit bis zur EU-Integration zu Grunde. Calleo thematisiert die Suche eines Staates nach seiner Rolle in der globalen Weltordnung. Für jede einzelne Variante, die der Staat in seiner Rolle einnehmen kann, wird die Bedeutung herausgestellt, die Beziehungen zu bestimmten Staaten neu zu regeln um die eigene Position zu legitimieren. Bei der geopolitischen Neupositionierung sind dabei sowohl innerstaatliche Entwicklungen als auch außenpolitische Dynamiken relevant (Calleo 1978).

EU Beitritt – South East Europe Energy Community Treaty (SEEECT) – Energiekapitel

Im Rahmen der Energiekooperation zwischen der EU und der Türkei galt die Unterzeichnung des IGA als sehr bedeutend für den Fortschritt des Nabucco-Projekts. Dabei war die EU in den IGA-Verhandlungen bestrebt, die Energieangelegenheit mit der Türkei auf bilateraler Ebene zu behandeln. Zu diesem

Zweck forderte die EU von Ankara die Ratifizierung des SEEECT[1], wodurch die Übernahme einschlägigen EU-Energierechts gewährleistet und der Gastransit über das türkische Territorium gesichert werden sollte. Im Gegensatz dazu forderte die Türkei, Energieangelegenheiten im Rahmen der Beitrittsverhandlungen zu behandeln. Ankara strebte an, das Energiekapitel, welches durch das Veto der zypriotischen Regierung blockiert wurde, zu öffnen. Zumal das *Screening* des Kapitels bereits erfolgreich abgeschlossen worden war, und somit offen für die Verhandlungen stehen würde. Aus türkischer Sicht hätte die Öffnung des Energiekapitels auch symbolische Wirkung gehabt und hätte vor allem als ein wichtiger Fortschritt in den Verhandlungen gegolten (European Policy Center Online 2009).[2] Ankara versuchte in diesem Zusammenhang das Nabucco Pipeline Projekt als Argument für die Eröffnung des Energiekapitels zu nutzen.

Es überrascht nicht, dass die türkische Regierung einen solchen politischen Kurs verfolgt hat, während sie gleichzeitig versuchte diplomatische Mechanismen, wie z.B. das bilaterale Abkommen SEEECT, die augenscheinlich außerhalb des EU-Beitrittsprozesses liegen, zu vermeiden. Denn aus der Sicht der Türkei kam die Einwilligung zum SEEECT der Vorstellung gleich, einem großen und bedeutsamen Teil des *Acquis*, einseitig zuzustimmen, ohne etwas fordern zu können. Dabei sieht Ankara das Abkommen nicht zwingend als ein trojanisches Pferd, durch das die EU-Mitgliedschafts-Bestrebungen sabotiert werden. Da das SEEECT allerdings auch für Nicht-EU-Staaten offen steht, sieht Ankara das Abkommen für Staaten geeignet, die für eine EU-Mitgliedschaft überhaupt nicht in Frage kommen. Sie befürchtet somit in der Folge eine Verminderung ihrer EU-Beitritts-Chancen (Tekin/Williams 2011: 172,179,184, Barysch 2007: 6). Der Widerstand das SEEECT zu unterzeich-

---

[1] Das SEEECT ist ein von der EU geführtes Energie Rahmenwerk, welches beabsichtigt, den Energiehandel mit den Vertragsstaaten zu vereinheitlichen. Dabei erfordert das SEEECT, dass Drittstaaten mit dem *Acquis Communautaire* für Energie in Einklang gebracht und somit in den EU Binnenmarkt für Energie eingegliedert werden (Pollak 2010: 147, Barysch 2007: 6).

[2] Auch weil das Energiekapitel von Zypern blockiert wird. Die Öffnung des Kapitels hätte aus türkischer Sicht bedeutet, dass man den Zypernkonflikt, der die EU-Türkei Beziehungen belastet, umgehen kann (siehe Beitrag von Hakan Akbulut in diesem Band).

nen ist auf die Skepsis zurückzuführen, Vereinbarungen einzugehen, die eine Vollmitgliedschaft gar nicht als Ziel haben, und somit den Status Quo für längere Zeit zementieren (Tekin/Williams 2011: 179). Nachdem das SEEECT auch im Rahmen der Europäischen Nachbarschaftspolitik Staaten wie der Ukraine und Moldawien, die keinen Kandidatenstatus haben, angeboten wurde, sah sich die türkische Regierung in ihren Argumenten bestätigt (Barysch 2007: 7). Ankara betrachtet sich als EU-Beitrittskandidat und möchte nicht als „Privilegierter Partner" im Energiebereich „abgespeist" werden. Außerdem genießt die Türkei bereits die Vorzüge einer „Privilegierten Partnerschaft" mit der EU. So trat die Türkei bereits im Jahre 1996 der Zollunion bei, nimmt an von der EU geführten Friedensmissionen als NATO Mitglied teil und ist in viele europäische Institutionen integriert. Die Türkei betrachtet eine privilegierte Partnerschaft, so wie sie immer wieder durch Nicolas Sarkozy und Angela Merkel vorgebracht wurde, als eine Mitgliedschaft zweiter Klasse und lehnt diese deshalb ab (Bürgin 2007: 86ff.).

Tekin und Williams (2011: 175ff.) zufolge, war die Rolle der Türkei in den Energiesicherheits-Überlegungen der EU-Kommission einer der Gründe für den Beginn der Beitrittsverhandlungen, weshalb die türkische Regierung erwartete, auf den strategischen Motiven beruhend, in Energiefragen als Beitrittskandidat behandelt zu werden um eine Energiekooperation im Interesse der EU zu fördern. Im Gegensatz dazu scheuten jedoch viele Akteure innerhalb der EU, wie z.B. die EU-Kommission sowie gewichtige Mitgliedstaaten wie Deutschland und Frankreich, davor zurück offen eine direkte Verbindung zwischen der Energiekooperation und dem EU-Beitritt der Türkei herzustellen. Neben den allgemeinen Hindernissen, des türkischen EU-Beitritts wie z.B. die Furcht vor einer Machtverschiebung innerhalb der EU sowie Masseneinwanderung türkischer StaatsbürgerInnen (Bürgin 2007: 88f.), haben einige Akteure auch Bedenken, dass den Bewerberländern aufgrund einer einzigen, wenn auch entscheidenden, Sachdimension die EU-Mitgliedschaft gewährt werden könnte (Tekin/Williams 2011: 178).

Nicht nur die Überbetonung der EU, dass die Türkei aufgrund ihrer „einzigartigen" geographischen Lage unentbehrlich sei, sondern auch die Bestrebungen der Türkei eine Regionalmacht zu werden, die dabei mehrdimensionale außenpolitische Ziele verfolgt, nährt die Vorstellung, dass die Türkei

sich nicht wie andere EU-Beitrittskandidaten verhält. Vielmehr ist die türkische Regierung darauf bedacht, beim Dialog mit Brüssel als gleichwertiger
Partner wahrgenommen zu werden. Sie möchte, dass in den Beziehungen
mit der EU, die besonderen Umstände sowie die multi-regionalen Interessen
der Türkei berücksichtigt werden. Ein Resultat dieser Selbstwahrnehmung
spiegelt sich im Versuch der türkischen Regierung, den EU-Beitritt nicht nur
durch innerstaatliche Reformen, sondern ebenso durch *strategic-level-
bargaining* zu erlangen, wider (Kardas 2011: 36f.).

Aus der Sicht Ankaras ist das Einfrieren des Energiekapitels ein Symbol für
die Ungleichbehandlung der Türkei durch die EU. Es hat das Vertrauen in die
EU untergraben (Tekin/Williams 2011: 179, Kardas 2010). Da die EU keine
klare Beitrittsperspektive in den Beitrittsverhandlungen anbot, verlor die
Energiekooperation mit der EU aus der Sicht Ankaras an Attraktivität. So
konnte die EU in den letzten Jahren weder für die Durchsetzung innerstaatli-
cher Reformen noch für die Kooperationen im Energiesektor als ein externer
Anker dienen. Das Fehlen einer Perspektive auf Mitgliedschaft verringerte
die Bedeutung der Nabucco-Pipeline als gemeinsame strategische Priorität.
In weiterer Folge trat die Türkei aus der Sicht der EU in den IGA-
Verhandlungen fordernd auf und war nicht kooperativ (Winrow 2009: 8ff.,
Kardas 2011: 47f.).

Zypernkonflikt: Hindernis für die Kooperation

Hinter Ankaras Widerstreben, das SEEECT in Bezug auf die Energietransit-
regelungen zu unterzeichnen und sich um die Öffnung des Energiekapitels zu
bemühen, stand das Zypern-Problem. Dass die zypriotische Regierung das
Energiekapitel blockiert, ist auf den Widerstand der Türkei zurückzuführen,
die sich gegen die Gas- und Öl-Ausbeutung durch die griechischen Zyprioten
in umstrittenen Territorialgewässern im östlichen Mittelmeer stemmt
(Winrow 2009: 7, AG Friedensforschung Online 2011). Demnach kann das
Energiekapitel voraussichtlich so lange nicht geöffnet werden, bis Ankara
von dem Anspruch, dass die Hoheitsmacht über die nördliche Meereszone,
der türkischen Behörde des nördlichen Teils der Insel obliegt, abweicht
(Tekin/Williams 2011: 181f.). Aus der Sicht Ankaras ist die Ressourcenaus-

beutung nur nach einer politischen Einigung der Insel zulässig, damit sowohl die griechischen als auch die türkischen ZypriotInnen des Inselstaates von den Ressourcen profitieren können (AG Friedensforschung Online 2011).

Die türkische Regierung sieht die EU in Geiselhaft Zyperns. Ankara sieht die EU in der Pflicht, auf Zypern einzuwirken, um das Veto aufzuheben. Um den Zypernkonflikt beizulegen hat die türkische Regierung selbst bisher wenig unternommen. Sie erwartet sich vor allem von der EU dem Versprechen nachzukommen, die internationale Isolation des nördlichen Teils der Insel aufzuheben.[3] Da die EU dieser Zusage nicht nachgegangen ist, hat sie aus Sicht Ankaras an Glaubwürdigkeit verloren (Oğuzlu 2012: 234, Euractive Online 2009). Andererseits scheint es so, dass das Zypernproblem für viele EU Staaten einen guten Vorwand für ihre Positionierung hinsichtlich der türkischen Beitrittsfrage geboten hat (Bürgin 2007: 98). Vor allem angesichts des Umstandes, dass ein Türkei-Beitritt in vielen europäischen Ländern, unter anderem in Schlüsselländern wie Frankreich und Deutschland, relativ unpopulär wäre.

Die Schwierigkeit für die türkische Regierung stellt sich folgendermaßen dar: ohne eine Zusicherungen der EU, die Isolation des nördlichen Teils der Insel aufzuheben, ist die Öffnung der türkischen Häfen für griechisch-zypriotische Schiffe angesichts der tendenziell nationalistischen Haltung gegenüber dem Zypernkonflikt innerhalb der türkischen Bevölkerung für die AKP-Regierung mit hohen politischen Kosten verbunden. Schon die ursprüngliche konstruktive Haltung der AKP, im Rahmen des Annan-Plans, den Zypernkonflikt beizulegen, ist sowohl bei Teilen der Elite als auch bei der politischen Opposition auf große Kritik gestoßen. Die Hauptoppositionspartei, die Cumhuriyet Halk Partisi (Republikanische Volkspartei, CHP), die sich als ein wichtiger Bestandteil des nationalistischen Blocks etabliert hat, versucht, basierend auf dem wachsenden Nationalismus aus dieser Situation Kapital zu schlagen. Die

---

[3] In der Erklärung des Europäischen Rates vom 26. April 2004 wurde beschlossen, dass der Isolation des türkischen Teils der Insel ein Ende gesetzt und gezielt dessen wirtschaftliche Entwicklung gefördert wird. Dieses Versprechen wurde als Belohnung für das positive Votum Ankaras bei der Abstimmung zur Wiedervereinigung der Insel im Rahmen des Annan-Plans ausgesetzt (Bürgin 2007: 94).

politischen Gegner der AKP stellen die Regierung als zu nachgiebig gegenüber Bedrohungen der nationalen Interessen, unter anderem im Hinblick auf den Zypernkonflikt, dar. Unweigerlich wird die AKP dadurch in die Defensive gedrängt (Avcı 2011: 413ff.). In der Folge ist auch die öffentliche Unterstützung für einen EU-Beitritt in den letzten Jahren drastisch zurückgegangen. Vor diesem Hintergrund nehmen die politischen Kosten der türkischen Regierung Kompromisse einzugehen merklich zu, da die politische Opposition, die zunehmend euroskeptischer wird, sie einfach ausnutzen kann und dabei als schädlich für die nationalen Interessen darstellt (Bürgin 2012: 886).

Für den Fall, dass Ankara das SEEECT ohne eine gleichzeitige Aufhebung der Blockade des Energiekapitels unterzeichnen würde, wäre dennoch zu erwarten, dass der Konflikt um Zypern weiterhin den EU-Beitrittsprozess der Türkei behindern würde. Dies würde von der AKP Regierung Zugeständnisse zum Konflikt abverlangen, was wiederum innenpolitisch mit zu hohen Kosten verbunden wäre (Avcı 2011: 412f.). Für die Opposition, die Milliyetci ve Hareket Partisi (Partei der Nationalistischen Bewegung, MHP) und die CHP, wäre dies eine Gelegenheit, im innenpolitischen Machtkampf einen Erfolg für sich zu verbuchen. Vor diesem Hintergrund ist Ankara bemüht, Zugeständnisse von der EU zu erhalten, bevor das SEEECT unterzeichnet wird. Gemäß dieser Linie vertritt die türkische Regierung die Ansicht, dass die Aufhebung des Vetos zum Energiekapitel den Weg für die Unterzeichnung des SEEECT ebnen würde. Somit ist die AKP-Regierung auf die Aufhebung der zypriotischen Blockade des Energiekapitels bedacht, um den Beitrittsprozess in Gang zu bringen (Turkish Ministry of Foreign Affairs 2011). Ohne die verlangten Zugeständnisse war die türkische Regierung bisher nicht gewillt, das SEEECT zu ratifizieren und hat bisher lediglich den Status eines Beobachters inne.

Energieinteressen der Türkei vs. EU-Energiediversifizierung

Aufgrund der Präferenz der EU, Energieangelegenheiten im Rahmen bilateraler Kooperationsmechanismen abseits des Beitrittsprozesses zu behandeln, war es für Ankara unerlässlich, sich der Energiekooperation mit Bedacht auf die nationalen Prioritäten zu nähern. Die energiepolitischen Zielsetzungen

Ankaras sind zum einen, den Staat langfristig als eine Energiehandelsmacht zu etablieren und zum anderen, die inländische Energieversorgung sicherzustellen (Winrow 2009: 18ff.). Mit Bedacht auf die nationalen Interessen betrachtete die Türkei die Nabucco-Pipeline zunehmend aus einem wirtschaftlichen Standpunkt. Dabei war sie bestrebt, ihren Nutzen zu maximieren und lehnte es ab den türkischen Energiemarkt zu liberalisieren (Kardas 2011: 48). Dieser Umstand führte zu einer angespannten Atmosphäre zwischen Brüssel und Ankara. Die energiepolitischen Prioritäten Ankaras weichen von den Interessen der EU ab. Angesichts des Umstandes, dass ein EU-Beitritt aus heutiger Sicht unwahrscheinlich scheint, benötigt die Türkei mehr Sicherheit für die eigene Energieversorgung, sie strebt aber auch nach einer neuen Rolle in der globalen Weltordnung.

Die Bemühungen der EU, einen direkten Zugang zur kaspischen Region herzustellen, widersprechen generell der energiepolitischen Zielsetzung Ankaras, kostengünstiges Gas für den türkischen Energiebedarf bereitzustellen. Die geographische Nähe zu den Gaslieferstaaten in Zentralasien und Iran sollte nicht nur für die eigene Rolle als Energiedrehscheibe förderlich sein, sondern auch zu kontinuierlichen sowie kostengünstigen Gaslieferungen für den türkischen Energiebedarf dienen. Die Türkei befürchtete durch das Eindringen der EU in die Region einen Nachteil, da sie den eigenen Zugang zu kaspischen Energieressourcen nicht selbst regeln könnte. Im Falle, dass die europäischen KonsumentInnen das Gas direkt von der Region zu gleichen Konditionen wie die Türkei bekämen, würde der Preis für Gas aus dem kaspischen Raum steigen. Vor dem Hintergrund dieser Überlegungen war die türkische Regierung bestrebt, die eigene Energieversorgung sicherzustellen ehe der EU ein direkter Zugang in die kaspische Region ermöglicht wird (Kardas 2011: 47f., Winrow 2009: 18-21). Dieses Anliegen der Türkei erklärt auch die Erschwernisse, die die IGA-Verhandlungen in Bezug auf die Vorzugskonditionen, belastet haben. Darin stellte die Forderung Ankaras, 15% des Nabucco-Gases zu Vorzugskonditionen zu erhalten bzw. wahlweise 4 bis 8 Mrd. Kubikmeter Gas pro Jahr aus der zweiten Phase des Shah Deniz Feldes zu beziehen, eine Hürde dar und blockierte den Projektfortschritt (Winrow 2009: 18-21).

In weiterer Folge verfolgte die Türkei das Ziel sich als Energiedrehscheibe zwischen den Nachfrage- und Lieferantenstaaten zu etablieren. Dadurch sollte die Türkei nicht nur ein Transitland sein, das vergleichsweise niedrige Gebühren einheben kann, sondern ein Zwischenhändler sein, der eine Gewinnspanne beansprucht (Socor 2009, Kramer 2010: 22). Im Gegensatz dazu war die EU darauf bedacht, das Monopol des staatlichen Energiekonzerns, Petroleum Pipeline Corporation (Boru Hatları ile Petrol Taşıma Anonim Şirketi, BOTAS) einzugrenzen bzw. die Rolle BOTAS auf die Gasdurchleitung über das türkische Territorium zu begrenzen. Eine Energiepartnerschaft mit der EU würde zum einen klare und durchsetzbare Regelungen zur Gasdurchleitung über das türkische Territorium voraussetzen. Zum anderen würde sie die Liberalisierung des türkischen Gasmarktes mit sich bringen (Kardas 2011: 47f., Winrow 2009: 26). Die Präferenz der Türkei als Energiedrehscheibe ihren wirtschaftlichen Gewinn zu maximieren und dabei verschiedene Optionen zwischen rivalisierenden Projekten offen zu halten, minderte den Anreiz, das Regelwerk der EU in Bezug auf das Transitregime zu übernehmen. Demnach hätte das EU-Regelwerk den geopolitische Einfluss der Türkei in ihrer Nachbarschaft eingeschränkt (Triantaphyllou/Fotiou 2010b: 58f., Kardas 2011: 47f.). Offenbar wollte sich die türkische Regierung gegen ein mögliches Scheitern sowohl des Nabucco-Projektes als auch des EU-Beitritts absichern. So eröffnete sich für Ankara durch die South-Stream Pipeline die Möglichkeit, dennoch eine wesentliche Rolle innerhalb der europäischen Energieversorgung einzunehmen (Kramer 2010: 32).

Türkische Regionalmachtambitionen und der Südkorridor

Einem Staat der sich als Energiekorridor positioniert, ist es möglich, Energie politisch zu instrumentalisieren und somit in Verhandlungen als Machtfaktor einzusetzen. So eröffnet sich für die Türkei durch die Energiefrage eine weitere Möglichkeit sich als Regionalmacht zu etablieren (Coskun/Carlson 2010: 214). In diesem Zusammenhang weist Alihuseynov (2010: 238f.) darauf hin, dass die Türkei bereits in den Verhandlungen mit Aserbaidschan, dem Energieanbieter, sowie der EU, dem Energieabnehmer, als Akteur der „Energie-Geopolitik" gewichtig aufzutreten versuche. Die South-Stream Pipeline wiederum bietet für die Türkei die Möglichkeit, ihre geo-strategische Rolle als Energiebrücke gegenüber Russland aufzuwerten und Moskau zumindest theoretisch in ein Transitabhängigkeitsverhältnis zu bringen. Dadurch wird die geopolitische Rolle gegenüber Russland als auch gegenüber den EU-Staaten aufgewertet. In diesem Sinne scheint das Engagement in South-Stream auch als Zeichen der multivektoralen Ausrichtung der türkischen Außenpolitik zu sein.

Die Bestrebungen Ankaras eine Energiedrehscheibe zu werden, bergen allerdings auch Spannungen in ihren Beziehungen zur Russischen Föderation. So weist Frank Umbach (2011: 31) darauf hin, dass die Vorhaben der EU über die Türkei eine alternative Energielieferroute nach Europa zu bilden, die geopolitischen und energiepolitischen Interessen Moskaus bedrohen. Denn traditionell nimmt Russland bei der Belieferung Europas eine „Monopolstellung" ein, woraus sich eine starke geopolitische Einflussmöglichkeit ergibt (Coskun/Carlson 2010: 215). In diesem Kontext ist auch die strategische Bedeutung, die der South-Stream Pipeline aus der Sicht Moskaus zukommt, zu betrachten. Nachdem Russland durch South-Stream beabsichtigt hat, das Nabucco-Projekt zu sabotieren, sollte dadurch auch sichergestellt werden, dass die Stellung Moskaus als Hauptenergielieferant der EU nicht gefährdet wird. Darüber hinaus sollte dadurch weiterhin die Machtstellung gegenüber kaspischen Energieproduzenten erhalten bleiben, da die South-Stream Pipeline auch auf die Nabucco-Gaslieferanten abzielt (Balcer 2009: 86f.). In Anbetracht der dargestellten Sachlage steht somit die Türkei im Zuge ihrer Regionalmacht-Bestrebungen, eine alternative Energieroute für kaspische und zentralasiatische Energierohstoffe zu bilden, in direkter Konkurrenz mit Russland um den europäischen Markt.

Zwischen der Türkei und Russland gibt es zwar seit einigen Jahren eine beachtliche Annäherung (Ersen 2011: 94ff., Sidar/Winrow 2011, Bagci 2009: 7), allerdings sind auch in den bilateralen Beziehungen Hindernisse vorhanden. So weist Kogan (2008: 4) darauf hin, dass dabei insbesondere das Nabucco-Projekt die Beziehungen belastet. Durch die Unterstützung der South-Stream Pipeline, schafft die Türkei somit die Voraussetzungen für Moskau, die „Monopolstellung" weiterhin über die EU erhalten zu können. Es wird deutlich, wenn die Türkei bereits im Nabucco-Projekt beteiligt ist, und nun der Russischen Föderation für die South-Stream Pipeline ihre Zusage erteilt, dies ihre Vorsicht widerspiegelt, die Interessen Moskaus nicht zu gefährden. Die Türkei als aufstrebende Regionalmacht, der die EU-Mitgliedschaft verwehrt bleibt, ist nicht geneigt die Interessen Moskaus zu ignorieren. Angesichts der schwierigen Beziehungen mit der EU, kann die Bereitschaft der Türkei mit Russland in Bezug auf den Südkorridor zu kooperieren dahingehend gewertet werden, dass ihre neue Rolle als Regionalmacht eine Legitimation durch die Weltmacht Russland erfordert. Denn Ankara kann nicht an Russland vorbei zu einer Energiehandelsmacht aufsteigen.

Es ist auch notwendig, das Engagement der Türkei im South-Stream Projekt vor dem Hintergrund der Annäherung zwischen Moskau und Ankara zu betrachten. Erstens stellt Moskau als Gegenleistung für das Engagement der Türkei in South-Stream weitere Energieprojekte in Aussicht. Darunter befindet sich das Gemeinschaftsprojekt, die Samsun-Ceyhan Pipeline, welches dem türkischen Ziel dient, in der Mittelmeer-Hafenstadt Ceyhan ein Energiehandelszentrum zu errichten. Dadurch soll die eigene Position auf dem Ölmarkt gestärkt werden (Ersen 2011: 108). Zweitens deuten die in den letzten Jahren vertieften Wirtschafts- und Energiebeziehungen auf die Erwartungshaltung Ankaras hin, in regionalen Angelegenheiten einen kooperationsbereiten Partner zu haben (Kardas 2012: 94f.). Die Türkei als aufstrebende Regionalmacht spielt bereits in der Schwarzmeer-Wirtschaftskooperation sowie in der Caucasus Stability and Cooperation Platform[4] (CSCP) eine bedeutende Rolle (Fotiou 2009: 19). Bisher werden diese von Moskau mitgetragen, und stellen für Ankara ein Mittel dar, um interdependente Beziehungen zur umliegenden Region aufzubauen und dadurch ihr Einflussgebiet zu sichern (Bagci 2009: 7f.). Insgesamt reflektiert die empfängliche Haltung Ankaras gegenüber den russischen Energiekooperationsangeboten auch die positive Entwicklung der Türkei-Russland-Beziehungen.

---

[4] Das Caucasus Stability and Cooperation Platform wurde von der Türkei auf den Georgien-Konflikt 2008 folgend initiiert und sah die Einbeziehung Aserbaidschans, Armeniens, Georgiens sowie Russlands vor. Das Ziel des CSCP liegt darin, künftige sicherheitspolitische Krisen vorzubeugen.

Schlussbetrachtung

Die Türkei hat die Nabucco-Pipeline, die Hauptbestandteil der EU-Diversifizierungsvorhaben war, nicht in dem Maße gefördert, wie die EU es erhofft hatte. Zwar hat die Türkei das IGA unterzeichnet sowie von Forderungen abgesehen, das in die Nabucco-Pipeline einzuspeisende Gas zu Vorzugskonditionen zu erhalten bzw. es weiterzuverkaufen. Aber sie hat nicht, wie von der EU gefordert, einschlägiges EU-Energierecht auf bilateraler Basis durch den Beitritt zum SEEECT übernommen, womit die Gasdurchleitung über das türkische Territorium begünstigt worden wäre und das Nabucco-Projekt einen Schub erhalten hätte. Stattdessen forderte die Türkei im Bereich der Energiekooperation wie ein EU-Beitrittskandidat behandelt zu werden. Aufgrund der komplizierten Beitrittsverhandlungen gestaltet sich die Frage als schwierig. Angesichts der schwindenden Beitrittsperspektive benötigt die Türkei jedoch mehr Sicherheit für die eigene Energieversorgung als auch eine neue Rolle in der globalen Weltordnung.

In Anlehnung an die Interpretation der Politischen Geographie nach Calleo zu geopolitischen Positionierungen eines Staates wird ersichtlich, dass sich die Türkei verstärkt unter der AKP-Regierung von der einseitigen Ausrichtung an der EU-Integration wegentwickelt – in Richtung zu einem Land, das bestrebt ist als eigenständige Regionalmacht aufzutreten und sich demnach auch mehrere Optionen nach Interessenslage offen hält. Für den Beitrittsprozess blieb diese Entwicklung natürlich nicht ohne Konsequenzen. Die Türkei, die auf ihre eigenen Stärken vertraut, möchte der EU auf Augenhöhe begegnen und ist tendenziell weniger bereit sich EU Prioritäten unterzuordnen. Vor allem nicht, wenn EU Schlüsselländer wie Deutschland und Frankreich eine Gegenleistung in Form eines EU-Beitritts ablehnen. So hielt Ankara an dem Vorhaben fest, eine Energiedrehscheibe zu werden und somit künftig Erdgas nach einem Preisaufschlag als Zwischenhändler an diverse Konsumentenstaaten zu re-exportieren. Im Einklang mit den Regionalmachtambitionen wäre sie als Energiedrehscheibe gleichzeitig in der Lage, den inländischen Energiebedarf zu decken sowie einen Einfluss auf Gaspreise herzustellen.

Zur geopolitischen Positionierung der Türkei sind die Beziehungen zu Russland von großer Bedeutung. Denn die türkischen Bestrebungen haben Implikationen für ihre Beziehungen zu Moskau. Die Türkei als alternative Energieroute stellt für Russland, das traditionell bei der Belieferung Europas eine „Monopolstellung" einnimmt, eine Konkurrenz um den europäischen Markt dar. Die Türkei schafft somit durch ihr Engagement in South Stream die Voraussetzungen für Moskau, die Kontrolle über europäische Energieverbraucher erhalten zu können. Denn falls der Türkei der Beitritt verwehrt bleibt, erfordert ihre neue Rolle als eigenständiger Regionalakteur und Energiedrehscheibe eine Legitimation durch Russland. Aus der Sicht Ankaras ist es nicht möglich an Russland vorbei zu einer Energiedrehscheibe aufzusteigen. Vielmehr bedarf es zwischen der Türkei und Russland einer Neuregelung der Beziehungen und somit einer Einigung im Südkorridor.

Literatur

AG Friedensforschung (2011), „Eskalation im Mittelmeer – Türkei und Zypern streiten um Erdgasvorkommen." 05-11-11, Eckert Dirk, verfügbar auf: http://www.ag-friedensforschung.de/regionen/Zypern/gas.html, [Stand: 01-12-13].

Alihuseynov, Taleh (2010), „Die Rolle und Position der Türkei im umstrittenen Erdgasprojekt Nabucco." In *Die Beziehungen der Europäischen Union mit Osteuropa: Energie – Sicherheit – Stabilität,* herausgegeben von Olaf Leiße, Berlin: Nomos, 223-242.

Avcı, Gamze (2011), „The Justice and Development Party and the EU: Political Pragmatism in a Changing Environment." *South European Society and Politics*, 16:3, 409-421.

Bagci, Hüseyin (2009), „Changing Geopolitics and Turkish Foreign Policy." Sozialwissenschaftliche Schriftenreihe Reihe Studien Juni 2009. Wien: Internationales Institut für Liberale Politik Wien.

Balcer, Adam (2009), „The future of turkish-russian relations: a strategic perspective." *Turkish Policy Quarterly*, 8:1, 79-90.

Bürgin, Alexander (2012), „European Commission's agency meets Ankara's agenda: why Turkey is ready for a readmission agreement." *Journal of European Public Policy*, 19:6, 883-899.

Bürgin Alexander (2007), „Beitrittsverhandlungen auf Sparflamme – die EU-Mitgliedschaft und die innenpolitische Krise der Türkei." *Zeitschrift für Internationale Politik und Gesellschaft*, 3/2007, 84-100.

Calleo, David (1978), *The German Problem Reconsidered: Germany and the World Order 1870 to the Present.* Cambridge, UK: Cambridge University Press.

Coskun Bezen, und Carlson Richard (2010), „New Energy Geopolitics: Why does Turkey Matter?" *Insight Turkey*, 12:3, 205-220.

Ersen, Emre (2011), „Turkish-Russian Relations in the New Century." In *Turkey in the 21st Century: Quest for a New Foreign Policy,* herausgegeben von Zeynep Oktay Özden, Farnham: Ashgate, 95-113.

Euractive Online (2009), „Türkei setzt bei blockierten EU-Beitrittsgesprächen auf Energie-Karte." Ohne Verfasser, 20-01-09, http://www.euractiv.com/node/254710, [Stand: 20-07-12]

European Policy Center Online (2009), „Turkey as an energy hub for Europe: prospects and challenges." Policy Dialogue. European Politics and Institutions, 04-03-09, http://www.epc.eu/prog_details.php?cat_id=6&pub_id=987&prog_id=1, [Stand: 01-12-13]

Fotiou, Eleni (2009), *Caucasus Stability and Cooperation Platform: What is at Stake for Regional Cooperation?* Policy Brief No. 16/2009. Athens: International Centre for Black Sea Studies.

Kramer , Heinz (2010), *Die Türkei als Energiedrehscheibe:Wunschtraum und Wirklichkeit.* SWP-Studie April 2010. Berlin: Stiftung Wissenschaft und Politik Deutsches Institut für Internationale Politik und Sicherheit.

Kardas, Saban (2010), „Turkey Signals a Shift on French Participation in Nabucco." *Eurasia Daily Monitor,* 7:51, 16-03-2010. http://www.jamestown.org/single/?no_cache=1&tx_ttnews[tt_news]=36159 [Stand: 01-12-13]

Kardas, Saban (2011), „Geo-strategic position as leverage in EU accession: the case of Turkish-EU negotiations on the Nabucco pipeline." *Southeast European and Black Sea Studies,* 11:1, 35-52.

Kardas, Saban (2012), „Turkey-Russia Energy Relations: The Limits of Forging Cooperation through Economic Interdependence." *International Journal,* 67:81, 81-100.

Kogan, Eugene (2008), *Military and Energy – Security Situation Around the Black Sea Area.* Sozialwissenschaftliche Schriftenreihe Reihe Studien November 2008. Wien: Internationales Institut für Liberale Politik Wien.

Oğuzlu, Tarik H. (2012), „Turkey and the European Union: Europeanization Without Membership." *Turkish Studies,* 13:2, 229-243.

Pollak, Johannes, Samuel R. Schubert, und Peter Slominski (2010), *Die Energiepolitik der EU.* Wien: Facultas WUV.

Sidar, Cenk, und Gareth Winrow (2011), „Turkey & South Stream: Turco-Russian Rapprochement and the Future of the Southern Corridor." *Turkish Policy Quarterly,* 10:2, 51-61.

Socor, Vladimir (2009), „Turkey: a Bridge or Bottleneck for Caspian Gas to Europe?" *Eurasia Daily Monitor,* 6:193, 21-10-2009. http://www.jamestown.org/programs/edm/single/tx_ttnews[tt_news]=35628&tx_ttnews[backPid]=485&no_cache=1 [Stand: 01-12-13]

Tekin, Ali, und Paul Andrew Williams (2009), „EU-Russia Relations and Turkey's Role as an Energy Corridor." *Europe-Asia Studies,* 61:2, 337-356.

Tekin, Ali, und Paul Andrew Williams (2011), *Geo-politics of the Euro-Asia energy nexus – The European Union, Russia and Turkey.* New York, NY: Palgrave.

Triantaphyllou, Dimitrios, und Eleni Fotiou (2010a), „Assessing Turkey's Soft Power Role: Rhetoric versus Practice." *The International Spectator: Italian Journal of International Affairs*, 45:1, 99-113.

Triantaphyllou, Dimitrios, und Eleni Fotiou (2010b), „The EU and Turkey in energy diplomacy." *Insight Turkey*, 12:3, 55-62.

Turkish Ministry of Foreign Affairs (2011), „Turkey's Energy Strategy." http://www.mfa.gov.tr/turkeys-energy-strategy.en.mfa [Stand: 01-12-13]

Umbach, Frank (2011), „Energy security in Eurasia: clashing interests. " In *Russian Energy Security and Foreign Policy*, herausgegeben von Adrian Dellecker und Thomas Gomart, London: Routledge, 23-38.

Winrow, Gareth M. (2009), „Problems and Prospects for the 'Fourth Corridor': The Position and Role of Turkey in Gas Transit to Europe." Oxford Institute for Energy Studies, NG 30.

Winrow, Gareth M. (2011), „Turkey: An emerging energy transit state and possible energy hub." *The International Spectator: Italian Journal of International Affairs*; 46:3, 79-91.

The Shifting Balance of Power in Central Asia

Bernardo Mariani

Introduction

Played out in the growing international spotlight on Central Asia, Xi Jinping's September 2013 tour of Turkmenistan, Kazakhstan, Uzbekistan and Kyrgyzstan threw into sharp relief the region's growing strategic importance. The Chinese President signed deals worth dozens of US$ billions in the space of his week-long visit. Although the details behind such figures remain to be clarified, it is clear that the overall trade volume between China and Central Asia is bound to increase substantially in years to come; these new agreements come on top of a one hundred-fold increase in trade in the two decades since the dissolution of the Soviet Union, and Beijing's forging of diplomatic relations with the Central Asian states.

Against the looming backdrop of NATO's 2014 withdrawal from Afghanistan, the evolving relationship between China and Central Asia prompts a number of questions about the shifting balance of power in this region. Is China's engagement driven primarily by its economic development needs, or more by security concerns – specifically the impact that instability in Central Asia may have on China's north-western region of Xinjiang? And what of the traditional regional hegemon, Russia, which has dominated security management in Central Asia? What is the outlook for Sino-Russian relations, especially if Beijing shifts gear from a primarily economic to a more proactive political and even security role? Does China have a grand strategy to reorient Central Asia towards Beijing and away from other major powers?

Nor is shifting geopolitics in Central Asia just about the balance of power between China and Russia. The United States, India, Iran and Turkey rank amongst the actors aspiring to a larger role on the Central Asian stage, as does the European Union, which has in recent years stressed the growing importance of Central Asia for its energy security, strategic security, and political dialogue. Just how successful have these initiatives been, and what are the promises and challenges ahead?

What follows is an initial attempt to answer these questions. This paper outlines the economic, political, security and energy dimensions of the shifting balance of power in Central Asia, focusing in turn on the evolving roles of China, Russia, India and Turkey. It concludes with an eye to the EU's own aims in the region, offering a brief assessment of its potential and comparative advantage. It should be acknowledged throughout that the Central Asian states themselves are by no means pawns in a "new great game"; the analysis here aims very simply to lay the ground for more in-depth research on these dynamics and their implications for the region and its communities.

China

China has an increasingly significant and influential presence in Central Asia. This revival of the "economic belt along the Silk Road", as it has been termed in official parlance (MFA PRC 14-09-13), has seen massive investments in oil and gas pipelines, in roads and tunnels, as well as in mineral extraction and in communication and trade. In 2012, China's trade with the region totalled almost USD 46bn (Xinhua 15-10-13). Hundreds of Chinese companies already operate in Central Asia, while a significant supply of low-interest loans has helped encourage development in its growing markets. China's attention has been warmly welcomed by the region's political elites: its assistance is bolstering foreign currency reserves and government finances, without making demands on recipients for political concessions.

China's foreign policy approach to Central Asia, as elsewhere, has officially adhered to the five Principles of Peaceful Coexistence: respect for territorial integrity and sovereignty, non-aggression, non-interference, equality and mutual benefit, and peaceful coexistence. It is emphatically stressed in official discourse that the relationship is one of "good neighbourly friendship, mutual benefits, and win-win cooperation" (MFA PRC 14-09-13); relatedly, China's responsibility as a great power is to respect that each national government has the right and ability to properly handle domestic matters – including political conflict.

From this viewpoint, claims that China is pursuing a grand geopolitical strategy aimed at ultimate control and dominance of Central Asia are somewhat exaggerated. China has neither the capacity nor the intention to be a regional hegemon. Its engagement with Central Asia, while having accelerated in the past decade, must be put into perspective: Central Asia simply does not lie at the forefront of China's main international, economic, and security concerns. Still, the lack of a grand design does not mean that Chinese foreign policy in Central Asia is not realistic or strategic, nor that it lacks any geopolitical connotation.

To be sure, analysts studying China's engagement in Central Asia do not always concur on its main driver, in particular, whether economic issues – especially natural resource extraction, or internal security issues, i.e. the Xinjiang question – are the main priority. What is clear is that both sets of interests have a direct relationship to China's domestic issues and that they are interdependent.

Energy cooperation is an obvious highlight in China-Central Asia relations. China is the world's second-biggest consumer of oil, but possesses only one percent of the world's reserves. Central Asia, and particularly those countries rich in hydrocarbon reserves and mineral deposits, provides China with the opportunity to secure high-volume imports of oil and gas whilst minimising its reliance on maritime routes and an unstable Middle East. China now sources over 10% of its oil and gas imports from Central Asia. Through these resource extraction projects, investments in infrastructure, and low interest loans, China has become a major – if not the leading – economic partner of each of the five republics.

However, the China-Central Asia policy transcends a mere quest for resources and other economic interests. Firstly, the region's economic development, and – ideally, concomitant – political and social stability is in Beijing's interests; Central Asian underdevelopment, instability and conflict risks severely undermining its efforts to develop, "pacify" and more strongly bind Xinjiang to the rest of China. For Beijing, it is critical that its Central

Asian neighbours play a more active part in fighting Uyghur separatism. Additionally, a long list of security threats potentially affects China's investments, including domestic grievances, pervasive corruption, transnational crime, and socio-economic problems. Coupled with "rising nationalism, ingrained suspicions about Chinese expansionism and few tangible grassroots benefits" for the general public, Chinese investments risk "becoming targets for local residents voicing a variety of complaints" (ICG 2013: 14, see Beshimov/Satke 13-11-13). In the longer term, there is real concern regarding NATO's 2014 withdrawal from Afghanistan – specifically, that separatist organisations operating in Xinjiang may find financial, technical and training support there, and in Pakistan (ICG 2013: 27).

Despite its vigorous economic expansion and pressing security concerns, however, China's direct engagement in the region's security has been limited, and it has shown no willingness to intervene or mediate in major crises. Essentially leaving security and military issues to be dealt with by Russia, China has expressly stated that it will not deploy its military in Central Asia, regardless of the threat (ICG 2013: 6). Its only real mechanism for involvement in security issues is the Shanghai Cooperation Organisation (SCO), a framework for fighting the "three evil forces" of terrorism, separatism and extremism; collaboration on tackling drug trafficking and organised crime; and for natural disaster response. Although China has carried out over 20 joint anti-terror exercises with other SCO member states, there are as yet effectively no structures or mechanisms within the SCO for dealing with serious threats, disputes and major crises – a failing evidenced by the SCO's failure to act during the 2010 unrest in Kyrgyzstan.

Establishing military bases in Central Asia, let alone a muscular military intervention, would run contrary to China's principle of non-interference, and has been categorically rejected. As its economic engagement in a still-insecure region visibly deepens, however, China may not be able to fully protect its interests without a more proactive engagement in Central Asian security. Yet, China's future role in the security of Central Asia may ultimately depend on its relationship with Russia. The effectiveness of the SCO, whilst ambitious on paper, will remain limited by Sino-Russian relations and rivalry. The last two decades have seen great strides in economic, diplomatic and military cooperation between Beijing and Moscow, but the reality stands that Central Asia remains firmly within Russia's proverbial backyard.

Russia

While Russia has somewhat struggled with its diminished influence in the former Soviet Union, it has been working to strengthen its role in Central Asia – if in a selective, and often bilateral, fashion. In most calculations, Russia still remains the most prominent external power in Central Asia, enjoying high-level political relationships, security cooperation, and a range of investment projects in the region.

Official statistics suggest that economic engagement with the region has been visibly revived under President Vladimir Putin, with Russia-Central Asia trade tripling to US$21 billion between 2003 and 2007, and growing to US$27 billion in 2011 (Oliphant 2013: 3). Though these figures pale in comparison to the region's trade figures with China, Russia's economic engagement is more multi-faceted: it has a dominant energy presence, but its involvement also spans mining, construction, the military-industrial complex, telecommunications, transport, and agriculture. Soviet-era debt has also provided an additional opportunity for Russian leverage, with debt cancellation being used more or less indirectly to secure military-security arrangements, as in Tajikistan and Kyrgyzstan. Russia's economic engagement with Central Asia also encompasses a very modest degree of development aid, some of this channelled through the multilateral frameworks of the Eurasian Economic Community (EurAsEC) and the Commonwealth of Independent States (CIS). A more vital and substantial component of the relationship is that of labour migration and regional remittances. Reliable data is not easily obtainable, but the Russian Federation (RF) Ministry of Foreign Affairs suggests there may be up to "4.5 million" Central Asian labour migrants living and working in Russia, remitting up to US$9 billion to their home countries (Blagov 02-08-13). These remittances are enormously significant – particularly for the economies of Tajikistan, Kyrgyzstan, and Uzbekistan – as is, in many respects, a sizeable low-paid labour force for Russia's own economy.

Although supplanted by China as the leading trade partner of the region, Russia remains Central Asia's eminent external security actor. Observers concur that security is Russia's primary driver in its engagements. This is seen less as a matter of "imperialism" than sheer pragmatism: the 7,000 km Russo-Kazakh border is virtually impossible to fully control, and the region is therefore viewed as a buffer zone increasingly subject to strategic uncertainty and non-traditional threats (Peyrouse et al 2012: 8). It is recognised in the National Security Strategy to 2020 and in the 2013 RF Foreign Policy Concept that there is a role in security for multilateral arrangements to which Moscow is a party – the SCO, for example, and the Collective Security Treaty Organisation (CSTO). The latter, as the main Russian-Central Asian multilateral framework, makes provision for Russian sales of military materiel, combined military exercises, and a Collective Rapid Deployment Force (CRDF).

There is a strong and growing move, however, towards bilateral security arrangements, leveraging off economic aid for military cooperation. To this end, Russian military and research facilities have been retained in Kazakhstan, Kyrgyzstan and Tajikistan, constituting vital elements in the Russian defence system. Crucially, however, and despite its not insignificant capacity, "Russia is more inclined to deal with its own interests in Central Asia rather than expose itself to risks that would arise if it really took on the role of regional 'policeman'" (Oliphant 2013: 12). Moscow's reluctance in 2010 to actively intervene under CSTO auspices in Kyrgyzstan shows that Russia remains cautious and prudent – viewing Central Asia "as a set of risks to be contained rather than as an opportunity for new inroads or expansion" (Oliphant 2013: 12).

India

India's primary drivers in Central Asia bear strong similarities to China's: the need to ensure and diversify its energy supplies; to develop a market for its own goods and services; and to keep a check on the rise of radical Islamist groups that may pose a threat to domestic security. To this end, the last decade has seen a modest but steady rise in India's efforts to engage with Central Asia, culminating in the 2012 launch of the "Connect Central Asia" policy, a "broad-based approach incorporating political, security, economic and cultural connections" (MEA GOI 12-06-12). Most analysts, however, admit that India has yet to translate these aspirations into strategic policy action, and that it remains a minor player in the region, unable to compete with China or Russia in energy or regional security matters respectively (Blank 11-06-13, Campbell 2013: 9).

"India's delivery mechanism" has been seen as painfully slow, especially when compared with China's rapid economic penetration (Chaudury 13-10-13); indeed, "it is not yet apparent that India is willing and able to invest the considerable amounts of economic, military, and diplomatic capital" required to realise its ambitions (Campbell 2013: 10). China has so far outpaced India in energy acquisitions and in its capture of Central Asian trade markets, with its $46 billion trade volume in 2012 dwarfing India's $500 million. Some experts take the view that India's potential could lie in complementing China's larger-scale engagement, by plugging gaps in the goods and services market in areas in which it has developed expertise, such as IT, banking, and food processing (ibid: 8).

Kazakhstan's oilfields have been of particular interest for India, but it has yet to gain a firm foothold in the sector. Attempts to enhance its presence were thwarted in September 2013 when the Kazakh government blocked the sale of US oil company ConocoPhillip's stake in the Kashagan oil field to Indian state-owned ONGC Videsh Ltd; to add insult to injury, this was subsequently awarded to China National Petroleum Company. There have also been protracted talks around a gas pipeline linking Turkmenistan to India via Afghanistan and Pakistan (TAPI), but most Turkmen gas is already committed to Russia and China; the security risks associated with the proposed route have also raised questions over its implementation. With the appointment of the Asian Development Bank (ADB) as transaction advisor for the project, TAPI does now appear to be grinding into motion. Earmarked for completion in 2017, it will export a projected 33 billion cubic metres of natural gas a year to India, Afghanistan and Pakistan (The Express Tribune 21-11-13).

India has also sought a larger role in Central Asia's security matrix – again, with mixed outcomes. Much of India's political attention is drawn towards Afghanistan where, like in the case of China, NATO's withdrawal has been cause for alarm. It is feared not only that a resurgent Taliban will be counter to India's interests post-withdrawal, but that insecurity may spill over to destabilise other Central Asian states (Campbell 2013: 4). For New Delhi, religious extremism in the region is a prime concern: the rise of jihadist groups in Central Asia, linked to the Taliban, poses a potential threat to India's own security, particularly in Kashmir. India's concerns are compounded by spiralling drug production and trafficking in Central Asia, with these profits also providing significant funding for jihadist groups.

Unlike China, India has not shied away from the prospect of military deployment in Central Asia. In 2004, it began upgrading an airbase in Tajikistan amidst media speculation that there were to be Indian MiG29 bombers stationed there. The Tajik government eventually succumbed to pressure from Moscow, however, by closing the door on India's aspirations there. Lower-profile initiatives to enhance bilateral military ties have enjoyed more success, with plans to cooperate with the Kyrgyz military on research, military hospitals, and training for UN peacekeeping missions. Joint anti-terror working groups have also been established with Kazakhstan and Tajikistan. At the multilateral level, India does participate in the SCO, but only as an observer at present. Given Beijing's relative dominance, together with the presence of Pakistan – also an observer – India is unlikely to be able to make any serious use of this platform for its own security interests.

Turkey

A rising power and an increasingly active player in the international arena, Turkey has long seen itself as occupying a uniquely "central" position in its wider vicinity. Perceiving deep cultural, religious, ethnic and historical bonds with the Central Asian states, diplomatic efforts were channelled in the 1990s towards mentoring the newly-independent "Turkic sister republics", but Ankara's ambitions were forestalled by domestic crises. Today there appears to be no coherent or concerted foreign policy agenda towards Central Asia – certainly none that would match the bold vision of the immediate post-Soviet era – but there are steady efforts to maintain diplomatic relations and economic ties with the region. Ultimately, "Central Asia is, to some extent, a crowded and competitive field for a middle-tier power", and Turkey's economic, security and diplomatic presence remain, on balance, very modest (Wheeler 2013: 11). This is borne out in observations of Turkey's aid and economic relations with the region. Whilst Turkey's role as an international donor has expanded considerably, available figures suggest that aid to Central Asia as a share of total Turkish aid has in fact shrunk (Wheeler 2013: 9).

However, Turkey's economic engagement with Central Asia has noticeably deepened across the trade, infrastructure, energy, and communications sectors. Official statistics value trade volume with the region at US$6.5 billion in 2010, with total Turkish foreign direct investment (FDI) exceeding US$4.7 billion (MFA ROT 2013c). Economic ties have perhaps been most extensively developed with Kazakhstan: a Strategic Partnership treaty was signed in October 2009, and Ankara has actively supported Kazakhstan's bid to join the World Trade Organisation (WTO), and its desire to take the rotating lead of the Organisation for Security and Cooperation in Europe (OSCE). There is no real evidence, however, that Turkey's economic ties with any Central Asian country have deepened more rapidly than anywhere else, nor that Turkish firms dominate regional economies; conspicuously, no Central Asian country lies within the list of Turkey's top 20 trading partners (Efegil 2008).

One area that may become more significant is energy. As its economy grows, Turkey will likely look to diversify its range of energy suppliers beyond its current overreliance on Russia. Ambitions to become a regional energy terminal (MFA ROT 2013b) also render imperative extensive energy cooperation with Central Asia. In 2007, Turkey suggested that an institution similar to the Organisation for Petroleum Exporting Countries could be created between Turkey and the Central Asian states, but there appears to have been little progress on this front (Efegil 2008).

Turkey does seek to play an active role in the region's security and stability, though current evidence of its activity in this area appears less substantive than the official line would indicate. An explicit focus on its support for peace figures strongly in Turkey's foreign policy discourse, with "special importance" attached to "preventative diplomacy" and mediation (MFA ROT 2013a). It is unclear, however, that this will translate into Turkey taking on a conflict management role in the region – though a significant deepening of

Turkish economic involvement could well force a more proactive role. For now, Turkey's security role has remained limited to military-to-military ties – providing military aid to Kyrgyzstan to fight terrorism, drug trafficking and illegal migration – and the funding of police training programmes in Kyrgyzstan, Uzbekistan, and Kazakhstan. Turkey's membership of the Cooperation Council of Turkic-Speaking States (CCTS) also provides for its participation in regional institutions that could stand for it to play a greater role therein. References have been made to matters of conflict and security, though it is less clear what practical initiatives these have led to (MFA ROT 16-09-10). Should it choose a more proactive role – whether by choice or by circumstance – Turkey's manifold links with Central Asia may ultimately provide room for constructive engagement.

European Union

Relations between Central Asia and the EU are also intensifying, most palpably in its 2007 Strategy for a New Partnership with Central Asia. As a concerted regional approach, its scope is wide-ranging and comprehensive, identifying seven priority areas: human rights; rule of law; good governance and democratisation; youth and education; economic development; trade and investment; energy and transport links; environmental sustainability and water; common threats and challenges; and intercultural dialogue (EC 2007). These have since been reinforced in the 2012 Council Conclusions on Central Asia as "proven ... and ... valid", the only key shift noted being the repositioning of Afghanistan to the centre of the Strategy (Melvin 2012: 1).

In some respects, the EU's interests in Central Asia are not entirely dissimilar to those of the other core actors: the stability and security of the region are very important, as is energy cooperation for the diversification of Europe's energy supplies (de Jong/Wouters 2011). What is distinct, however, is the emphasis the EU places on democratic values and human rights; security, moreover, is defined in "soft", or "human security" terms. The EU's Central Asia Strategy is – at least in theory – more "values-based" – and in that respect, more ambitious. What is less clear, as some commentators have observed, is the extent to which these elements have been a success.

To be sure, progress has been made. Diplomacy has developed positively, with the recent establishment of EU delegations to four of the five countries, and progress also made towards opening a delegation to Turkmenistan. The extension of the Council of Europe's European Neighbourhood Policy to the Caspian region represents a window to Europe for the Central Asian countries: an invitation to look west for support in modernisation and reform. Political dialogue on sensitive issues such as Afghanistan has also deepened, reflected in the Partnership and Co-operation Agreement signed with Tajikistan in 2011.

The EU is a visible partner to the region on the security issues of border definition and control, terrorism, and drug trafficking, with member states increasingly engaged in several security initiatives, including regular high-level security dialogues; the implementation of the UN Global Counter-Terrorism Strategy; agreement on an updated EU-Central Asia Drug Action Plan; BOMCA (Border Management in Central Asia); CADAP (Central Asia Drug Action Programme); CABSI (Central Asian Border Security Initiative); the EU-UN Joint Plan of Action on UN Counter-Terrorism in Central Asia; and the MIEUX (Migration EU Expertise) programme against illegal migration.

The EU has also positioned itself as an active player in the region's development. For the period 2007-2013, the EU committed €750m to co-operation with Central Asia under the Development Co-operation Instrument (DCI), with the European Investment Bank's (EIB) support for sustainable economic development projects contributing to modernisation and best practice along EU lines. It has been observed that the assistance provided through the DCI has been spread rather thinly across the seven priority areas identified in the strategy document (Boonstra 2011: 9), but it remains true that this, too, has helped shift some Central Asian attention from its immediate neighbours to the north and east. The EU's shift towards differentiated bilateral aid programmes, particularly in the region's lowest income economies of Kyrgyzstan and Tajikistan, has also been well received (Peyrouse et al 2012: 17-18).

European energy cooperation has also deepened, if only gradually, and largely at a bilateral level. The extension of the EIB's mandate to include Central Asia helped facilitate investment, particularly in the Kazakh oil sector; progress also appears to have been made with Kazakhstan and Turkmenistan on the long anticipated Trans-Caspian pipeline, which – despite opposition from Russia and Iran – is once again formally on the table (Hasanov 30-11-13). Regional initiatives to play a larger role in water management and hydroelectric power have proved rather more challenging (Boonstra 2011: 17-18).

For some, these achievements are "modest at best", with Europe remaining "a marginal player in Central Asia, operating significantly below its potential" (Melvin 2012: 1). The democracy and human rights elements of the EU Strategy have been especially closely monitored. Commentators note not only that "there has been little evidence of any substantial progress on human rights, governance, democracy and civil society in the countries of Central Asia as a result of EU activity", but that there may even have "been a further rolling back of these issues under the EU watch" (Peyrouse et al 2012: 2). It is noted that the drive to secure energy resources has in some cases been at the expense of the EU's normative emphases – the apparent relaxation of human rights and rule of law pressure on Turkmenistan, for example, to secure its participation in the Southern Corridor gas pipeline.

These apparently conflicting logics will not be easily reconciled, particularly with the ready option of Chinese or Russian support for Central Asian political elites. Still, "there is a unique role in Central Asia for EU diplomacy, development policies and European civil society" (Melvin 2012: 5). A 2006 survey indicated a majority of citizens in Kazakhstan, Kyrgyzstan, Tajikstan and Uzbekistan prefer democracy "as an ideal form of government" (Nikolayenko 2011: 191). With deepened civil society engagement and people-to-people contact (Boonstra 2011), Central Asians may well look to the EU for inspiration and assistance in these endeavours, through its Rule of Law Initiative and engagement of the Venice Commission. Similarly, Central Asia's push towards global standards on education, human rights and penal system reform increasingly favours and benefits from EU structures including Erasmus and the European Training Foundation, with Kazakhstan now a member of the Bologna process and European Education Area. The EU has also committed to assist Central Asia in developing environmentally sustainable industries, committing under the Kazakh government's Green Bridge initiative to innovative technology transfers (Ospanova 09-10-13).

Conclusions

A balance sheet of the foregoing would suggest that China and Russia will dominate Central Asian foreign policy options for some time to come. China and Russia, put plainly, "are 'total' actors in Central Asia, not in the sense that they shape the local realities on the ground, but that they have the capacity to engage on all fronts" (Peyrouse et al 2012: 21). China, in particular, seems increasingly capable of outbidding or outmanoeuvring all other countries when securing energy acquisitions in the region. Geographically, too, Beijing has the clear advantage of direct borders with three of the five countries concerned, enabling a whole new Silk Road of transport infrastructure. India and Turkey simply lack the resources, and even Europe's capacity is limited, not only by the lack of territorial contiguity, but also by an "inability to concurrently influence the political, security, economic and cultural realms" it aspires to (ibid). Set against China's economic muscle, it appears even Russia may lag behind.

Much will hinge on decisions to collaborate or compete. Recent and unprecedented dialogue between Beijing and New Delhi indicate a positive movement towards cooperation in Central Asia, but it is likely that China will continue to leverage its present advantage to gain greater economic predominance. China's future role in the security of Central Asia, however, may well depend on its relationship with Russia. It remains unclear if Central Asia will see further collaboration between Russia and China, or whether the region will serve as a field of confrontation, in particular around the envisaged Russian plan of a customs union that would involve Kyrgyzstan and Tajikistan (beyond Kazakhstan and Belarus). What is certain is that it will become increasingly important for China to maintain influence in the region and to protect its interests as these deepen. China will inevitably have to become more involved in Central Asia's peace and security and move beyond anaemic crisis reaction to a more proactive strategy for peace, security and stability.

It certainly appears unlikely that Russia will allow India to project meaningful military power in the region. Some analysts point to US geo-strategic interests favouring a stronger Indian presence in Central Asia, thereby increasing India's influence. However, while "Washington's presence allows India to play, or at least aspire to, a greater Central Asian role than it could achieve on its own" (Blank 2003: 141), New Delhi does not yet appear to have capitalised on this. And with the prospect of waning US influence in the region, India is likely to remain an essentially minor power.

Turkey, too, has US backing, but may have a strategic advantage: its trade relations with China, energy dependence on Russia, and cultural affinities with the region could potentially position Ankara as a "pivot power" in a crisis (Wheeler 2013).

Yet, the "hard security" so often taken as default in these discussions of Central Asian security ought not obscure useful questions of development, human security, and longer-term conflict prevention. After all, and "beyond the contradictory or complementary nature of these external actors, Russia's and China's primary interest is to protect their domestic situation from any destabilisation coming from Central Asia. Their economic strategies are proactive … but their security policies are mostly reactive and defensive" (Peyrouse et al 2012: 23). How might these political positions and diplomatic initiatives affect conflict management in a region still threatened by manifold security concerns?

How will the EU and Turkey each balance their stated support for democratic institutions with an apparently pragmatic approach, focused on economic and energy cooperation with non-democratic regimes? To what extent will Central Asia be brought "on board" with EU and international conventions, to modernise, globalise, and stabilise? As one analyst deftly puts it, "if the EU wishes to be engaged in Central Asia it must understand the possibilities of the relationship, but also its limitations" (Akiner 2010: 39). The same might be asked of all the cast on the Central Asian stage.

References

Akiner, Shirin (2010), "Partnership Not Mentorship: Re-appraising the Relationship Between the EU and the Central Asian States." *China and Eurasia Forum Quarterly*, 8:4, 17-39.

Beshimov, Baktybek, and Ryskeldi Satke (2013), "China extends grip in Central Asia." *Asia Times*: 13-11-13. Available at: http://www.atimes.com/atimes/Central_Asia/CEN-01-131113.html.

Blagov, Sergei (2013), "Russia eyes stronger economic engagement with Central Asia." *Eurasian Daily Monitor*, 08-02-13. Available at: http://www.ocnus.net/artman2/publish /International_3/Russia-Eyes-Stronger-Economic-Engagement-with-Central-Asia_prin ter.shtml.

Blank, Stephen (2013), "India's Strategic Failure in Central Asia." *The Diplomat*, 11-06-13. Available at: http://thediplomat.com/2013/06/indias-strategic-failure-in-central-asia/?allpages=yes.

Blank, Stephen (2003), "India's Rising Profile in Central Asia." *Comparative Strategy*, 22:2, 141.

Boonstra, Jos (2011), "The EU's Interests in Central Asia: Integrating Energy, Security and Values into Coherent Policy." Working Paper, No 9, January 2011. Bonn: EADI.

Boonstra, Jos (2012), *Democracy in Central Asia: Sowing in unfertile fields?* Policy brief, No 23, May 2012. Brussels: EUCAM.

Campbell, Ivan (2013), *India's role and interests in Central Asia.* Briefing, October 2013. London: Saferworld.

Chaudury, Dipanjan Roy (2013), "Economic Relations with Central Asia: China steals a march, but India undeterred." *The Economic Times*, 13-10-13. Available at: http://articles.economictimes.indiatimes.com/2013-10-13/news/42993222_1_connect-central-asia-shanghai-cooperation-organisation-energy-hungry-india.

De Jong, Sijbren, and Jan Wouters (2011), *Central Asia and the EU's Drive Towards Energy Diversification.* Working Paper, No 64, June 2011. Leuven: Leuven Centre for Global Governance Studies.

EC – European Council (2007), *Regional Strategy Paper for Assistance to Central Asia for the period 2007-2013.* Brussels: EC.

Efegil, Ertan (2008), "Turkish AK Party's Central Asia and Caucasus Policies: Critiques and suggestions." *Caucasian Review of International Affairs*, 2:3, 166-172.

Hasanov, Huseyn (2013), 'Turkmenistan, EU will discuss Trans-Caspian pipeline project in Ashgabat." Trend, 30-11-13. Available at: http://en.trend.az/capital/energy/ 2216957.html.

ICG – International Crisis Group (2013), *China's Central Asia Problem.* Asia Report, No 244, 27 February 2013. Brussels: ICG.

Melvin, Neil (2012), *The EU Needs a New Values-Based Realism for its Central Asia Strategy.* Policy brief, No 28, October 2012. Brussels: EUCAM.

MEA GOI – Ministry of External Affairs Government of India (12-06-12), Keynote address by MOS Shri E. Ahamed at First India-Central Asia Dialogue, http://www.mea.gov.in/Speeches-Statements.htm?dtl/19791/ Keynote+address+by+ MOS+Shri+E+Ahamed+at+First+IndiaCentral+Asia+Dialogue.

MFA PRC – Ministry of Foreign Affairs of the People's Republic of China (2013), "Jointly Build Silk Road in the New Era with Mutual Learning of Civilization and Common Development", Available at: http://www.fmprc.gov.cn/eng/topics/xjpfwzysiesg jtfhshzzfh/t1078943.shtml.

Bernardo Mariani

MFA ROT – Ministry of Foreign Affairs Republic of Turkey (2010), Declaration of 10th Summit of the Heads of the Turkic Speaking States. Available at: http://www.mfa.gov.tr/declaration-of-10th-summit-of-the-heads-of-the-turkic-speaking-states-_istanbul_-16-september-2010_.en.mfa.

MFA ROT – Ministry of Foreign Affairs Republic of Turkey (2013a), "Resolution of Conflicts and Mediatio." Available at: http://www.mfa.gov.tr/resolution-of-conflicts-and-mediation.en.mfa.

MFA ROT – Ministry of Foreign Affairs Republic of Turkey (2013b), "Turkey's Energy Strategy". Available at: http://www.mfa.gov.tr/turkeys-energy-strategy.en.mfa.

MFA ROT – Ministry of Foreign Affairs Republic of Turkey (2013c), "Turkey's Relations With Central Asian Republics." Available at: http://www.mfa.gov.tr/turkey_s-relations-with-central-asian-republics.en.mfa.

Oliphant, Craig (2013), *Russia's role and interests in Central Asia*. Briefing, October 2013. London: Saferworld.

Ospanova, Rufiya (2013), "Central Asia, EU agree to work together on Green Bridge initiative." *The Astana Times*, 09-10-13. Available at: http://www.astanatimes.com/2013/10/central-asia-eu-agree-to-work-together-on-green-bridge-initiative/.

Nikolayenko, Olena (2011), "Support for Democracy in Central Asia." *International Journal of Public Opinion Research*, 23:2, 191-204.

Peyrouse, Sebastien, Jos Boonstra and Marlene Laruelle (2012), *Security and development approaches to Central Asia: The EU compared to China and Russia*. Working Paper, N° 11, May 2012. Brussels: EUCAM.

The Express Tribune (2013), "One step closer: ADB selected transaction adviser on TAPI pipeline." The Express Tribune, 21-11-13. Available at:http://tribune.com.pk/story/634534/one-step-closer-adb-selected-transaction-adviser-on-tapi-pipeline/.

Wheeler, Thomas (2013), *Turkey's role and interests in Central Asia*. Briefing, October 2013. London: Saferworld.

Wood, Barry D. (2013), "China stakes out Silk Road riches as deal maker Xi charms Central Asia." *Huffington Post*, 30-09-13. Available at: http://www.huffingtonpost.com/barry-d-wood/china-stakes-out-silk-roa_b_4008437.html.

Xinhua (2013), "China-central Asia trade accelerates." Available at: http://english.people.com.cn /90883/8426220.html.

Yavobashvili, Temuri (2013), "A Chinese Marshall Plan for Central Asia?" *The Central Asia-Caucasus. Analyst,* 16-10-13. Available at: http://www.cacianalyst.org/publications/analytical-articles/item/12838-a-chinese-marshall-plan-for-central-asia.

Unreif für die Insel?
Die EU und die Implikationen des Zypernkonflikts

Hakan Akbulut

Einleitung

Die Verhandlungen zur Wiedervereinigung der seit nunmehr knapp einem halben Jahrhundert geteilten Mittelmeerinsel Zypern sollten nach einer Unterbrechung von eineinhalb Jahren im Herbst 2013 wiederaufgenommen werden. Zumindest Anfang Dezember 2013 war dies jedoch nicht der Fall. Beide Seiten – griechische und türkische Zyprioten – konnten sich bis dato nicht auf einen Text für eine gemeinsame Erklärung einigen, der die Grundlage für die Verhandlungen bilden und somit das Ziel und die Modalitäten der Gespräche vorgeben sollte. Egemen Bağış, der türkische Minister für EU Angelegenheiten, kommentierte diesen Umstand während einer Tagung des Gemischten Parlamentarischen Ausschusses (GPA) EU-Türkei am 5. Dezember 2013 mit dem Hinweis, dass das bekannteste Tier auf der Insel das für seine Sturheit und Dickköpfigkeit berüchtigte Maultier sei. Diese Sturheit habe wohl auch auf die Menschen der Insel abgefärbt. Dieser undiplomatischen Bemerkung von Bağış folgten die dreisten Aussagen von Takis Hadjigeorgiou, einem griechisch-zypriotischen Mitglied des Ausschusses, der sich darüber erzürnte, dass Bağış das Treffen vorzeitig verlassen hatte (HDN 06-12-13). Bağış wiederum entgegnete später, dass die Aussagen bzw. Gedanken eines so genannten Parlamentariers eines aus türkischer Warte nicht-existenten Staates genauso nicht-existent oder aber belanglos seien, wie auch der Parlamentarier selbst (Sabah 06-12-13).

Diese Geschehnisse und Wortgefechte im Rahmen des GPA sagen bereits viel über die Qualität der Beziehungen zwischen der Türkei und den griechischen Zyprioten sowie über die Vereinnahmung von EU-Foren in diesem

Kontext aus. Dass Bağış bzw. die Türkei die Republik Zypern – de facto den griechisch-zypriotischen Teil der Insel – offiziell nicht anerkennen, ändert zweifelsohne nichts daran, dass das Zypernproblem in den letzten Jahren den Beitrittsprozess der Türkei massiv behindert hat und ein Dauerthema in den EU-Türkei-Beziehungen darstellt. So hatte auch der Stellvertreter von Bağış, Alaattin Büyükkaya, während der zuvor genannten Tagung beklagt, dass das Thema Zypern bei der Zusammenkunft des GPA in den Vordergrund gerückt werde. Dies stelle einen Fehler dar (Kıbrıs Gazetesi 06-12-13). Büyükkaya erinnerte daran, dass das Treffen im Rahmen der EU-Türkei-Beziehungen stattfinde und das Zypernthema lediglich eines von vielen zu behandelnden Themen sei. In Richtung der griechischen und griechisch-zypriotischen Mitglieder des Ausschusses hielt er zudem fest, dass sie sich der Frage stellen müssten, ob diese sich dem Zypernthema als Repräsentanten des EU-Parlaments annäherten oder in dieser Frage stattdessen den griechischen Teil der Insel oder Griechenland repräsentierten (ebd.).

Die negativen Implikationen der Zypernfrage beschränken sich jedoch nicht auf die Beziehungen der Union mit der Türkei. Nachdem die Türkei ein NATO-Mitgliedsland ist, hätte es wohl mehr als eine Überraschung dargestellt, wenn nicht auch die Beziehung zwischen den beiden Institutionen – also zwischen der EU und der NATO – in Mitleidenschaft gezogen worden wäre. In der Praxis bedeutet dies, dass die EU, die sich als globaler Sicherheitsakteur profilieren möchte, mit der wohl stärksten militärischen Organisation der Welt, die noch dazu ihr Hauptquartier – salopp ausgedrückt – vor ihrer Haustüre hat und mit der sie auch die Mehrzahl ihrer Mitglieder teilt, nur sehr begrenzt kooperieren kann.

Die hier einleitend angeschnittenen Implikationen des EU-Beitritts der griechischen Zyprioten für die Beziehungen der Union sowohl zur Türkei als auch zur NATO werden im Folgenden ausführlicher dargestellt und erläutert. Es gilt hierbei, das Element der „institutional capture", also der Instrumentalisierung, und das „Kapern" von internationalen Institutionen und Foren durch einzelne Mitglieder für ihre spezifischen nationalen Interessen und Belange (siehe dazu Krebs 1999: 355-356) herauszuarbeiten und hervorzuheben. Da sich Debatten über „global shifts" auch auf die Frage konzentrieren, wie die EU oder die NATO auf diese reagieren sollten bzw. inwieweit sie in diesem Rahmen gestalterisch einwirken, könnten die Erfahrungen aus den hier behandelten Fällen als eine Art Warnhinweis vor übersteigerten Erwartungen an die EU oder die NATO verstanden werden, die vor dem Hintergrund abweichender nationaler Interessen und Präferenzen agieren und global operieren müssen. Es geht also nicht um die Übertragbarkeit oder eine Verallgemeinerung dieser Erfahrungen, sondern um ein „in Erinnerung rufen" von Herausforderungen und Schwierigkeiten, mit denen solche Akteure konfrontiert sind, und einen Verweis darauf, wie schnell sie selbst zum Teil des Problems werden können.

Ein schwieriges Beziehungsgeflecht

Will man die Komplikationen, die sich im EU-Kontext aufgrund des Zyperndisputs ergeben, verstehen, so muss zumindest ein Beziehungsgeflecht aus fünf unterschiedlichen Akteuren beleuchtet werden. Mit der EU im Zentrum dieses Beziehungsgeflechts war es Griechenland, das bereits 1961 mit der damaligen Europäischen Wirtschaftsgemeinschaft (EWG) ein Assoziierungsabkommen abschloss und 1981 den Europäischen Gemeinschaften (EG) beitrat. Eine wesentliche Motivation für den Beitritt Griechenlands stellte damals auch der Konflikt mit der Türkei dar.

Die Enosis-Bewegung auf Zypern, die nach einer Vereinigung der Mittelmeerinsel mit Griechenland trachtete, hatte in den späten 1940er Jahren an Intensität gewonnen und Griechenland unvermeidlich auf einen Kollisionskurs mit der Türkei gebracht. Schließlich war die Insel über Jahrhunderte hinweg unter osmanischer Kontrolle gewesen, bevor sie 1878 von den Briten okkupiert und nach dem Ausbruch des Ersten Weltkriegs annektiert wurde. Schließlich erhielt Zypern 1925 den Status einer Kronkolonie (Akbulut 2005: 27). Auf der auch aus strategischer Perspektive bedeutsamen Insel machten die Inseltürken ca. 20 % der Gesamtbevölkerung aus. So sprach sich die Türkei zuerst für eine Beibehaltung des Status quo aus und stellte später der Enosis-Forderung das Konzept von Taksim, also einer Teilung Zyperns in einen griechischen und einen türkischen Teil, entgegen. Eine Ära der Annäherung zwischen Griechenland und der Türkei, die in den 1920er Jahren nach der Unterzeichnung des Vertrags von Lausanne ihren Anfang genommen und sogar zu einem gegenseitigen Beistandspakt geführt hatte (Fırat 2001: 355), sollte also aufgrund der Geschehnisse auf und rund um Zypern Mitte der 1950er ein Ende finden.

Der Kompromiss lautete schließlich weder Enosis noch Taksim, sondern die Gründung eines „unabhängigen" Staates Zypern auf der Grundlage eines Proporzsystems, in dem u.a. die Regierungsämter sowie die Sitze im Parlament und die Posten in der Polizei zwischen den InselgriechInnen und -türkInnen aufgeteilt wurden. Zudem wurden neben der ehemaligen Kolonialmacht Großbritannien Griechenland und die Türkei als Garantiemächte etabliert. Diese sollten die Unabhängigkeit, territoriale Integrität und Souveränität der Insel sowie den Erhalt des geschaffenen Staatssystems gewährleisten und zu diesem Zweck wenn notwendig auch intervenieren können – falls möglich gemeinsam, falls nicht, auch im Alleingang.

Die neugeschaffene Ordnung erwies sich tatsächlich als sehr kurzlebig – das System brach bereits drei Jahre später zusammen. Es folgten gewalttätige Auseinandersetzungen zwischen den beiden Gemeinschaften, wobei sich ein Großteil der TürkInnen in bewaffnete Enklaven zurückzog (Brus et al. 2008: 25). Damit nahm auch die de facto Teilung der Insel ihren Anfang. Immer wieder aufflammende Kämpfe zwischen den beiden Bevölkerungsgruppen in den Folgejahren belasteten dementsprechend auch die Beziehungen der NATO-Partner Griechenland und der Türkei, wobei die Türkei bereits 1964 und 1967 mit einer militärischen Intervention drohte. Sie machte diese Drohung jedoch erst 1974 wahr, als auf der Insel ein von der Junta in Athen dirigierter Staatreich verübt wurde. Im Sommer 1974 eroberten türkische Truppen in zwei Etappen rund 36 % der Insel und schufen die Situation, wie wir sie heute kennen. Die griechischen Zyprioten im Norden der Insel flüchteten in den Süden, während die türkischen Zyprioten nun im türkisch kontrollierten nördlichen Teil Zuflucht suchten. Hier sollten sie zuerst eine eigene Administration aufbauen und 1983 sogar einen eigenen Staat ausrufen – die Türkische Republik Nordzypern (TRNZ), die jedoch lediglich von der Türkei anerkannt wurde.

Aus Protest dagegen, dass die NATO und vor allem die USA die türkische Invasion nicht verhindert hatten, verließ Griechenland den militärischen Arm der NATO (Varvaroussis 1979: 112-114). Im Bemühen, den Konflikt mit der

Türkei zu internationalisieren und dadurch die Unterstützung anderer Staaten zu erlangen, wurde auch ein EU-Beitritt als ein wesentliches Instrument identifiziert (Stephanou/Tsardanides 1991: 223, Meinardus 1982: 445). So trugen der Zypernkonflikt und in diesem Zusammenhang die Spannungen mit der Türkei[1] wesentlich zur Entscheidung Griechenlands, den Europäischen Gemeinschaften beizutreten, bei.

Der Türkei, die eigene Beitrittsambitionen in die Europäischen Gemeinschaften hegte, wurde kommuniziert, dass die Aufnahme Griechenlands die Beziehungen zu ihr nicht berühren werde (Stephanou/Tsardanides 1991: 210). Dies stellte natürlich ein in der Praxis nicht einzuhaltendes Versprechen dar. So blockierte das EG-Mitglied Griechenland lange Zeit die Reaktivierung des Assoziationsabkommens der Türkei mit der EWG aus dem Jahr 1963, das aufgrund des Militärputsches vom September 1980 ausgesetzt worden war. Griechenland sollte zudem in den 1980er und 1990er Jahren die Auszahlung von Finanzhilfen an den östlichen Nachbarn blockieren (Nachmani 2001: 84, Akbulut 2005: 112).[2] Ein EG-Beitritt war also für die Türkei neben all den anderen Aspekten auch zur Aufhebung des strategischen Vorteils, den Griechenland aufgrund seiner Mitgliedschaft genoss, erstrebenswert. Ihr Beitrittsgesuch vom Jahr 1987 wurde von der Gemeinschaft jedoch abgelehnt. Grund hierfür waren natürlich nicht nur die Konflikte mit Griechenland und Zypern, sondern u.a. auch demokratiepolitische und wirtschaftliche Unzulänglichkeiten.

Auf der anderen Seite beantragten die zypriotischen Griechen im Jahr 1990 die Aufnahme in die Europäischen Gemeinschaften. Sie genossen dabei eine privilegierte Stellung und waren im Vergleich zur Türkei im Vorteil, da sie erwartungsgemäß von Anfang an Schützenhilfe aus Athen erhielten. So

---

[1] Diese beschränkten sich inzwischen nicht mehr nur auf die Zypernfrage. Die Abgrenzung des Festlandsockels sowie der territorialen Gewässer und Lufträume in der Ägäis, der militärische Status von manchen griechischen Inseln und darüber hinaus Minderheitenfragen lieferten u.a. zusätzlichen Konfliktstoff (siehe dazu Akbulut 2005).

[2] Griechenland vollzog jedoch 1999 eine Kehrtwende in seiner Türkei-Politik, stimmte der Verleihung des Kandidatenstatus an die Türkei sowie der Auszahlung von Finanzhilfen an das Land zu.

machte Athen beispielsweise seine Zustimmung zum Abschluss einer Zollunion zwischen der Union und der Türkei von der Zusage von Aufnahmege-
sprächen mit den griechischen Zyprioten abhängig (vgl. Axt 1995: 259,
Riemer 2000: 88). Letztendlich erhielten die griechischen Zyprioten im Dezember 1997 auf dem Gipfel von Luxemburg gemeinsam mit zehn mittel-
und osteuropäischen Staaten den Status eines Beitrittskandidaten, wobei die
Verhandlungen 1998 beginnen sollten. Diese wurden 2002 abgeschlossen.
Später sollte der frühere EU-Erweiterungskommissar Günter Verheugen festhalten, dass die Union von der ursprünglichen Position, Zypern nur nach einer Lösung des Konflikts aufzunehmen, abgehen musste, weil Griechenland
ankündigte, die gesamte Ostweiterung zu blockieren, sollte nicht auch Zypern beitreten dürfen (siehe Deutschlandfunk 16-04-04, Reuters 04-02-13).[3]

Die Türkei hingegen ging auf dem Gipfel von Luxemburg leer aus. Es wurde
ihr lediglich bescheinigt, dass sie für einen Beitritt in Frage käme; auch
diesmal stellte die Zypernfrage natürlich nicht den alleinigen Grund dar. Da-
raufhin setzte Ankara den politischen Dialog mit der EU aus und machte sich
daran, den Beitrittsprozess der Inselgriechen mit unterschiedlichen Maßnahmen und Drohungen zu torpedieren. So erklärte der damalige Anführer der
Inseltürken, Rauf Denktaş, augenblicklich die kurz nach der türkischen Invasion aufgenommenen interkommunalen Gespräche für beendet (Akbulut
2013: 13). Darüber hinaus kündigten die Türkei und die Inseltürken an, die
Integration Nordzyperns mit dem „Mutterland" (also der Türkei) zu forcieren
und gründeten zu diesem Zweck auch einen „Assoziierungsrat" (Kramer
2000: 178).

Die Türkei zog ihr Beitrittsgesuch jedoch nicht, wie nach dem Gipfel von
Luxemburg angedroht, zurück und wurde im Jahr 1999 auf dem Gipfel von
Helsinki zum EU-Beitrittskandidaten gekürt. Hierbei wurde sie auch mit der
Forderung konfrontiert, auf eine Lösung der Probleme mit Griechenland hin-
zuarbeiten, und sollten diese bis 2004 nicht gelöst sein, sie vor den Internati-

---

[3] Auf der anderen Seite hatte 1997 die damalige türkische Außenministerin, Tansu Çiller,
gedroht, die Osterweiterung der NATO zu blockieren, sollte die Türkei nicht in die EU
aufgenommen werden. Die Drohung wurde jedoch nicht wahrgemacht (Bağcı 1999: 585).

onalen Gerichtshof in Den Haag zu bringen, und den Wiedervereinigungs-prozess auf Zypern zu unterstützen (Akbulut 2005: 23). Während sich die Beziehungen zu Griechenland nach 1999 tatsächlich deutlich verbesserten (wenngleich keiner der wesentlichen Streitpunkte bis dato gelöst wurde), hielt dies die Türkei indes nicht davon ab, weiterhin einen harten Kurs in der Frage des EU-Beitritts der Republik Zypern zu fahren. So drohte der türki-sche Premier Bülent Ecevit, der 1974 die türkischen Truppen auf die Insel beordert hatte, dass eine Aufnahme des griechischen Teils Zyperns in die EU die nähere Anbindung der TRNZ an die Türkei oder sogar eine Annexion zur Folge haben würde (Milliyet 04-11-01). Er war nach eigenen Aussagen be-reit, die Perspektive einer türkischen Mitgliedschaft für die Causa Zypern zu opfern.

Die Regierungsparteien sollten jedoch bei den Wahlen vom November 2002 aus dem türkischen Parlament gefegt werden. Die neugewählte AKP[4]-Regierung leitete eine Wende in der Zypernpolitik ein. Von nun an wurde auf eine Lösung des Konflikts auf der Grundlage eines vom damaligen UN-Generalsekretär Kofi Annan vorgelegten und mehrmals revidierten Plans noch vor einem EU-Betritt des griechischen Teils Zyperns hingearbeitet. Damit sollte einerseits sichergestellt werden, dass die Insel geeint der EU bei-treten kann, andererseits sollte damit auch ein großer Stolperstein auf dem Weg der Türkei in die EU ausgeräumt werden. Bedeutsam in diesem Zu-sammenhang ist auch, dass bei einer Großdemonstration im Jahr 2002 60.000 BewohnerInnen des türkischen Teils der Insel auf die Straße gingen und von der politischen Führung eine baldige Lösung verlangten, um gemeinsam mit dem griechischen Teil der EU beitreten zu können (Axt 2009: 60). Am Ende wurde der Annan-Plan bei getrennten Abstimmungen von 65 % der türki-schen Bevölkerung angenommen, während ihn 76 % der BewohnerInnen des griechischen Teils ablehnten (n-tv.de 25-04-04).

Somit trat im Mai 2004 die Republik Zypern der EU bei. De facto bedeutete dies lediglich den Beitritt des griechischen Teils der Insel. Da die EU die TRNZ nicht anerkennt, stellt aus EU-Perspektive auch der Nordteil der Insel

---

[4] Gerechtigkeits- und Fortschrittspartei

EU-Territorium dar, in dem das Gemeinschaftsrecht ausgesetzt ist. Türkische Zyprioten haben allerdings wiederum den Status von EU-Staatsbürgern (EC o.J.). Faktisch änderte dies jedoch nichts an der Isolation der türkischen Zyprioten. Nach dem positiven Votum der Inseltürken hatte die EU-Kommission eine Finanzhilfe in Höhe von € 259 Mio. sowie die Wiederaufnahme des Direkthandels zu vergünstigten Konditionen mit Nordzypern in Aussicht gestellt (vgl. Akbulut 2011: 7). Während die Gelder nach zwei Jahren freigegeben wurden, haben die griechischen Zyprioten eine Wiederaufnahme des Direkthandels zwischen der EU und den Inseltürken bis dato blockiert. Sie sehen darin eine Aufwertung des Status der Inseltürken, gar eine de facto Anerkennung, und verweisen in diesem Zusammenhang auf die Möglichkeit der Inseltürken, ihre Produkte über griechisch-zypriotische Häfen in die EU zu verbringen (siehe dazu auch Brus et. al 2008: 8, ICG 2011: 7). Dies stößt jedoch zumeist auf administrative Hürden oder bleibt aufgrund sozialen Drucks und psychologischer Barrieren (insbesondere die Angst davor, die eigene Gemeinschaft zu hintergehen) eine ungenutzte Option (siehe auch ICG 2009: 27).

Während die Inseltürken also nach wie vor keinen direkten Handel mit der EU betreiben können und auch keine internationalen Flüge über den Flughafen Ercan in Nordzypern zugelassen werden, wurde die Türkei nach der Aufnahme der Republik Zypern mit der Notwendigkeit konfrontiert, den Geltungsbereich ihres Zollabkommens mit der Union auf die neuen Mitgliedsländer und somit auch auf die griechischen Zyprioten auszudehnen, was eine Öffnung ihrer Häfen und Flughäfen für griechisch-zypriotische Schiffe und Flugzeuge miteinschließt. Die Türkei hat dies jedoch bis dato abgelehnt und verlangt im Gegenzug eine Beendigung der Isolation der Inseltürken.

In Reaktion hierauf hat die Union 2006 die Verhandlungen mit der Türkei in acht Kapiteln ausgesetzt und darüber hinaus verfügt, dass keine Verhandlungskapitel provisorisch abgeschlossen werden dürfen. Zusätzlich zu diesen acht von der EU eingefrorenen Kapiteln werden sechs weitere (darunter etwa das Energiekapitel) von den griechischen Zyprioten unilateral blockiert. Hinzu kommen Kapitel, die von Frankreich mit der Begründung blockiert werden, diese seien nur im Kontext einer Vollmitgliedschaft relevant, was zumindest Frankreich selbst im Falle der Türkei nicht anstrebt (vgl. Günay

2010). Unter Präsident Hollande hat Frankreich jedoch der Öffnung eines Kapitels zugestimmt, sodass die Verhandlungen in Fragen der Regionalpolitik und Koordinierung der strukturellen Instrumente im November 2013 aufgenommen werden konnten. Insgesamt ändert jedoch auch der Umstand, dass nach drei Jahren erstmals wieder ein Verhandlungskapitel geöffnet werden konnte, nichts daran, dass der türkische Beitrittsprozess nur schleppend voranschreitet und nicht unbedingt in einer Aufnahme des Landes in die EU enden muss, zumal die Verhandlungen mit einem offenen Ende geführt werden und Länder wie Österreich angekündigt haben, ihre Zustimmung zu einer endgültigen Aufnahme der Türkei in letzter Instanz von einem Volksentscheid abhängig zu machen.

Vor diesem Hintergrund ist weder eine Lösung des Zyperndisputs noch ein EU-Beitritt der Türkei in absehbarer Zeit wahrscheinlich. Dies bedeutet eine Beibehaltung eines zumindest „sonderbar" anmutenden Status quo im oben geschilderten Beziehungsgeflecht: Was de jure EU-Territorium darstellt, bleibt dennoch isoliert und darf nicht einmal zu vergünstigten Konditionen direkten Handel mit der Union betreiben. Zudem ist dieses Territorium – zumindest aus der Warte der Republik Zypern – unter der Besatzung eines Beitrittskandidaten[5], der diesen Status bereits vor 14 Jahren erhalten hat, sich aber noch nicht einmal heute ausmalen kann, was am Ende dieses so genannten Beitrittsprozesses stehen wird. Aufgrund der fehlenden Problemlösung auf Zypern erscheint auch eine vollständige Normalisierung in den Beziehungen zwischen diesem Beitrittskandidaten und dem EU-Mitglied Griechenland vorerst unmöglich. All dies findet auch seinen Niederschlag in den Beziehungen zwischen der EU und der NATO.

Die Zypernfrage und die EU-NATO Beziehungen

Als Zypern 1960 unabhängig wurde, stellte sich natürlich die Frage nach der außenpolitischen Ausrichtung dieses neuen Staates. Nachdem die drei Garan-

---

[5] Die EU spricht in diesem Zusammenhang von "areas of the Republic of Cyprus in which the Government of the Republic of Cyprus does not exercise effective control" (EC o.J.).

tiemächte Großbritannien, Griechenland und die Türkei NATO-Mitglieder waren, wäre nach Ansicht von Ker-Lindsay (2010: 68) ein Beitritt Zyperns zur NATO naheliegend gewesen. Die neue Republik entschied sich jedoch für die Blockfreiheit und wurde zu einem Gründungsmitglied der Blockfreienbewegung (Non-Aligned Movement, NAM). Auch hier spielte die Konstante „Türkei" eine wichtige Rolle. Die griechisch-zypriotische Politelite stand einem NATO-Beitritt ablehnend gegenüber, da sie befürchtete, dass die Allianz bei Interessenskonflikten aufgrund ihrer strategischen Bedeutung immer der Türkei den Vorzug geben und sich stets auf ihre Seite stellen würde (ebd.: 68). Später sollte sich die NAM-Teilnahme auch als ein sehr nützliches Instrument erweisen, um einer Anerkennung der TRNZ durch andere NAM-Mitglieder (unter ihnen viele muslimische Länder) entgegen zu wirken (ebd.: 69). Nicht einmal die Türkei selbst wollte Zypern in der NATO sehen, da sie befürchtete, das könnte ihre vertraglich verbrieften Rechte als Garantiemacht unterminieren. Ein NATO-Betritt Zyperns hätte zur Folge haben können, dass NATO-Partner wie die USA im Falle einer drohenden militärischen Eskalation einschreiten würden, um eine türkische Intervention zu verhindern und so einen potentiellen Konflikt zwischen NATO-Staaten und eine damit einhergehende Schwächung der Allianz zu verhindern (ebd.: 68).

Als im Winter 1963 gewalttätige Auseinandersetzungen zwischen den beiden Gemeinschaften ausbrachen und die Beziehungen zwischen den NATO-Partnern Griechenland und der Türkei auf die Probe stellten, wäre Zypern sogar beinahe zum ersten Schauplatz einer NATO-Operation außerhalb des Vertragsgebiets (also „out of area") geworden. Großbritannien warf dazu die Idee einer NATO-Friedenstruppe auf. Als diese abgelehnt wurde, schlug London die Bildung einer internationalen Truppe vor, die von NATO-Ländern beschickt werden sollte (Nicolet 2001: 316-317). Diese Pläne konnten allerdings u.a. aufgrund der ablehnenden Haltung der Inselgriechen, die in der NATO keinen neutralen Akteur sahen, nicht umgesetzt werden.

Nichtsdestotrotz hatte das Zypernproblem stets Relevanz für die NATO. Schließlich belastete es die Beziehungen zwischen zwei Mitgliedsländern und, in weiterer Folge, die Zusammenarbeit dieser Länder mit den USA und mit der Allianz an sich. Welche Ausmaße das Zypernproblem haben würde, wurde der NATO nach der Landung der türkischen Truppen auf Zypern im

Sommer 1974 vor Augen geführt. Griechenland verließ aus Protest den militärischen Arm der Allianz. Zudem wurde die Türkei, ein an der Grenze zur Sowjetunion gelegenes Mitgliedsland, vom US-Kongress für mehr als drei Jahre mit einem Waffenembargo belegt.

Während auf das türkische *Fait accompli* von 1974 eine vergleichsweise ruhigere, „stabilere" Phase auf Zypern folgte, sollte die Zypernfrage vor allem gegen Ende der 1990er Jahre verstärkt wieder zu einem Problem für die NATO werden. Von der Raketenkrise gegen Ende der 1990er Jahre abgesehen[6], trug der Zypernfaktor wesentlich zur türkischen Blockadehaltung in der Frage der EU-NATO-Kooperation bei. Auf dem Weg, sich als autonomen und fähigen Akteur im Bereich der Konfliktprävention und des Krisenmanagements zu etablieren, beschloss die EU auf dem Gipfel von Köln (1999), die für die Erfüllung der Petersberger Aufgaben (humanitäre Einsätze, Rettungseinsätze, friedenserhaltende und -schaffende Maßnahmen) relevanten Funktionen und Fähigkeiten der Westeuropäischen Union (WEU) in die Union zu transferieren und die hierfür notwendigen Entscheidungen bis Ende 2000 zu fällen (Council of the EU 1999). Somit würde die WEU zu diesem Datum ihren Zweck als Organisation erfüllt haben (ebd.)[7]. Für die Türkei bedeutete dies, dass sie die Rechte und Möglichkeiten, die sie im Rahmen der WEU als assoziiertes Mitglied genossen hatte[8], verlieren und auf die neu geschaffenen

---

[6] Die griechischen Zyprioten bestellten S-300 Boden-Luft-Raketen aus Russland. Die Türkei drohte mit Luftschlägen, sollten diese Raketen tatsächlich auf der Insel stationiert werden. Letztendlich wurden die Raketen auf der griechischen Insel Kreta stationiert (Akbulut 2005: 31).

[7] Die WEU wurde jedoch erst im Juni 2011 aufgelöst.

[8] Als assoziiertes Mitglied der WEU, konnte die Türkei beispielsweise an den Tagungen des Rats der WEU teilnehmen, hier das Wort ergreifen und Vorschläge einbringen. Von einer Teilnahme konnte sie nur auf Verlangen der Mehrheit der Vollmitglieder oder der Hälfte der Mitglieder inklusive der Ratspräsidentschaft ausgeschlossen werden (zum Folgenden vgl. Cebeci 2009). Sie konnte sich darüber hinaus mit Ausnahme des Sicherheitskomitees an allen Arbeitsgruppen der WEU beteiligen. Was Operationen und Übungen betrifft, so konnten assoziierte Mitglieder „participate fully and on the same basis as full members in WEU operations, unless a majority of full members or half the Member States including the Presidency decide[d] otherwise" (ebd.). Zudem genossen die assoziierten Mitglieder im Rahmen der Westeuropäischen Rüstungsgruppe (Western European Arma-

Strukturen und Fähigkeiten keinen Einfluss haben würde (vgl. dazu Cebeci 2011: 94-98, Cebeci 2009). Abgesehen von der Sorge, dass die Aneignung von militärischen Fähigkeiten durch die EU zu einem Bedeutungsverlust der NATO führen könnte, war somit die Eventualität eines Einsatzes dieser EU-Fähigkeiten gegen türkische Interessen etwa in der Ägäis oder auf Zypern für das anfängliche türkische Veto gegen ein automatisches Zugriffsrecht für die EU auf NATO-Kapazitäten und -Fähigkeiten verantwortlich[9]. Im Endeffekt einigten sich die EU und die NATO (mitunter auf einer Vereinbarung zwischen den USA, Großbritannien und der Türkei vom Dezember 2001 aufbauend) auf die Berlin-Plus-Regelungen[10], die der Türkei zwar nicht die gewünschten Mitsprache- und Mitwirkungsrechte einräumen, aber zumindest im Hinblick auf den Zypernkonflikt und die Streitigkeiten mit Griechenland wichtige Elemente erhalten (zum Folgenden vgl. Cebeci 2011, Açıkmeşe/ Triantaphyllou 2012). Es wurde beschlossen,

- dass die EU-Fähigkeiten nicht gegen NATO-Länder eingesetzt werden (und vice versa),

- dass Länder, die keine NATO-Mitglieder sind und weder an der Partnerschaft für den Frieden (Partnership for Peace, PfP) teilnehmen noch ein Sicherheitsabkommen mit der Allianz unterzeichnet haben, an keinen EU-geführten Operationen teilnehmen können, wenn diese unter Heranziehung von NATO-Kapazitäten und -Fähigkeiten stattfinden,

- dass die EU Wege und Möglichkeiten entwickeln wird, um eine weitestmögliche Einbindung von europäischen NATO-Partnern, die keine EU-Mitglieder sind, in ihre Operationen zu gewährleisten,

---

ment Group, WEAG), dem „Vorläufer" der heutigen Europäischen Verteidigungsagentur, etwa auch dieselben Rechte und Verpflichtungen wie Vollmitglieder der Union.

[9] Aufgrund der türkischen Blockadehaltung konnte die EU-Operation Concordia in Mazedonien nach Angaben von Hofmann (2009: 50) erst nach einer Verzögerung von einem Jahr anfangen.

[10] „Berlin-Plus" bezeichnet ein Sammelsurium von mehreren Übereinkommen zwischen der NATO und der EU, die die Formen und Prinzipien der Kooperation zwischen den beiden Institutionen festlegen und in einem geheimen Briefwechsel zwischen dem NATO-Generalsekretär und dem Hohen Außenpolitischen Repräsentanten der EU im März 2003 bestätigt wurden (vgl. Günay 2010).

- dass die EU darüber hinaus diese Staaten im Falle von Operationen in ihrer geographischen Nähe oder von sicherheitspolitischer Relevanz für sie vorab konsultieren wird,

- und dass diese NATO-Partner selber entscheiden dürfen, ob sie an EU-geführten Operationen teilnehmen möchten, wenn zur Realisierung dieser auf NATO-Kapazitäten und -Fähigkeiten zurückgegriffen wird.

Auf dieser Grundlage war aus türkischer Warte sichergestellt, dass EU-Fähigkeiten nicht auf Zypern oder in der Ägäis eingesetzt werden können. Zudem kann gemäß den getroffenen Vereinbarungen die Republik Zypern nicht an Berlin-Plus-Operationen – also an EU-Operationen, die unter Rückgriff auf NATO Kapazitäten und Fähigkeiten erfolgen – teilnehmen (Cebeci 2011: 100). Darüber hinaus ist die Republik Zypern von jeglicher Zusammenarbeit zwischen der EU und der NATO ausgeschlossen, weil sie kein Sicherheitsabkommen mit der Allianz hat, dessen Zustandekommen von der Türkei blockiert wird. In Reaktion hierauf blockiert die Republik Zypern die Behandlung von anderen Themen als Operation Althea – der einzigen laufenden Berlin Plus Operation – bei gemeinsamen Tagungen des Nordatlantikrats und des Politischen und Sicherheitspolitischen Komitees (Cebeci 2011: 100, Açıkmeşe/Triantaphyllou 2012: 564). Andere relevante Sicherheitsfragen konnten bis dato nur im Rahmen von informellen Treffen erörtert werden (Hofmann 2009: 47, Graeger/Haugevik 2011: 744).

Während die Türkei den Abschluss eines Sicherheitsabkommens zwischen der NATO und der Republik Zypern blockiert, verweigert auf der anderen Seite die Republik Zypern ihre Zustimmung zu einem Sicherheitsabkommen zwischen der Türkei und der EU und verhindert darüber hinaus die Annahme des Implementationsdokuments, das die Grundlage für die Zusammenarbeit zwischen der Europäischen Verteidigungsagentur und der Türkei bilden würde (Türkisches Außenministerium o.J.).

Vor diesem Hintergrund kann eine engere EU-NATO-Zusammenarbeit zumindest vorerst ausgeschlossen werden. Solange das Zypernproblem nicht gelöst ist, gibt es auch keinen Grund anzunehmen, dass sich an der Haltung der Republik Zypern oder der Türkei etwas ändern wird. Die türkische Seite hält auf den Seiten des Außenministeriums in diesem Sinne unmissverständlich fest, dass „if there is no movement in Cyprus and if there is no movement on Turkey's concerns in the EU with regard to our participation in the Common Security and Defense Policy, no further movement should be expected on the NATO-EU dossier" (Türkisches Außenministerium o.J.).

Fazit und Ausblick

Institutionen sind Akteure, aber zugleich auch Instrumente im Dienste nationaler Vorhaben und Strategien. So kann ihre Reaktion auf eine sich verändernde Welt schlüssig und nachvollziehbar sein – oder auch widersprüchlich und ambivalent. Sie können helfen, Probleme zu lösen, oder auch bestehende Probleme verschärfen. Somit dürfte es auch keine Überraschung darstellen, dass die oben genannten Länder und Gemeinschaften versucht haben, ihren Einfluss oder ihre Mitgliedschaft in der EU oder der NATO dafür zu nutzen, um ihren Positionen im Rahmen ihrer Konflikte zur Geltung zu verhelfen, aber auch um die „gegnerische Seite" unter Druck zu setzen und Kompromisse und Zugeständnisse zu erzwingen.

All dies geschah oder geschieht natürlich nicht in Isolation vor den anderen Mitgliedsländern dieser Institutionen. Sie sind in diesem Sinne keine unbeteiligten Zuschauer, die lediglich die Herausforderungen zur Kenntnis nehmen müssen, die z.B. eine Aufnahme der griechischen Zyprioten in die EU für die EU-Türkei-Beziehungen oder für die Zusammenarbeit zwischen der EU und der NATO mit sich gebracht hat. Nachdem nach so vielen Jahren keine Einigung in der Frage herrscht, ob und wann die Türkei in die Union aufgenommen werden sollte, sollte die „zypriotische Hürde" jenen Ländern, die gegen einen Beitritt der Türkei sind, nicht ganz „ungelegen" sein. Das Zypernproblem bietet in Abwesenheit einer klaren Zielsetzung und Strategie einen Ausweg, um den türkischen Beitrittsprozess zu verlangsam oder endgültig einzufrieren[11].

---

[11] Das heißt natürlich nicht, dass die Türkei alles Notwendige tut und nur aufgrund des Zypernproblems nicht der EU beitreten kann. Hier wird lediglich der für die Ziele dieser Ar-

Ähnliches gilt für die Beziehungen zwischen der EU und der NATO. Sie ergeben sich nicht lediglich aus dem Zyperndisput. Auch hier fehlt eine handlungsleitende Vision und Strategie. Es ist nach wie vor unklar, wie autonom die EU in militärischen Fragen sein sollte, über welche Kapazitäten sie verfügen und, vor allem, wie sehr sie sich von der NATO und den USA „abkoppeln" sollte. Es ist ein ständiger Ausgleich zwischen den Interessen jener, die an der NATO und den USA festhalten und den transatlantischen Link nicht geschwächt sehen wollen, und jenen, die die EU als einen zur Gänze eigenständigen und fähigen Akteur im Sicherheitsbereich sehen wollen, zu finden (siehe dazu auch Hofmann 2009: 45). Mit der Lösung des Zypernproblems wäre zwar ein wichtiges Hindernis aus dem Weg geräumt, aber auch dies allein würde keine effektive und sinnvolle Kooperation zwischen den beiden Institutionen garantieren. Die Lösung des Zypernproblems stellt lediglich einen notwendigen, aber keinen hinreichenden Faktor für eine effektive EU-NATO-Kooperation dar.[12] Was genauso benötigt wird, sind klare Zielvorgaben und Strategien. Kurzum, um die Zusammenarbeit zwischen der EU und der NATO auf klare Bahnen lenken zu können, müssen zuvor ganz grundlegende Fragen geklärt werden: Was will die EU sein und welche Rolle will sie in der Welt spielen?

Solange die oben angesprochenen Fragestellung nicht geklärt sind, wird wohl sowohl in der Frage des türkischen Beitrittsprozesses als auch in der Frage der EU-NATO Kooperation weiterhin die Strategie des „nach vorne Wurschtelns" verfolgt werden. Dies ist weder gut noch schlecht. In manchen Fällen erweist es sich als nützlich, in anderen als hinderlich. Manche Länder profitieren hiervon, andere bedauern es. Ob eine EU, die mit einer Stimme spricht, in eine klar vorgegebene Richtung marschiert, und sich die notwendigen Kapazitäten und Fähigkeiten angeeignet hat, um global „handlungsfähig" zu sein – was dies im Konkreten auch immer bedeuten mag – so gut für ihre

beit wichtige Aspekt betont, zumal hier keine ausführliche Auseinandersetzung mit dem Beitrittsprozess der Türkei angestrebt wird.

[12] Für eine ähnliche Sichtweise siehe u.a. Graeger/Haugevik 2011 und Açıkmeşe/Trianaphyllou 2012.

Hakan Akbulut

Mitglieder und die Welt wäre oder nicht, darüber kann ohnehin nur spekuliert werden.

Literatur

Akbulut, Hakan (2005), *NATO's Feuding Members: The Cases of Greece and Turkey.* Wien [u.a.]: Peter Lang.

Akbulut, Hakan (2011), *Der Zypernkonflikt und seine Auswirkungen auf die EU-Ambitionen der Türkei.* oiip Kurzanalyse, Nr. 2011/2. Wien: oiip.

Akbulut, Hakan (2013), *Die zypriotische Hürde: Stand und Perspektiven des Zypernkonflikts und die Implikationen für den EU-Beitrittsprozess der Türkei.* oiip Arbeitspapier, Nr. 70/2013. Wien: oiip.

Açıkmeşe, Akgün, und Dimitrios Triantaphyllou (2012), „The NATO-EU-Turkey Trilogy: The Impact of the Cyprus Conundrum." *Southeast European and Black Sea Studies*, 12:4, 555-573.

Axt, Heinz-Jürgen (1995), „Zypern – ein Beitrittskandidat der Europäischen Union. Implikationen für die Insel, die Region und die Union." *Südosteuropa*, 44:5, 259-279.

Axt, Heinz-Jürgen (2009), „Zypern: Konfliktbeilegung durch Europäisierung? – Jüngste Erfahrungen und Perspektiven." *Südosteuropa Mitteilungen*, 49:6, 49-65.

Bağcı, Hüseyin (1999), „Türkische Außenpolitik nach dem Luxemburger EU-Gipfel vom Dezember 1997: Europäisch ohne Europa?" In *Jahrbuch für internationale Sicherheitspolitik 1999*, herausgegeben von Erich Reiter, Hamburg: E.S. Mittler & Sohn, 579- 602.

Brus, Marcel, Mensur Akgün, Steven Blockmans, Sylvia Tiryaki, Theo Van Den Hoogen, und Wybe Douma (2008), *A Promise to Keep: Time to End the International Isolation of the Turkish Cypriots.* Istanbul: TESEV.

Cebeci, Münevver (2009), *A Delicate Process of Participation: The Question of Participation of WEU Associate Members in Decision-Making for EU-led Petersberg Operations, with Special Reference to Turkey.* EUISS Occasional Paper, No. 10/1999, Paris: EUISS.

Cebeci, Münevver (2011), "NATO-EU Cooperation and Turkey." *Turkish Policy Quarterly*, 10:3, 93-103.

Council of the EU [Council of the European Union] (1999): Presidency Conclusions. Cologne European Council. 3 and 4 June 1999. http://consilium.europa.eu/ueDocs/ cms_Data/ docs/pressData/en/ec/ kolnen.htm [Zugriff: 14-12-12].

EC – European Commission [o.J.], Turkish Cypriot Community. http://ec.europa.eu/cyprus /turkish_cypriots/ [Zugriff: 06-02-10].

Fırat, Melek (2001), „Yunanistan'la İlişkiler [1923-1939]." In *Türk Dış Politikası. Kurtuluş Savaşından Bugüne Olgular, Belgeler, Yorumlar*, Band I, herausgegeben von Baskın Oran, İstanbul: İletişim, 325-356.

Graeger, Nina, und Kristin M. Haugevik, (2011), „The EU's Performance with and within NATO: Assessing Objectives, Outcomes and Organisational Practices." *Journal of European Integration*, 33:6, 743-757.

Günay, Cengiz (2010), *Die Türkei als Regional Player?*, Studie im Auftrag des Bundeskanzleramtes. Wien: oiip. [nicht veröffentlicht]

Hofmann, Stephanie C. (2009), „Overlapping Institutions in the Realm of International Security: The Case of NATO and ESDP." *Perspectives on Politics*, 7:1, 45-52.

ICG – International Crisis Group (2009), *Cyprus: Reunification or Partition*. Europe Report No. 201 – 30 September 2009. Nicosia, Istanbul, Brussels: ICG.

ICG – International Crisis Group (2011), *Cyprus: Six Steps Toward a Settlement*. Europe Briefing No. 61 – 22 February 2011. Nicosia, Istanbul, Brussels: ICG.

Ker-Lindsay, James (2010), „Shifting Alignments: The External Orientations of Cyprus since Independence." *The Cyprus Review*, 22:2, 67-74.

Kramer, Heinz (2000), *A Changing Turkey: The Challenge to Europe and the United States.* Washington, DC: Brookings.

Krebs, Ronald R. (1999), „Perverse Institutionalism: NATO and the Greco-Turkish Conflict." *International Organization*, 53:2, 343-377.

Meinardus, Roland (1982), *Die Türkei-Politik Griechenlands – Der Zypern-, Ägäis-, und Minderheitenkonflikt aus der Sicht Athens (1967-1982).* Frankfurt/Main: Peter Lang.

Nachmani, Amikam (2001), „*What says the Neighbor to the West? On Turkish – Greek Relations.*" In *Turkey in World Politics. An Emerging Multiregional Power*, herausgegeben von Barry Rubin und Kemal Kirişci, Boulder, CO: Lynne Rienner, 71-89.

Nicolet, Claude (2001), „American and British NATO-Plans for Cyprus, 1959-1964." *Thetis*, 8/2001, 314-318.

Riemer, Andrea K. (2000), *Griechenland und die Türkei im neuen Millennium – Stabilisierer versus Regionalmacht.* Frankfurt/Main: Peter Lang.

Stephanou, Constantine, und Charalambos Tsardanides (1991), „The EC Factor in the Greece – Turkey – Cyprus Triangle." In *The Greek – Turkish Conflict in the 1990s. Domestic and External Influences,* herausgegeben von Dimitri Constas, London: Macmillan, 207-230.

Türkisches Außenministerium [Rebuplic of Turkey, Ministry of Foreign Affairs, o.J.]: III. The European Union Common Security and Defence Policy (CSDP) and NATO-EU Strategic Cooperation. http://www.mfa.gov.tr/iii_-turkey_s-views-on-current-nato-issues.en.mfa [Stand: 08-12-13].

Varvaroussis, Paris (1979), *Konstellationsanalyse der Außenpolitik Griechenlands und der Türkei (1974-75: seit der Invasion der Türkei in Zypern).* München: Uni-Druck.

Kampf der Subkulturen?
„Muslime" versus „Schwule" in westeuropäischen Homonationalismen

Sarah Ponesch

„Was guckst du? Bist du schwul?" lautet der Titel eines in der taz erschienenen Artikels, welcher sich mit der Problematik homophober Angriffe auseinandersetzt, diese jedoch – wie die Überschrift bereits vermuten lässt – auf eine ganz bestimmte Täter-Opfer-Konstellation einengt.[1] Einleitend erklärt Feddersen, Redakteur bei der taz und selbst offen homosexuell: „Ein hoher Prozentsatz der Gewalt gegen Schwule wird von Menschen aus dem islamischen Kulturkreis verübt. Das Problem wird tabuisiert, seine Thematisierung ist politisch nicht korrekt. Stattdessen wird gefragt: Sind die Angegriffenen zu offen mit ihrer sexuellen Identität umgegangen?" (taz 08-11-03). Das hier zugrunde liegende reduktionistische und essentialisierende Islamverständnis in Zusammenhang mit der unbelegten Behauptung des hohen Prozentsatzes homophober Gewalttaten von Seiten muslimischer Menschen könnte genauso gut dem rechten politischen Spektrum zugerechnet werden. Es handelt sich jedoch keinesfalls um einen einzelnen journalistischen „Ausrutscher". Vielmehr lässt sich der Beitrag in eine lange Reihe unterschiedlicher Publikationen, Tagungen, Mottos und Artikel zur Thematik erhöhter Homophobie innerhalb der (implizit) muslimischen „Einwanderungsgesellschaft" einreihen, welche vom linken bis zum rechten politischen Rand reichen und die gesellschaftliche Spaltung in der Identifizierung eines gemeinsamen „Feindbildes"

---

[1] Besonders wichtig zu betonen ist, dass die Problematik homophober Gewalttaten keinesfalls durch diesen Artikel in Frage gestellt oder bagatellisiert werden soll, im Gegenteil. Der Text macht es sich zum Ziel, die mannigfaltigen Diskriminierungen und reduktionistischen Stereotypisierungen von LSBTIQ (Lesben, Schwulen, Bisexuellen, Trans*-Menschen, Intersexuellen und Queers, im Englischen LGBTIQ) sichtbar zu machen und ihre Verschränkung mit weiteren Ebenen wie *race*, Klasse, Behinderung oder anderer gesellschaftlicher „Marker" im Sinne der Intersektionalität ins Zentrum zu rücken.

zumindest rhetorisch überwinden.[2] Wie lassen sich also diese unreflektierten und verallgemeinernden Zuschreibungen von Seiten unterschiedlicher politischer Lager erklären? Welche stereotypen Bilder werden dabei gezeichnet und welche Funktionen erfüllen sie?

Licht auf diese paradoxen Verhältnisse vermag das von Jasbir Puar (2007) eingeführte Konzept des „Homonationalismus" zu werfen. Das oben angeführte Zitat kann dabei exemplarisch für jene Prozesse verstanden werden, welche die Inkorporation (bestimmter) ehemals exkludierter homosexueller Subjekte in die Nation markieren, jedoch gleichzeitig mit der dualen Gegenüberstellung rassialisierter – und hier zumeist orientalisierter – „Anderer" arbeiten und diese in diskursiven Verhandlungen als Bedrohung für erstere festschreiben.

„The Muslim or gay binary mutates form a narrative of incommensurate subject positionings into an 'Islam versus homosexuality' tug of populations war: a mutation that may reveal the contiguous undercurrents of conservative homonormative ideologies and queer liberalism" (Puar 2007: 19).

In Weiterführung der populären Prämisse des „Kampfs der Kulturen" wird damit der „Kampf der Subkulturen" (Heidenreich 2005) verkündet, welcher in orientalistischer Tradition eine inhärente Dichotomie zwischen „dem Westen", verkörpert durch „die Homosexuellen", und „dem Orient", dargestellt durch „die Muslime", voraussetzt und durch kontinuierliche Wiederholungen verfestigt.[3] Ganz im Sinne der von Edward Said (1978) begründeten Theorie

---

[2] Als Negativbeispiele aus dem linken politischen Spektrum können u.a. folgende Veröffentlichungen angeführt werden: Bozic (2008), Bündnis 90/Die Grünen (2008), LSVD (2004). Das wohl prominenteste Beispiel für rechten Homonationalismus stellte der mittlerweile verstorbene niederländische Politiker Pim Fortuyn dar. Für ausführliche Kritiken homonationalistischer Diskurse siehe u.a. Ahmed (2011) für GB, Bracke (2012), El-Tayeb (2012) für die NL, Haritaworn/Petzen (2010) für D.

[3] Ich verzichte hier absichtlich auf die Verwendung des Binnen-Is, da sich die Zuschreibungen von Muslimen als Täter (nicht nur) im Kontext homophober Angriffe zumeist (implizit) auf muslimische Männer beziehen und diese auf einen bestimmten „Prototypen" des als „archaisch, rückständig, patriarchal und fundamentalistisch" identifizierten „Muslims" reduzieren und festschreiben, was in den nachfolgenden Ausführungen weiter präzisiert werden soll (siehe u.a. Petzen 2005, Scheibelhofer 2011).

des Orientalismus wird eine Art „innereuropäischer Orient" geschaffen, welchem identifizierte Problemfelder zugeschrieben und im Prozess der diskursiven Gegenüberstellung aus dem „abendländischen Europa" exkludiert werden. Ähnlich wie zu Zeiten des Kolonialismus erschafft sich das „neue Europa" durch den Orientalismus und als Verfechter der Menschenrechte selbst und sichert damit seine Vormachtstellung in Abgrenzung zu den problematisierten rassialisierten „Anderen" ab, die es sowohl nach außen als auch nach innen zu bekämpfen gilt (vgl. Ahmed 2011, Bracke 2012, El-Tayeb 2012, Haritaworn 2009, Petzen 2005).

Der vorliegende Artikel macht es sich zur Aufgabe, die wirkungsmächtigen Mechanismen des *otherings*[4] hinter der Fassade des scheinbaren Dualismus von „Muslimen" versus „Schwulen" sichtbar zu machen und hinsichtlich ihrer politischen Implikationen und Verwertungen zu untersuchen. Die politisierten Spannungsfelder zwischen „morgenländischer Rückständigkeit" und „abendländischer Moderne" sollen dabei anhand ihrer konkreten Ausformungen in den Ver*körperungen* homosexueller Männer als „akzeptable Andere" sowie muslimischer Männer als „inakzeptable Andere" aufgezeigt werden. Erstere werden im Modus des Homonationalismus als lebende bewegte „Beweise" westeuropäischer Fortschrittlichkeit verhandelt und spiegeln damit das „Negativ" der orientalisierten „Anderen", die erstarrt auf der Stufe des „Vormodernen" verharren.

Islam und Europa – Wie Öl und Wasser?

Die beschriebenen Entwicklungen lassen sich in einen größeren Diskurs über „gescheiterten Multikulturalismus", „fehlende Integration(-swilligkeit)", die Bildung von „Parallelgesellschaften" sowie der „Selbstghettoisierung" rassialisierter „Anderer" einreihen und verfolgen – ähnlich der konstanten und ein-

---

[4] Das so genannte *othering* bezeichnet einen Prozess identitärer Abgrenzung gegenüber einer als „anders" und „fremd" klassifizierten Person oder Gruppe, welcher gleichzeitig mit einer Hierarchisierung einhergeht und die somit erschaffenen „Anderen" als minderwertig gegenüber dem „Eigenen" festschreibt.

dimensionalen Thematisierung der „Kopftuchdebatte" in der muslimische Frauen als kollektive Opfer „ihrer Kultur" stilisiert werden – einen bestimmten politischen Zweck.

Fatima El-Tayeb argumentiert, dass das *othering* von MuslimInnen im westeuropäischen Kontext auf einer transnationalen Islamophobie basiert, die durch das *framing* innereuropäischer „Anderer" als Bindeglied für die fortschreitende Europäisierung und den Abbau innerer Beschränkungen gegenüber der als „richtig" klassifizierten „EuropäerInnen" dient.[5] Die Europäisierung der einzelnen Nationalstaaten wird somit durch die Wahrnehmung einer gemeinsamen Bedrohung durch (implizit oder explizit) nicht-*weiße*[6] Migration – und hier, wenn nicht ausschließlich so doch vermehrt jene von MuslimInnen – vorangetrieben (El-Tayeb 2012: 80f.). Balibar bezeichnet diese Entwicklung als „Neo-Rassismus", einen „Rassismus ohne Rassen", in welchem ein reduktionistisches und eindimensionales Kulturverständnis die biologistisch ausgerichteten „Rassentheorien" ablöst (Balibar 1990). Statt eine „Rasse" einer anderen gegenüberzustellen und ihre natürliche Gegensätzlichkeit zu behaupten, wird dasselbe Muster auf die (unterstellte) „Kultur der Anderen" übertragen und im Prozess der Rassialisierung/Kulturalisierung verallgemeinert.

Da sich das vereinte postnationale Europa in seiner Repräsentation nach innen und außen als Verteidiger von Menschenrechten und Toleranz definiert, werden Problematiken der Exklusion und Diskriminierung rassialisierter Minderheiten (auch von staatlicher Seite) unter Bezugnahme auf die erklärte „Andersartigkeit" (ewig) migrantischer Gruppierungen und „ihrer Kultur"

---

[5] Als Beispiel führt El-Tayeb (2012) die Bewegung der „Cities against Islamization" an, einem Netzwerk rechter Parteien aus Belgien, Deutschland, den Niederlanden, Österreich und Spanien, die exemplarisch für die verstärkte internationale Kooperation eigentlich nationalistischer Bewegungen gelesen werden kann, siehe unter http://www.stedentegenislamisering.be/De/.

[6] Unter Bezugnahme auf die Theorien der Critical Whiteness Studies wird „*weiß*" als gesellschaftlicher Marker, welcher mit Mechanismen der In- und Exklusion einhergeht, kursiv geschrieben. Damit soll auf seine soziale Konstruktion hingewiesen werden, die allerdings im Zuge gesellschaftlicher Aushandlungsprozesse weitreichende Wirkungsmacht erlangt und somit reale Ungleichheiten widerspiegelt.

sowie deren Unvereinbarkeit mit „unserem" europäischen Wertesystem legitimiert und den Betroffenen selbst zugeschrieben (vgl. El-Tayeb 2012, Haritaworn 2009, Haritaworn et al. 2008, Petzen 2005).

Besonders MuslimInnen – oder, wie El-Tayeb treffend erklärt, als solche *identifizierte* Personen(-gruppen), seien sie nun laut Selbstdefinition muslimisch oder einfach nur dem „suspekten Wirkungsbereich Islam" zugeordnet – verkörpern hierbei die orientalisierten „Anderen" im „neuen Europa" (El-Tayeb 2012: 80). Islam wird dabei weniger als Religion sondern vielmehr als allumfassende Kultur, beziehungsweise als gesellschaftliches Ordnungsprinzip im Sinne einer allumfassenden Determinierung verstanden (vgl. Dirlik 2007, Krämer 2008, Volpi 2010). MuslimInnen werden aus diesem verkürzten Verständnis heraus oftmals nicht in ihren vielfältigen Lebensentwürfen anerkannt sondern als sinnbildliche *Verkörperungen* „des Islams" verstanden und auf die damit einhergehenden stereotypen Zuschreibungen reduziert.

> *„[T]he perception [is] that Muslims and Europeans are like oil and water, unable to mix and merge; instead archaic Muslim enclaves, separate qua space and time, are supposedly surviving unchanged within the larger European societies, which in turn are forced to push these resisting populations into modernity through increasingly punitive measures (see e.g. the expanding anti-hijab legislation)"* (El-Tayeb 2012: 81).

Zur diskursiven Herstellung „muslimischer Patriarchen" und „schwuler Weltenbürger"

In Zusammenhang mit dem beschriebenen Phänomen des Homonationalismus entstehen aus dem dargelegten Verständnis von Islam und „seinen Gläubigen" mehrere Problematiken: Erstens wäre es den identifizierten Muslim(Inn)en aus dieser verkürzten Interpretation heraus gar nicht möglich, *nicht* homophob zu sein, ohne sich von ihrem Glauben – und im Sinne dieser reduktionistischen Sichtweise auch von ihrer als homogen verstandenen *einen* Kultur – zu verabschieden sowie sich in die als weltoffen und tolerant charakterisierte „Mehrheitsgesellschaft" zu assimilieren. Zweitens wären damit Lebensformen, die zugleich lsbtiq[7] *und* muslimisch sind weder denk- noch lebbar, weshalb jene Personen sich ebenfalls vom islamischen Glauben – und auch hier ist zumindest implizit Kultur gemeint – abwenden müssten. Wird dieser Gedanke noch weiter gesponnen, so resultierte daraus nur ein logischer Schluss, nämlich der, dass es sich bei MuslimInnen und LSBTIQ um zwei grundlegend verschiedene Gruppierungen handle, die sich gegensei- tig ausschließen. Die einzige und damit auch unausweichliche Möglichkeit, diese „Kluft" zu überwinden und vom „Dunklen Zeitalter" in die „Moderne" einzutreten, bestünde demnach in der Abkehr vom Islam (und „seiner Kul- tur") sowie der vollständigen Assimilation in die als fortschrittlich, frei und weltoffen verstandene „Mehrheitsgesellschaft" (vgl. Ahmed 2011, El-Tayeb 2012, Haritaworn 2009, Jivraj/de Jong 2011, Puar 2007).

Wie bereits angesprochen spielen vor allem muslimische und homosexuelle Männer, beziehungsweise stereotype Männlichkeits*bilder* über diese beiden als grundverschieden kategorisierten Gruppen eine zentrale Rolle in den pro- zessualen Aushandlungen homonationalistischer Diskurse.[8]

(Homophobe) Gewalt wird dabei als Problem der „anderen" Männer, ihrer im Singular verstandenen „muslimischen Männlichkeit", dargestellt. Im *othering* erhält sie einen „Körper", wird verdichtet in einem bestimmten Männlich- keitstypus, der nicht „unserer", sondern ein „fremder" ist (vgl. Scheibelhofer 2011). Ich verwende hier den Begriff Typus im Gegensatz zu Connell's (2006) Vorschlag der „Handlungsmuster" zur Erklärung von Männlichkei*ten* ganz bewusst, da den aufgezeigten Zuschreibungen exakt jene unterstellte Unbeweglichkeit und Homogenität der identifizierten stereotypen „muslimi-

---

[7] Klein geschrieben steht der Begriff „lsbtiq" für die jeweiligen Adjektive. An der Verwen- dung wird allgemein kritisiert, dass durch das einfache Hinzufügen weiterer Buchstaben Benachteiligungen und Marginalisierungen innerhalb dieser heterogenen „Gruppen" ver- schleiert werden.

[8] Dem vorliegenden Artikel liegt der Ansatz zu Grunde, dass Geschlecht sozial konstruiert ist, weshalb weder „Mann"/„Männlichkeit" noch „Frau"/„Weiblichkeit" als „natürlich" gegeben, sondern sowohl gesellschaftlich determiniert als auch im Sinne der Performativi- tät erst *hergestellt*, verstanden wird (siehe u.a. Butler 1990, Butler 1993).

schen Männlichkeit" bereits innewohnt. Für die Konstruktion der „ganz anderen Männlichkeit" ist diese Charakterisierung als „statisch" und „unbelehr-
bar" von zentraler Bedeutung, worauf später noch genauer eingegangen wird.

Als Effekte dieser stereotypen Darstellungen sind hier mehrere zu nennen. Es
ergibt sich, dass die „eigenen" Problematiken hinsichtlich gesellschaftlicher,
bis hin zu staatlicher und institutioneller Diskriminierungen entlang von Geschlecht und Sexualität und den damit verbundenen Gewaltausübungen nicht
mehr diskutiert werden (müssen). Die immanente Krisenhaftigkeit von
Männlichkeit (Pohl 2011) wird durch ihre Reduktion auf eine *bestimmte*
Männlichkeitsform – die nicht „unsere" sondern eine, oder genauer *die,* „andere" ist – ausgelöscht. In der dichotomen Gegenüberstellung von „muslimischer Männlichkeit" als negativem und (implizit *weiß* gedachter) „westeuropäischer" Männlichkeit als positivem Pol wird diese „reingewaschen" und
erscheint neben der hyperproblematisierten „anderen Männlichkeit" regel-
recht „unschuldig" (vgl. Scheibelhofer 2011).

Der „muslimische Mann" ist dadurch problem-*behaftet* im wahrsten Sinne
des Wortes. Sara Ahmed (2004) weist daher auf das „*sticken*" bestimmter
(nicht nur negativer) Begriffe hin, indem sie beispielsweise erklärt wie durch
den kontinuierlichen Gebrauch der wörtlichen Verbindung von Islam mit
Terrorismus der eine Terminus an den anderen gebunden wird. Dem „Is-
lami(sti)schen" haftet also bereits das „Terroristische" an, selbst wenn nicht
mehr der direkte Begriff „islamistischer Terrorismus" gebraucht wird, so
klebt das eine dennoch am anderen und muss nicht mehr explizit gemacht
werden. Die Verbindung wurde durch beständige mediale, politische und öffentliche Wiederholungen bereits von den AdressatInnen verinnerlicht und
„naturalisiert", sie bedarf daher keinerlei Erklärung mehr. Dies gilt, wie bereits erklärt, nicht nur für Begrifflichkeiten sondern auch für Körper, weshalb
„dem Muslim" auch bereits „der Terrorist" anhaftet.

Problematiken des strukturellen Rassismus werden in den beschriebenen homonationalistischen Diskursen nicht einfach nur negiert sondern erlangen
(nicht nur, aber auch) durch sie breitenwirksame Zustimmung. Die Figur des
„muslimischen Mannes" kann daher im eurozentristischen Bedrohungsszena-
rio des „Kampfs der (Sub-)Kulturen" (Heidenreich 2005), einmal politisch
aufgeladen, auch politisch verwertet werden (vgl. El-Tayeb 2012).

Sein konstitutives „Gegenüber" wird dabei vom „homosexuellen Mann" dargestellt. Wieso auch an dieser Stelle nicht von LSBTIQ gesprochen wird, wurde zwar bereits zu Beginn des Abschnitts kurz angesprochen, soll hier jedoch noch einmal präzisiert werden. Die Gründe für diese männliche Dominanz sind andere als bei jenen des identifizierten „Täters". Angesichts gängiger Vorstellungen von Geschlecht und Sexualität könnten eigentlich viel eher Frauen, Trans*-Menschen, Intersexuelle oder andere weitaus marginalisiertere Gruppierungen im Vergleich zum „schwulen Mann" als Prototyp des „Opfers" gehandelt werden.

Die „klassische" Viktimisierung bezieht sich nämlich zumeist auf Frauen. Ihnen wird in historischer Tradition ein beinahe „natürliches" Opfersein zugesprochen (vgl. Moser 2005). Wieso ist dies also gerade nicht der Fall? Obwohl der Terminus LSBTIQ mittlerweile weit verbreitet ist und auch von politischen Institutionen wie der EU[9] verwendet wird, so wird in konkreteren Beschreibungen und „Analysen" bezüglich homophober Angriffe schwulen Männern oftmals eine dominante Position zugesprochen. Dies drückt sich beispielsweise darin aus, dass häufig nur von Homophobie und nicht, oder nur eingeschränkt, von Transphobie die Rede ist. Ein anderes Beispiel liegt in der Bezeichnung „schwul" oder „homosexuell" anstatt „lsbtiq" oder indem entweder implizit durch die alleinige Verwendung der männlichen Form oder explizit indem nur von Schwulen gesprochen wird, nur Männer als Opfer heterosexistischer Gewalttaten positioniert werden (vgl. Haritaworn 2009: 53f.).[10]

Unter anderem kann dies durch die generelle männliche Dominanz westeuropäischer Vergesellschaftungen erklärt werden, welche sich nicht nur entlang

---

[9] Diese gebraucht den Begriff LGBT, siehe unter http://fra.europa.eu/sites/default/files/eu-lgbt-survey-results-at-a-glance_en.pdf.

[10] Als Beispiel führt Haritaworn (2009) einen Artikel der Jungle World mit dem Titel „Das große Schweigen" an, in dem Homo- (und Trans)phobie seitens „türkischer Jugendlicher" thematisiert wird und findet dabei folgendes heraus: „«Schwul» findet im Leitartikel der *Jungle World* 21 Erwähnungen, «lesbisch» dagegen nur acht, und immer nur im Tandem mit «schwul». Bisexualität erscheint gar nicht. Transphob/ie wird nur einmal erwähnt, Homophob/ie, Schwulen- und Homosexuellenfeindlich/keit dagegen 22 Mal. (Hervorhebung im Original, Haritaworn 2009: 53)

heterosexueller Geschlechterbeziehungen erstreckt, sondern ihre Wirkung auch in nicht-heterosexuellen Verhältnissen entfaltet. Die „patriarchale Dividende" (Connell 2006) bleibt damit auch homosexuellen als „untergeordneten" Männlichkeiten – wie Connell sie (in der Einzahl) nennt – erhalten, wenn auch mit einigen Vorbehalten und Abstrichen. Überspitzt erklärt Böhnisch deshalb: „Auch wenn du der letzte underdog bist, ausgegrenzt und niedergehalten, bist du immer noch ein Mann und damit im Prinzip mehr wert als jede Tussi" (Böhnisch nach Cremers 2007: 41). Allerdings möchte auch ich ähnlich wie Rieske betonen, dass diese Aussage in ihrer Pauschalisierung auch das Potential zur Verharmlosung und Missachtung anderer Problematiken, verschränkt mit verschiedenen Formen intersektioneller[11] Diskriminierung, in sich birgt und deshalb mit Vorsicht zu betrachten ist (Rieske 2011: 47f).

Anders gesagt können Männer zwar sehr wohl vielfältigen Diskriminierungen ausgesetzt sein, diese beziehen sich jedoch nicht auf ihr „Mann-sein" *per se*, sondern sind immer mit anderen Dimensionen wie *race*, Klasse, Sexualität, Religion oder Behinderung verschränkt. Dabei kann (zugeschriebene) Männlichkeit zwar sehr wohl negativ identifiziert werden, diese wird jedoch erst in Rückkoppelung zu anderen marginalisierenden „Markern" politisch aufgeladen und problematisiert. Soll heißen, dass sich das *othering* „des muslimischen Mannes" nicht primär in seiner „anderen *Männlichkeit*" sondern in seiner „*anderen* Männlichkeit" manifestiert. „Seine" (zugeschriebene) Männlichkeit wird also erst in ihrer Orientalisierung problem-*behaftet*.

Trotz der polemischen Formulierung vermag das obige Zitat daher dennoch zu zeigen, weshalb homosexuelle Männer im Vergleich zu Frauen oder Personen, die sich weder in den Mann-Frau- noch in den Homo-Hetero-Binarismus einordnen lassen, in homonationalistischen Opfer-Täter-

---

[11] Der Begriff „Intersektionalität" wurde von Kimberlé Crenshaw eingeführt und bezeichnet die mehrdimensionale Verschränkung gesellschaftlicher „Marker" wie *race*, Klasse, Geschlecht, Sexualität, Behinderung, Religion und weiteren. Dabei wird betont, dass beispielsweise eine Frau *of colour* nicht nur auf der Ebene der Rassialisierung oder des Geschlechts diskriminiert wird, sondern in der *Verflechtung* der beiden Felder, weshalb diese anstatt gesondert, zusammen betrachtet werden müssen.

Sarah Ponesch

Diskursen sichtbarer sind. Vereinfacht gesagt werden sie schlichtweg aufgrund der „Ressource Männlichkeit" (ebd.) als gesellschaftlich „wertvoller", als „bedeutender" stilisiert, womit bereits der Übergang zu einer weiteren Ebene anklingt.

Die vorangegangenen Ausführungen allein reichen nicht aus um die starke Fokussierung auf homosexuelle Männer zu erklären. Vielmehr muss hinter diese überhöhte Position geblickt werden um zu erkennen, was genau der „schwule Mann" *repräsentiert*. Ehemals ausgegrenzt, erlangt er im Homonationalismus einen Status, welcher ihm lange Zeit aktiv verwehrt, ja, welchem er selbst konträr gegenübergestellt wurde: jenen des souveränen westeuropäischen Subjekts, das es vor dem „Anderen" im Inneren zu schützen gilt. Durch die zentrale Bedeutung von Menschenrechtsdiskursen in der Selbstdarstellung (West-)Europas als Hort von Demokratie, Pluralismus und Toleranz wird der „homosexuelle Mann" von seiner vormaligen „Devianz" befreit und rückt in den Mittelpunkt der Gesellschaft (vgl. El-Tayeb 2012). Trotzdem auch Trans*- und intersexuelle Menschen von den Rändern westeuropäischer Gesellschaften stärker in ihre Mitte aufgenommen werden, wird ihnen dennoch nicht dieselbe „Eignung" der Verkörperung „des westeuropäischen Subjekts" in homonationalistischen Diskursen zugesprochen. Dies lässt sich unter anderem durch folgende Ausführungen erklären.

Um „das moderne westeuropäische Subjekt" verkörpern zu können werden dem „schwulen Mann" bestimmte Eigenschaften auf den Leib geschrieben, die ihn klar vom identifizierten „Negativ", dem „muslimischen Mann", abgrenzen. Ein bedeutendes Element nimmt dabei sein implizites *Weiß-sein* ein, das dichotom zum rassialisierten „Anderen" steht.

Zu beachten ist, dass sich das *Weiß-sein* des hier nachgezeichneten stereotypisierten westeuropäischen „schwulen Mannes" im größeren Kontext von *White Supremacy*[12] abspielt, sich dieser bedient und sie gleichzeitig wieder

---

[12] *White Supremacy* als Ansatz der Critical Whiteness Studies bezeichnet ein System hegemonialer Gesellschaftsverhältnisse, die *weiße* im Gegensatz zu *nicht-weißen* Menschen sowohl höherstellt als auch als Norm, gegen die die „Anderen" gelesen werden, positioniert.

unterfüttert. Ähnlich der Funktion „hegemonialer Männlichkeit" (Connell 2006) positioniert sich *Whiteness* als unmarkierte Norm, welche im „Verborgenen" operiert. *White Supremacy* funktioniert daher nur in der Weise als sie un- oder nicht vollständig bewusst beziehungsweise un- oder nur oberflächlich besprochen bleibt. Ihre Macht, ja ihre gesamte Existenz, bezieht sich implizit auf ihr Bleiben, auf die Verschleierung ihrer Wirkungsmacht und die Negierung beziehungsweise Ignoranz ihrer normierenden und normalisierenden Effekte zwischen Ausschluss und Inkorporation. Auch hier handelt es sich um hegemoniale und äußerst effektvolle Aushandlungsprozesse westlicher/westeuropäischer Vergesellschaftungen, die einer ständigen performativen Reproduktion bedürfen. Die Suprematie von *Whiteness* vereint somit sowohl Elemente von Struktur als auch Handlung und umschließt durch staatliche, institutionalisierte, politisierte, soziale sowie ökonomische Verflechtungen die Gesamtheit westeuropäischer Bevölkerungen (vgl. Bérubé 2001).

Whiteness wird damit zur „Neutralität" erhoben, folglich stellt sie den Anspruch keine „Farbe", sondern die unmarkierte Norm, gegen die all die „anderen" Hautfarben gelesen werden, zu sein. Dies drückt sich sowohl in Alltags- als auch in medialen, wissenschaftlichen, wirtschaftlichen oder vielen weiteren Diskursen aus. „For many white owners, managers, and patrons of gay bars, only a white bar can be *just* gay; a bar where men of color go is seen as racialized" (Hervorhebung im Original, Bérubé 2001: 257). Aus dieser „Logik" folgt, dass *weiße* Menschen, und hier wie bereits gezeigt besonders Männer, in Westeuropa die „Allgemeinheit" verkörpern, sie repräsentieren *den Menschen an sich*. All jene, die als *nicht-weiß* wahrgenommen werden, sind bereits markiert und werden durch unterschiedliche Formen des *otherings* zu den „Anderen" der Stadt/Nation/Region gemacht. Daher wird es ihnen auch beispielsweise nicht, oder nur sehr schwer, ermöglicht, als Sprecher für die „Allgemeinheit" zu dienen. Ihnen wird das „Spezielle" im Prozess der Rassialisierung bereits eingeschrieben[13] (vgl. ebd.). Was das Zitat zu

---

[13] Die Critical Whiteness Studies machen es sich daher zur Aufgabe, den Blickwinkel auf rassistische Strukturen und Praxen zu ändern. In diesem Sinne ist Rassismus nicht beim Adressaten, beim „Anderen" zu suchen, sondern soll bereits im (implizit *weißen*) „Ursprung" erkannt und aufgedeckt werden. Die Frage, die dabei gestellt wird, lautet daher

zeigen vermag, ist daher, dass diese Positionierung als „neutral" nur aus einer Art „*weißen* Blicks" heraus funktioniert, denn nur wer jene Privilegien die mit *Whiteness* einhergehen bereits besitzt, hat die Macht *nicht-Weiße* in Form überhöhter Selbstpositionierung als „Andere" darzustellen und festzuschreiben.

Strukturen und Handlungsmuster *weißer* Privilegien und Herrschaftsansprüche, seien diese nun implizit oder explizit, können daher benutzt werden, um Erfolge auf anderen Ebenen zu verzeichnen. Diese Mechanismen mögen dabei im Homonationalismus für einige Schwulen- und wohl auch für lbtiq-Vereine Vorteile erwirken können, grenzen dabei allerdings gleichzeitig mehrfach diskriminierte Personen aus und fügen sich somit in den machtvollen Nexus von *White Supremacy* ein (vgl. Massad 2007, El-Tayeb 2012, Haritaworn 2009, Puar 2007). Von Ignoranz oder Negierung bis hin zum aktiven Ausschluss unter (offen oder verborgen) rassistischen Vorzeichen werden so die mehrdimensionalen Verschränkungen von *race*, Geschlecht, Sexualität, Klasse und vielen weiteren Kategorien unsichtbar gemacht, was massive Auswirkungen für betroffene Personen nach sich zieht.

> „*[A] gay rights politics that is supposedly color-blind (and sex-neutral and classless) is in fact a politics of race (and gender and class). It assumes, without ever having to say it, that gay must equal white (and male and economically secure); that is, it assumes white (and male and middle-class) as the default categories that remain once one discounts those who as gay people must continually and primarily deal with racism (and sexism and class oppression), especially within gay communities. It is the politics that remains once one makes the strategic decision, as a gay activist, to stand outside the social justice movements for race, gender, or class equality, or to not stand with disenfranchised communities, among*

auch: Wer sind die kollektiven *VorteilsnehmerInnen* von Rassismus? Durch diesen veränderten Fokus kann es gelingen, Rassismus nicht mehr als etwas zu begreifen, das *weiße* Menschen nicht betrifft, sondern seine wirkungsmächtigen Verflechtungen mit westeuropäischen Formen von Vergesellschaftung zu erkennen, zu benennen und folglich auch bekämpfen zu können. Was von Menschen *of colour* betont wird, ist jedoch vor allem auch die Vorsicht davor, unter dem „Deckmantel" antirassistischer Critical Whiteness Studies den Blick wiederum nur auf *weiße* Personen zu lenken und damit einmal mehr Lebensrealitäten *of colour* auszublenden und zu marginalisieren.

*whom are lesbian, bisexual, gay, or transgender people who depend on
these movements for dignity and survival"* (Bérubé 2001: 266).

Es sollte damit gezeigt werden, welche Art von Phobie im Homonationalismus besondere Relevanz findet, nämlich hauptsächlich jene, die sich gegen
homosexuelle Männer richtet, die eine ganz bestimmte Form von (eindeuti-
ger) Männlichkeit verkörpern, welche sowohl Marker wie *weiß* als auch wirt-
schaftlich abgesichert, gebildet sowie geistig und körperlich „gesund" auf
sich vereint. All jene, die sich allerdings nicht in dieses äußerst exklusive
Raster einordnen lassen können oder wollen, werden damit einmal mehr unsichtbar gemacht. Richtigerweise merkt Ferry daher an, „[…] that the modern
movement often ignores many queer identities including transgendered and
transsexual individuals, people who express a genderqueer identity, the radically queer, queers of color, queers who do not identify with these particular
sexualities, and queers who are either homeless, of lower socio-economic status, old, and/or disabled" (Ferry 2012: 106). Von weiterem Interesse sind diese in westeuropäischen homonationalistischen Diskursen zumeist nur, wenn
sie als „Spektakel" in Abgrenzung zur norm(alis)ierten „homosexuellen
Männlichkeit" Verwendung finden können (vgl. Haritaworn 2009).

Verwertbare Körper – verkörperte Werte?

Die angeführten dichotomen Männlichkeitsbilder, welche in westeuropäischen Homonationalismen gezeichnet werden, erfüllen dabei unterschiedliche Funktionen und dienen als wortwörtliche Ver*körperungen* der behaupte-
ten Dichotomie zwischen „Islam" und „Europa" in den Aushandlungsprozes-
sen neoliberaler Vergesellschaftungen, welche von der Förderung und Propa-
gierung *einer bestimmten Form* von Diversität im Sinne ihrer ökonomischen
Verwertbarkeit geprägt sind.

Auf der Ebene politischer Regulierungen können diese Bilder daher verwendet werden, um auf der einen Seite spezielle Typen von „gay neoliberalism"
(Engel 2008: 50) zu propagieren und auf der (wortwörtlich) „anderen" Seite
einschränkende und diskriminierende Maßnahmen entlang rassialisierter
Trennlinien durchzusetzen und zu legitimieren. Dabei rückt auch die Frage

von Mobilität ins Zentrum. Während es zu einer massiv verstärkten innereuropäischen Mobilität kommt, werden den als „inakzeptabel" kategorisierten „Anderen" zur selben Zeit Restriktionen auferlegt. Einerseits werden MuslimInnen dabei auf rassistisch-ideologischer Ebene als „rückständig" und noch nicht oder niemals auf „unserer Stufe" imaginiert. Andererseits wird wiederum ihre reale Bewegung mit Bildern des „Terroristen", des „ungebildeten Arbeitsmigranten, welcher „uns" die Arbeitsplätze wegnimmt" oder anderen als gefährlich und unerwünscht eingestuften Stereotypen assoziiert. Diese Vorstellungen wirken wiederum legitimierend auf realpolitische Einschränkungen ihrer Mobilität durch polizeiliche Maßnahmen wie *ethnic profiling*, verstärkter internationaler Grenzüberwachung sowie bildungs-, wirtschafts- und sozialpolitischer Benachteiligungen die sich auf die monetären Voraussetzungen für Bewegung beziehen, aus und werden gleichzeitig wiederum in den orientalistischen Kreislauf eingespeist (vgl. Scheibelhofer 2011, Steyerl 2000).

> *„In other words, the construction of Muslim communities as static and repressive, preventing their members from moving – literally in case of women or intellectually in case of men – goes hand in hand with and hides legal, political and economic restrictions imposed on these communities, limiting their ability to move across borders between and within nations, often even within cities"* (El-Tayeb 2012: 81).

Im Zeitalter des postnationalen Europas erlangt die Frage nach Bewegung und Mobilität damit eine neue Dimension. Den Gesetzen des modernen „Weltenbürgertums" folgend, welches (dank des Zugangs zu ausreichend Kapital und der „richtigen StaatsbürgerInnenschaft") keine Grenzen mehr kennt, kann die absolute (Bewegungs-)Freiheit des „grenzenlosen Europas" gefeiert werden. Dieser dynamische Vorgang fußt speziell auf der wechselseitigen Beeinflussung von „KonsumbürgerIn" und urbanem Raum. Eingebettet in die globale Marktwirtschaft eröffnen sich Möglichkeiten des Transnationalen jenseits lokaler Bindungen. Werden die beiden diskursiv hergestellten Figuren des (implizit) *„weißen,* wohlhabenden, gebildeten Schwulen" gegenüber des (implizit) „orientalisierten, armen, ungebildeten Muslims" betrachtet, so lässt sich erkennen, dass diese eine gegensätzliche Form von „Zeit und Raum" verkörpern. Während „der Schwule" die „gute Diversität"

(Lentin/ Titley 2011) repräsentiert, welche „modern, beweglich, kosmopolitisch (jedoch nicht oder nur „passend" politisch aktiv) und kapitalistisch" verstanden wird, so markiert „der Muslim" die „schlechte Diversität" (ebd.), welche Elemente wie „vormodern, unbeweglich, traditionell und bedrohlich" auf sich vereint (vgl. El-Tayeb 2012, Haritaworn 2009).

Ein Blick hinter die Fassade dieses propagierten Modells macht ersichtlich, dass sich die Fragen rund um Mobilität und Diversität stark um die Möglichkeit ihrer ökonomischen Verwertbarkeit drehen und keineswegs als Selbstzweck betrachtet werden, sondern immer bereits (auch) wirtschaftspolitisch determiniert sind. Wie auch Lentin und Titley aufzeigen, überwindet die propagierte „Diversität" abermals nicht die dichotome Aufteilung des „Modernen" gegen das „Vormoderne", des (*weißen*, westeuropäischen) „Wirs" gegen das (rassialisierte) „Andere", sondern verfestigt und verwertet diese im Gegenteil.

> „*[It] draws on a shifting spectrum of old and new targets of racial stigmatization, mobilizing not just conventional, national insider/outsider distinctions, but increasingly the boundaries between the rational, self-managing citizen-subject and the willful, dependent, resource-heavy subject*" (Lentin/Titley 2011: 178).

Daher löst das hier gezeigte Diversitätsmodell etablierte Macht- und Ungleichverhältnisse nicht auf, sondern verpackt diese in „bunte" Repräsentationsfolien und verkündet seine Fortschrittlichkeit und Toleranz, während im Verborgenen nur allzu bekannte Herrschaftsmuster reproduziert werden (vgl. ebd., Duggan 2004, Puar 2007).

Es sind deshalb genau jene Modi der (oberflächlichen) Inklusion ehemals „devianter" Subjekte in den Mainstream, die Lisa Duggan (2002) als „neue Homonormativität" bezeichnet. Sie beschreibt damit jenen Prozess, welcher nicht-heterosexuelle Subjekte insofern akzeptiert als diese die Heteronormativität[14] nicht gefährden und den Ansprüchen des neoliberalen Staats und sei-

---

[14] „Die Heteronormativität drängt die Menschen in die Form zweier körperlich und sozial klar voneinander unterschiedener Geschlechter, deren sexuelles Verlangen ausschließlich auf das jeweils andere gerichtet ist. Heteronormativität wirkt als apriorische Kategorie des

ner kapitalistischen Ausrichtung gerecht, oder in anderen Worten, *verwertbar* gemacht werden können. Die starke Präsenz (implizit) *weißer* gebildeter wohlhabender geistig und körperlich „gesunder" Männer lässt sich deshalb zum einen durch die allgemeine Männerzentriertheit westeuropäischer Gesellschaftsstrukturen erklären und zum anderen dadurch, dass diese zwar „die Anderen", jedoch nicht „die ganz Anderen" – wie beispielsweise Trans*-Menschen oder queers *of colour* – repräsentieren und im Zuge von Diversität ökonomisch und gesellschaftlich verwertbar gemacht werden können, ohne dabei etablierte heteronormative Strukturen radikal aufzubrechen. Während der *weiße* schwule Mann inzwischen als „Musterschüler des Neoliberalismus" (Woltersdorff 2004: 146) inszeniert wird, verkörpert der rassialisierte heterosexuelle Muslim den notorischen „Fünfer-Kandidaten". Damit wird dem „Musterschüler" die Aufgabe der „Nachhilfe" übertragen, er wird zum „Klassensprecher" und zum „lebendigen Beweis" einer von „uns" geschaffenen „demokratischen, toleranten, bunten und vielfältigen Leitkultur".

Ehemals widerständische Subjekte sollen somit normiert und im Zuge homonationalistischer Diskurse in die Nation/die Metropole inkorporiert und ökonomisch verwertbar gemacht werden, was jedoch – und das ist wichtig zu betonen – keinen Garant für ihre zeitlich sowie räumlich unbegrenzte und allumfassende Inklusion bedeutet. Am Ende führt somit die im Homonationalismus (!) propagierte scheinbare Inklusion ehemals „devianter" Subjekte zu einer massiven Einschränkung alternativer Lebensformen von lsbtiq Menschen, seien diese nun *weiß* oder *of colour,* und legitimieren gleichzeitig rassistische Ausgrenzungsmechanismen von „MuslimInnen" im Zuge diskursiv hergestellter Dualismen. Möchte (West-)Europa dem geschaffenen Bild demokratischer und gerechter Gesellschaften selbst gerecht werden, bedarf es daher Alternativen im Sinne radikaler Solidarität, sozialer Gerechtigkeit und gesellschaftlicher Anerkennung jenseits ökonomischer Verwertbarkeit.

Verstehens und setzt ein Bündel von Verhaltensnormen. Was ihr nicht entspricht, wird diskriminiert, verfolgt oder ausgelöscht (so in der medizinischen Vernichtung der Intersexualität) – oder den Verhältnissen ästhetisch-symbolischer Verschiebung dienstbar gemacht" (Wagenknecht 2007: 17).

Literatur

Ahmed, Sara (2004), *The cultural politics of emotion*. Edinburgh: Edinburgh University Press.

Ahmed, Sara (2011), „Problematic proximities: or why critiques of gay imperialism matter." *Feminist legal studies*, 19:2, 119-132.

Balibar, Etienne (1990), „Gibt es einen »Neo-Rassismus«?" In *Rasse, Klasse, Nation. Ambivalente Identitäten*, herausgegeben von Balibar, Etienne und Immanuel Wallerstein, Hamburg/ Berlin: Argument, 23-38.

Bérubé, Allan (2001), „how gay stays white and what kind of white it stays" In *The making and unmaking of whiteness*, herausgegeben von Birgit Brandner Rasmussen (u.a.), Durham, NC: Duke University Press, 234-265.

Bozic, Ivo (2008), „Das große Schweigen: Homophobe türkische Jugendliche und die Angst vor Rassismusvorwürfen." *Jungle World*, 26-06-08.

Bracke, Sarah (2012), „From 'saving women' to 'saving gays': Rescue narratives and their dis/continuities." *European Journal of Women's Studies*, 19:2, 237-252.

Butler, Judith (1990), *Gender Trouble: Feminism and the Subversion of Identity*. New York, NY: Routledge.

Butler, Judith (1993), *Bodies that matter*. New York, NY: Routledge.

Bündnis 90/Die Grünen (2008), „Berliner Aktionsplan gegen die Homophobie." Abgeordnetenhaus Berlin, 16. Wahlperiode.

Connell, Raewyn W. (2006), *Die soziale Ordnung von Männlichkeit*. Opladen: Leske + Budrich, 87-107.

Cremers, Michael (2007), *Neue Wege für Jungs?! Ein geschlechtsbezogener Blick auf die Situation von Jungen im Übergang Schule – Beruf*. Bielefeld: Kompetenzzentrum Technik – Diversity – Chancengleichheit e.V.

Dirlik, Arif (2007), „Globalisierung heute und gestern: Widersprüchliche Implikationen eines Paradigmas" In *Globalgeschichte. Theorien, Ansätze, Themen*, herausgegeben von Sebastian Conrad, Andreas Eckert und Ulrike Freitag, Frankfurt, New York, NY: Campus Verlag, 162-187.

Duggan, Lisa (2002), „The new homonormativity: The sexual politics of neoliberalism." In *Materializing Democracy. Toward a Revitalized Cultural Politics*, herausgegeben von Ross Castronovo und Diana D. Nelson, Durham, NC: Duke University Press, 173–194.

Duggan, Lisa (2004), *The twilight of equality? Neoliberalism, cultural politics, and the attack on democracy*. Boston, MA: Beacon Press.

El-Tayeb, Fatima (2012), „'Gays who cannot properly be gay': Queer Muslims in the neoliberal European city." *European Journal of Women's Studies*, 19:1, 79-95.

Engel, Antke (2008), „Gefeierte Vielfalt. Umstrittene Heterogenität. Befriedete Provokation. Sexuelle Lebensformen in spätmodernen Gesellschaften." In *Heteronormativität und Homosexualitäten*, herausgegeben von Rainer Bartel (u.a.), Innsbruck, Wien, Bozen: Studien-Verlag, 43-63.

Sarah Ponesch

Ferry, Nicole C. (2012), „Rethinking the Mainstream Gay and Lesbian Movement Beyond the Classroom: Exclusionary Results from Inclusion-Based Assimilation Politics." *Journal of Curriculum Theorizing*, 28:2, 104-117.

Haritaworn, Jin, mit Esra Erdem und Tamsila Tauquir (2008), „Gay Imperialism: Gender and Sexuality Discourse in the 'War on Terror'." In *Out of place: Interrogating Silences in Queerness and Raciality*, herausgegeben von Adi Kuntsman und Esperanza Miyake, York: Raw Nerve Books, 71-98.

Haritaworn, Jin (2009), „Kiss-Ins und Dragqueens. Sexuelle Spektakel von Kiez und Nation." In *Verqueerte Verhältnisse: Intersektionale, ökonomiekritische und strategische Interventionen*, herausgegeben von AG Queer Studies, Hamburg: Männerschwarm, 41-65.

Haritaworn, Jin, und Jennifer Petzen (2010), „Invented Traditions, New Intimate Publics: Tracing the German 'Muslim homophobia' discourse" In *Islam in its International Context: Comparative Perspectives*, herausgegeben von Chris Flood und Stephen Hutchings, Cambridge, UK: Cambridge University Press, 48-64.

Haritaworn, Jin (2010), „Wounded Subjects. Sexual Exceptionalism and the Moral Panic on 'Migrant Homophobia' in Germany." In *Decolonizing European Sociology*, herausgegeben von Rodriguez Gutiérrez (u.a.), Farnham, Burlington: Ashgate, 135-151.

Heidenreich, Nanna (2005), „'Der Kampf der Subkulturen' Homophobie vs. Rassismus?" In *Quer durch die Geisteswissenschaften. Perspektiven der Queer Theory*, herausgegeben von Elahe Haschemi Yekani und Beatrice Michaelis, Berlin: Querverlag, 203-215.

Jivraj, Suhraiya, und Anisa de Jong (2011), „The Dutch homo-emancipation policy and its silencing effects on queer Muslims." In *Feminist Legal Studies* 19:2, 143-158.

Krämer, Gudrun (2008), „Vision und Kritik des Staates im Islamismus." In *Der Staat im Vorderen Orient. Konstruktion und Legitimation politischer Herrschaft*, herausgegeben von Peter Pawelka, Baden-Baden: Nomos Verlag, 167-185.

Massad, Joseph A. (2007), *Desiring Arabs*. Chicago, IL: University of Chicago Press.

Moser, Maria Katharina (2005), „Frauen – die paradigmatischen Opfer in Kriegssituationen? Konstruktionen von Geschlecht, Viktimisierung und Krieg." In *Krieg an den Rändern. Imperialismus und Gewalt von Sarajewo bis Kuito*, herausgegeben von Joachim Becker, Gerald Hödl und Peter Steyerl, Wien: Promedia, 108-123.

Lentin, Alana, und Gavan Titley (2011), *The crises of multiculturalism: Racism in a neoliberal age*. London: Zed Books.

LSVD Berlin-Brandenburg e.V. (2004), *Muslime unter dem Regenbogen. Homosexualität, Migration und Islam*. Berlin: Querverlag.

Petzen, Jennifer (2005), „Wer liegt oben? Türkische und deutsche Maskulinitäten in der schwulen Szene." In *Karriere eines konstruierten Gegensatzes: zehn Jahre «Muslime versus Schwule». Sexualpolitiken seit dem 11. September 2001*, herausgegeben von Koray Yilmaß-Günay, Berlin: o.V., 25-45.

Pohl, Rolf (2011), „Männer – das benachteiligte Geschlecht? Weiblichkeitsabwehr und Antifeminismus im Diskurs über die Krise der Männlichkeit." In *In der Krise? Männlichkeiten im 21.Jahrhundert*, herausgegeben von Mechthild Bereswill und Anke Neuber, Münster: Westfälisches Dampfboot, 104-135.

Puar, Jasbir (2007), *Terrorist Assemblages. Homonationalism in Queer Times*. Durham, NC: Duke University Press.

Rieske, Thomas Viola (2011), „Perspektiven auf Geschlechterverhältnisse in Bildungsinstitutionen." In *Bildung von Geschlecht. Zur Diskussion um Jungenbenachteiligung und Feminisierung in deutschen Bildungsinstitutionen*, Studie im Auftrag der Max-Traeger-Stiftung, Frankfurt am Main, 46-72.

Said, Edward W. (1978), *Orientalism*. New York, NY: Vintage Books.

Scheibelhofer, Paul (2011), „Intersektionalität, Männlichkeit und Migration. Wege zur Analyse eines komplizierten Verhältnisses." In *Intersectionality Revisited: Empirische, theoretische und methodische Erkundungen*, herausgegeben von Manuela Barth (u.a.), Bielefeld: transcript, 149-173.

Steyerl, Hito (2000), „Murphy's law: Politik statt Ontologie." *Vor der Information*. (Schwerpunktnummer Antirassistische Öffentlichkeiten, Feministische Positionen), 18-21.

Volpi, Frédéric (2010): „Locating Political Islam in Democratization Studies." In *Political Islam Observed*, herausgegeben von Frédéric Volpi, London: Hurst, 101-122.

Wagenknecht, Peter (2007), „Was ist Heteronormativität? Zu Geschichte und Gehalt des Begriffs." In *Heteronormativität*, herausgegeben von Jutta Hartmann, Wiesbaden: VS Verlag für Sozialwissenschaften, 17-34.

Woltersdorff, Volker (2004), „Zwischen Unterwerfung und Befreiung. Konstruktion schwuler Identität im Coming Out." In *under construction. Konstruktivistische Perspektiven in feministischer Theorie und Forschungspraxis*, herausgegeben von Urte Helduser (u.a.), Frankfurt am Main: Campus Verlag, 138-149.

Kurzzusammenfassungen

Heinz Gärtner: Where is Europe?

In dem Beitrag wird der Frage nachgegangen, welchen Stellenwert Europa in der akademischen Debatte in den USA über die neue Welt einnimmt. Die Auseinandersetzung wir vor allem von den großen Schulen der Realisten und liberalen Internationalisten geführt. Sie dreht sich um zentrale Frage, ob sich neue konkurrierende Pole herausbilden, oder ob sich eine liberale Weltordnung mit gemeinsamen Regeln und Normen (Ikenberry) durchsetzt. Offen ist, ob die Welt „post-American" (Zakaria), oder ob sie von einem amerikanischen Jahrhundert geprägt sein wird. China wird als die große Herausforderung gesehen. Europa wird als gegebene Größe angenommen, oder die Welt als „post-European" (Haass) bezeichnet. Eine neue Dynamik löste die Ankündigung von US-Präsident Obama zu Beginn 2013 aus, ein „Transatlantic Trade and Investment Partnership" (TTIP) zu verhandeln. Die USA und Europa könnten damit globale Prinzipien entwickeln, die autokratische Staaten wie China integrieren (liberale Internationalisten) oder isolieren (Realisten).

Kari Möttölä: Grand Strategy as a Syndrome: The United States' Review of Liberal Institutionalism

Die Komplexität des globalen Wandels mit dem relativen Niedergang der Vereinigten Staaten hat den liberalen Internationalismus als eine praktikable „Grand Strategy" in Frage gestellt. Der Artikel reflektiert amerikanische Debatten in Think Tanks und Akademia, die auf die Alternativen „deep engagement", „retrenchment" und „democratic ascendancy" fokussieren. Präsident Obamas Cross-Over-Strategie scheint Elemente aus allen drei Profilen zu verbinden. Der Artikel schließt mit Gedanken über die Folgen der amerikanischen strategischen Auseinandersetzungen für die Europäische Union, welche dabei ist, ihre globale Strategie zu entwerfen.

Jan Pospisil: At the End of Relief and Development? Assessing the EU Approach of Resilience in Crisis Prone Countries

Mit ihrem im Juni 2013 veröffentlichten Aktionsplan für Resilienz in von Krisen betroffenen Ländern hat die Europäische Kommission Dokument vorgelegt, das ein couragiertes und innovatives Politikkonzept vorschlägt. Der Aktionsplan soll vor allem die Politikbereiche der humanitären Hilfe und der Entwicklungspolitik bis zum Jahr 2020 ausrichten. Im Anschluss an erste konkrete Resilienz-Initiativen in der Sahel-Zone und am Horn von Afrika, welche die EU seit etwa zwei Jahren verfolgt, wird mit Hilfe dieses Aktionsplans eine Resilienz-Agenda entwickelt, das die LLRD-Agenda der Verbindung von Humanitärer Hilfe und Entwicklungspolitik voranbringen und damit der EU ein international unverwechselbares Profil geben soll.

Lisa Sigl und Carmen Heidenwolf: Scientists as Diplomats?! On the Challenges of Researching International Science, Technology and Innovation Policies

Die zunehmende Internationalisierung von Forschungs-, Technologie- und Innovations- (FTI-)politik wirft wichtige Fragen für das Verständnis internationaler Beziehungen auf. Zwar steht außer Zweifel, dass sie zunehmend die Art und Weise beeinflussen in der internationale Beziehungen aufgebaut und gepflegt werden. Welche globalen Machtdynamiken allerding entlang wissenschaftlicher und Technologiekooperationen entstehen, ist aber weithin unerforscht. Dieser Beitrag reflektiert, wie – zumindest diskursiv – diplomatische Verantwortlichkeiten an WissenschaftlerInnen und FTI-Stakeholder übertragen werden. Am Beispiel der Beziehungen zwischen der Europäischen Union (EU) und China wird nachgezeichnet, wie sich deren institutioneller Rahmen im Kontext von FTI-Kooperationen derzeit verändert. Die Analyse dieser Transformationsprozesse ist notwendige Voraussetzung für das Verständnis sich entfaltender Machtdynamiken im Kontext von FTI-Internationalisierung.

Cengiz Günay: Troubled Neighbourhood: The EU and the Transformations in the Arab World

Der Artikel diskutiert kritisch die EU-Nachbarschaftspolitik gegenüber den sich in einem Übergangsprozess befindlichen arabischen Ländern. Die Politiken der EU gegenüber der Region gehen weitgehend von europäischen Erfahrungen und Entwicklungsprozessen aus und erheben diese zur Norm. Dabei werden wichtige regionale Dynamiken und Diskurse ignoriert. Die EU versuchte zwar, durch die Steigerung der Förderungen für die Zivilgesellschaft in den arabischen Ländern und die in Aussichtstellung einer regionalen wirtschaftlichen Integration auf die Umbrüche zu reagieren, sie bleibt dabei aber in ihren eigenen Paradigmen gefangen und geht kaum auf die Bedürfnisse der einzelnen Gesellschaften ein. Anstatt die eigenen Rezepte auf die Region überzustülpen müssten neue Ansätze und Konzepte entwickelt werden. Dazu gehört es zum einen, die Natur der Beziehungen grundlegend zu überdenken, aber auch, neue Kontakte zu bislang vernachlässigten Akteuren des sozialen und politischen Wandels wie den Islamisten aufzubauen.

John Bunzl: Dilemmata europäischer Palästinapolitik

Der Text befasst sich mit der sinkenden Wahrscheinlichkeit einer Zweistaatenlösung des Israel-Palästina-Konflikts und mit sich daraus ergebenden gesteigerten Notwendigkeiten von alternativen Lösungsmodellen. Zunächst gilt es noch, die Bemühungen auf einen unabhängigen, souveränen palästinensischen Staat zu richten. Dies gilt auch für die EU. Die im vorliegenden Text erörterten neuen „Leitlinien" für die Vergabe von EU-Geldern an Forschungsprojekte, versuchen in diesem Sinn zu wirken; sie beschränken die Förderungswürdigkeit auf das israelische „Kernland" innerhalb der Grenzen bis 1967. Es ist dennoch unwahrscheinlich, dass solche Maßnahmen eine Zweistaatenlösung herbeiführen können. Anstatt eine bestimmte Lösungggsformel anzustreben, plädiert der vorliegende Text für die Hereinnahme bestimmter Prinzipien in den „Friedensprozess". Diese Prinzipien sollen das Kräfteverhältnis entschärfen und solche Lösungen befördern, die Prinzipien von individueller und kollektiver Gleichkeit entsprechen.

Ufuk Şahin: EU, Türkei und Russland: Eine Neubetrachtung des Südkorridors

Vor dem Hintergrund des türkischen Engagements in konkurrierenden Pipeline-Projekten, South Stream und Nabucco, wird in dem vorliegenden Artikel untersucht, welche Motive und Gründe den EU-Beitrittskandidaten und den „Energietransitstaat" Türkei dazu veranlasst hat, beide Pipeline-Projekte zu unterstützen. Darüber hinaus wird ausgearbeitet, was die Entwicklungen im Südkorridor über die künftige Rolle der Türkei in der Versorgungssicherheit der EU im Energiebereich verraten. Beruhend auf der Theorie der Geopolitik nach David P. Calleo wird argumentiert, dass vor dem Hintergrund der komplizierten Beitrittsverhandlungen die Anreize der EU nicht ausreichen, um die zunehmend selbstbewusste Türkei für eine Kooperation gemäß der Bestimmungen der EU-Energieversorgungssicherheit zu gewinnen.

Bernardo Mariani: The Shifting Balance of Power in Central Asia

Der massive Anstieg von chinesischem Handel und Investitionstätigkeit in Zentralasien wirft eine Reihe von Fragen über die Verschiebung des Machtgleichgewichts in dieser Region auf – nicht nur zwischen China und Russland, dem traditionellen Hegemon der Region. Türkei, Indien und auch die Europäischen Union ringen mit den neuen Anwärtern um eine größere Rolle auf der zentralasiatischen Bühne. Dieses Papier umreißt die wirtschaftlichen, politischen, sicherheits- und energiepolitischen Dimensionen des wechselnden Machtverhältnisses, verfolgt die sich verändernden Rollen von China, Russland, der Türkei und Indien, mit abschließendem Blick auf die EU und ihre Aussichten in der Region.

Hakan Akbulut: Unreif für die Insel? Die EU und die Implikationen des Zypernkonflikts

Von der EU und der NATO wird erwartet, dass sie als Kollektiv auf die globalen „shifts" reagieren und als aktive Mitgestalter fungieren. Dieses Papier greift vor dem Hintergrund der Komplikationen und Hindernisse, die sich durch die Zypernfrage ergeben, das Element des „institutional capture" auf und warnt vor einer überhöhten Erwartungshaltung. Der Zyperndisput und seine Auswirkungen auf den EU-Beitrittsprozess der Türkei sowie auf die Zusammenarbeit zwischen EU und NATO führen vor Augen, wie sehr spezifische Länderinteressen internationale Institutionen vereinnahmen können. Was für die Protogonisten des Zyperndisputs gilt, gilt auch für die anderen Mitgliedsländer dieser Organisationen, die unterschiedliche Vorstellungen darüber haben, ob die Türkei der EU beitreten sollte, welche Rolle die EU global spielen und wie sie sich im Verhältnis zur NATO positionieren sollte.

Sarah Ponesch: Kampf der Subkulturen? „Muslime" versus „Schwule" in westeuropäischen Homonationalismen

Dieser Beitrag macht es sich zum Ziel den Ansatz des „Homonationalismus", welcher 2007 von Jasbir Puar in den USA eingeführt wurde, aufzugreifen und in einen westeuropäischen Bezugsrahmen zu übersetzen. Vor diesem Hintergrund soll untersucht werden, wie Debatten über die angeblich erhöhte Homophobie seitens muslimischer Minderheiten und die Behauptung „ihrer" (und *nur* ihrer) damit einhergehenden Gefährdung homosexueller Staatsbürger(Innen) strukturiert sind und welche politischen Implikationen diese beinhalten. Dabei soll herausgearbeitet werden wie die diskursive Herstellung eines scheinbaren Dualismus zwischen „Muslimen" – als orientalisierte „Andere" – versus „Schwulen" – als „westeuropäisches Wir" – funktioniert, warum dieser männlich dominiert ist und diese Homonationalismen mit Fragen ökonomischer Verwertbarkeit verbunden sind und von einer bestimmten Vorstellung von Diversität unterfüttert werden. Im Sinne Heidenreichs kommt es dabei zur Proklamierung einer Art „Kampf der Subkulturen", welcher als Fortführung des populären „Kampfs der Kulturen" gelesen werden kann und sich somit in die lange eurozentristische „Tradition" des Orientalismus einreihen lässt.

Abstracts

Heinz Gärtner: Where is Europe?

In American academic debates, Europe plays only a marginal role. So far, the debate has been dominated by the view of US scholars. The discourse on the relative decline of the United States has called into question liberal internationalism as its long-term grand strategy and as a theory of the dynamics of world order; consequently, there are fundamental implications for the position of Europe in global change. Having significantly reduced its military footprint in Europe, the United States has now clearly signalled its intention to re-orientate its strategic focus to the Asia-Pacific region. Barack Obama announced a free trade agreement between the United States and the European Union in his State of the Union address in 2013. The "Transatlantic Trade and Investment Partnership" (TTIP) has introduced a new element into the debate, however. For liberal internationalists, the TTIP could provide a stable basis for market economies and liberal democracies to strengthen their global influence. Geo-strategists and realists would argue that, on a grand strategic level, closer US-European ties – the TIPP together with the "Transpacific Partnership" (TPP) – would enhance the West's leverage with China. Furthermore, it would isolate China's autocratic capitalist model, and the US and Europe would not only consolidate their status as leading economies, but also build a political bloc of liberal democracies.

Kari Möttölä: Grand Strategy as a Syndrome: The United States' Review of Liberal Institutionalism

Complexities of global change, including the relative decline of the United States, have called into question liberal internationalism as a workable grand strategy. This article reviews American think tank and academic debates, which propose deep engagement, retrenchment and democratic ascendancy as alternative routes, respectively, to recasting, replacing and bending liberal internationalism. President Obama's crossover strategy seems to combine elements from all three profiles. The article concludes with thoughts on the consequences of American strategic struggles for the European Union, which is in the process of charting its global strategy.

Jan Pospisil: At the End of Relief and Development? Assessing the EU Approach of Resilience in Crisis Prone Countries

With its "Action Plan for Resilience in Crisis Prone Countries" from June 2013, the European Commission has presented a document that proposes a courageous and innovative policy concept. The action plan intends to guide in particular the policy fields of humanitarian relief and development cooperation until the year 2020. Subsequent to the first two resilience initiatives in the Sahel region and in the Horn of Africa, which the EU has been pursuing for about two years now, the Action Plan develops resilience as a concept that is intended to follow up the LRRD approach in linking relief and development policies. Furthermore, it is designed to give the EU an internationally recognizable, distinctive profile.

Lisa Sigl and Carmen Heidenwolf: Scientists as Diplomats?! On the Challenges of Researching International Science, Technology and Innovation Policies

The internationalization of science, technology and innovation (STI) policies raises important questions for researching international relations. While STI policies seem to increasingly shape the ways in which the European Union (EU) and its member states forge international relations, it remains unclear how (far) STI collaboration will contribute to global power shifts. We will reflect on how diplomatic responsibility is – at least discursively – assigned to scientists and stakeholders in STI along the idea of "science diplomacy". By drawing attention to EU policies towards China, we then illustrate that international STI policies yield a dynamically changing institutional landscape. Understanding these transformations will be a precondition for an understanding of how (soft) power dynamics are unfolding in this context.

Cengiz Günay: Troubled Neighbourhood: The EU and the Transformations in the Arab World

The article critically examines the EU's neighbourhood policy towards Arab countries in transition. Trapped in its normative paradigm which suggests a linear line of development that puts democracy, as a genuinely Western value, at the top of an evolutionary civilizational process, the EU has failed to read regional dynamics and has omitted Arab discourses. In the wake of the uprisings, the EU promised to increase financial support for Arab civil society and to intensify economic integration with the region; it has, however, done little to listen to the needs and grievances of the Arab societies. In order to become an affective external actor, the EU needs to rethink the foundations of its relations with the region and to reach out to new and influential agents of social and political change in the region, such as Islamists.

John Bunzl: Dilemmata europäischer Palästinapolitik

This text results from the decreasing probability of a Two State solution to the Israel-Palestine conflict and the increasing search for alternative scenarios. The European Union promotes the creation of an independent Palestinian state in the West Bank, East-Jerusalem and Gaza. It has adopted several measures to discourage the building of Israeli settlements in the Occupied Territories. The "Guidelines" announced in July 2013 figure prominently in this text. Although there are reasonable doubts regarding the effectiveness of these measures, they do point in the direction of a more equitable relationship between Israelis and Palestinians. The measures taken should be evaluated according to their impact on this relationship. The "Peace Process" would benefit from the introduction of such and other principles and not only be dependent on the relationship of forces. The relevant principles can be found in the values of the EU itself.

Abstracts

Ufuk Şahin: EU, Türkei und Russland: Eine Neubetrachtung des Südkorridors

Against the background of Turkish involvement in competing pipeline projects, South Stream and Nabucco, this article examines the motives and reasons why Turkey supports both pipeline projects as an EU candidate country and possibly an "energy transit state". In addition, the article elaborates what the developments in the Southern Corridor reveal about the future role of Turkey for EU energy security. Based on the political geography theory of David P. Calleo, the article argues that – since accession negotiations are showing little progress – the EU offers few incentives to an increasingly assertive Turkey to consider EU provisions for energy diversification.

Bernardo Mariani: The Shifting Balance of Power in Central Asia

The massive increase in Chinese trade and investment in Central Asia, which consists of the former Soviet Union republics of Kazakhstan, Kyrgyzstan, Tajikistan, Turkmenistan and Uzbekistan, prompts a number of questions about the shifting balance of power in this region – and not just between China and Russia, the region's traditional hegemon. Turkey, India, and the European Union (EU), too, rank amongst the aspirants to a larger role on the Central Asian stage. Outlining the economic, political, security, and energy dimensions of the changing balance of power, this paper traces the evolving roles of China, Russia, Turkey and India, concluding with an eye to the EU, and its prospects in the region.

Hakan Akbulut: Unreif für die Insel? Die EU und die Implikationen des Zypernkonflikts

The EU and NATO are expected to respond to the emerging global shifts in the international order collectively and to shape them alongside other actors. Against the backdrop of difficulties and impediments caused by the Cyprus issue, this paper highlights the phenomenon of institutional capture and warns against exaggerated expectations. This is because the Cyprus dispute and its repercussions on Turkey's EU accession process, as well as on cooperation between the EU and NATO, clearly show to what extent international institutions can be held hostage to specific national interests. What applies to the protagonists of the Cyprus issue is also true for other members of those institutions that seem to hold diverging positions on whether Turkey should be admitted to the EU, what role the EU should play on the global scene and how it should position itself vis-à-vis NATO when embarking on such a role.

Sarah Ponesch: Kampf der Subkulturen? „Muslime" versus „Schwule" in westeuropäischen Homonationalismen

This article aims to take up the concept of "homonationalism", which was introduced in the USA by Jasbir Puar in 2007, and translate it into a Western European context. It will be examined how the debates around the allegedly higher levels of homophobia among Muslim minorities, accompanied by "their" (and *only* their) threat to homosexual European citizens, are structured and what kinds of political implications they include. It will be elaborated how this discursive production of the seeming dualism between "Muslims" – as orientalized "others" – versus "Gays" – as a "Western European we" – functions, why it is dominated by male actors and how those homonationalisms are connected with questions of economic applicability, which themselves are fed by a certain understanding of diversity. According to Heidenreich, there has been a proclamation of a sort of "Clash of Subcultures", which can be understood as a continuation of the popular "Clash of Civilizations" argument and can therefore be classified as being part of the long Eurocentric tradition of orientalism.

Liste der AutorInnen

Hakan Akbulut ist wissenschaftlicher Mitarbeiter am oiip und Lehrbeauftragter an der Universität Wien. Seine Arbeitsschwerpunkte bilden die türkische Außen- und Sicherheitspolitik, nukleare Non-Proliferation und Abrüstung sowie der Zypernkonflikt. Hakan Akbulut absolviert derzeit ein Doktoratsstudium der Politikwissenschaft an der Universität Wien.

John Bunzl ist im wissenschaftlichen Beratungsstab des oiip. Seine Forschungsschwerpunkte sind Israel/Palästina, Naher Osten, Islamophobie und Antisemitismus. Er ist Autor zahlreicher Publikationen.

Heinz Gärtner ist Direktor des Österreichischen Instituts für Internationale Politik (oiip) und Senior Scientist am Institut für Politikwissenschaft an der Universität Wien. Er hat regelmäßig Forschungs- und Lehraufenthalte an der Universität Stanford. Sein letztes Buch heißt „Der amerikanische Präsident und die neue Welt" (Lit.-Verlag), November 2012.

Cengiz Günay ist Senior Fellow am oiip und Lektor am Institut für Politikwissenschaft und dem Institut für Internationale Entwicklung der Universität Wien. Zu seinen Forschungsschwerpunkten gehören: Islamismus, Politische Reform, sozio-ökonomische Transformationsprozesse und die Frage der Demokratisierung im Kontext des Nahen Ostens und der Türkei und die Rolle von nicht-staatlichen Akteuren.

Carmen Heidenwolf ist seit März 2012 am oiip tätig und bringt ihre Erfahrung aus dem Bereich der transatlantischen Wissenschafts- und Technologiebeziehungen in das Team ein. Während ihres Studiums der Politikwissenschaft und der Bildungswissenschaft hat sie ein Forschungspraktikum am österreichischen Office of Science and Technology in Washington D.C. absolviert.

Bernardo Mariani ist als Konflikt-und Sicherheitsexperte bei Saferworld tätig. Seit 2008 leitet er das Saferworld China-Programm, das Grundlagen-forschung, Advocacy und die Fazilitierung eines Dialoges über Chinas wachsende internationale Rolle verbindet, insbesondere in Hinblick auf Konfliktprävention und Friedensförderung.

Kari Möttölä (geb. 1945) ist seit 2013 Gastlektor, Professor beim Netzwerk für Europäischen Studien, an der Universität von Helsinki. Er ist in einer Studie zur finnischen, regionalen und europäischen Sicherheit, der Europäischen Union und die transatlantischen Beziehungen beschäftigt. Von 1989 bis 2013 war er Sonderberater in der Abteilung für politische Planung und Forschung des finnischen Außenministeriums.

Sarah Ponesch ist Projektassistentin am oiip als Head of Network des österreichischen Netzwerks der Anna Lindh Stiftung. Zu ihren Forschungsschwerpunkten gehören feministische, postkoloniale und queere Theorien sowie Rassismus und politischer Islam. Ihr regionalspezifischer Fokus liegt vorwiegend auf der MENA Region.

Jan Pospisil ist Senior Fellow am oiip und Lehrbeauftragter an der Universität Wien. Seine Forschungsschwerpunkte liegen im Überschneidungsbereich von Entwicklungs- und Sicherheitspolitik mit dem Fokus auf fragiler Staatlichkeit und neuen Sicherheitskonzepten wie Resilienz sowie gesamtstaatlichen Ansätzen in der Sicherheitspolitik.

Ufuk Sahin ist Doktorand am Institut für Politikwissenschaft, Universität Wien. Seine Forschungsschwerpunkte sind: Türkische Geopolitik, Europäische Außen- und Energiepolitik, Türkei-Irak Beziehungen.

Lisa Sigl arbeitet seit Juni 2012 im Rahmen von Forschungsprojekten des oiip und leitet den Forschungsbereich Internationale Wissenschafts- und Technologiepolitik. Sie verfügt über einen interdisziplinären Hintergrund im Bereich der Naturwissenschaften, der Soziologie und der Wissenschafts- und Technologieforschung. Ihre Forschungsinteresse umfassen Forschungskulturen im Vergleich sowie die globale Entwicklung von Wissensgesellschaften und -ökonomien.

Notes on Contributors

Hakan Akbulut is Research Fellow at the Austrian Institute for International Affairs (oiip) and Lecturer at the University of Vienna. His areas of research include Turkish foreign and security policy, the Cyprus issue as well as nuclear non-proliferation and disarmament. Hakan Akbulut is a PhD candidate in Political Science.

John Bunzl is Scientific Advisor at the oiip. His main research areas cover Israel/Palestine, Middle East, Islamophobia and Antisemitism. He works at the oiip since 1980. He is the author of numerous publications.

Heinz Gärtner is Director of the oiip and Senior Scientist at the Institute of Political Science at the University of Vienna. He has held visiting fellowships at several international universities and research institutes, as, among others, in Stanford, Oxford, New York, Vancouver and Rome. His most recent book, "Der amerikanische Präsident und die neue Welt [The American President and the New World]" has been published in November 2012.

Cengiz Günay is Senior Fellow at the oiip and Lecturer at the Institute for Political Sciences and the Institute for International Development at the University of Vienna. His fields of research are Islamism, political reforms, socio-economic transformation processes and the question of democratization in the context of the Middle East and Turkey as well as non-state actors in international politics.

Carmen Heidenwolf is a member of the oiip since March 2012. She contributes in the team with an interdisciplinary background in international relations and educational science. In her diploma thesis she discussed the transatlantic science and technology relations as a field of cooperation and competition. Her practical experiences at the OST Washington D.C. and the European Commission contribute to the understanding of institutions in the S&T arena.

Bernardo Mariani is a conflict and security analyst. Since 2008, he has managed Saferworld's China Programme, which undertakes research, raises awareness and promotes dialogue on China's growing international role, particularly relating to conflict prevention and peacebuilding

Kari Möttölä (b. 1945) is Visiting Scholar, Professor at the Network for European Studies, the University of Helsinki since September 2013. He is engaged in the study of Finnish, regional and European security; the European Union; and transatlantic relations. From 1989 to 2013, he was Special Adviser at the Unit for Policy Planning and Research, the Finnish MFA.

Sarah Ponesch works as a project assistant at the oiip as the Head of Network for the Austrian network of the Anna Lindh Foundation. Her research interests include feminist, postcolonial und queer theory as well as racism studies and political Islam. Her regional focus primarily lies on the MENA region.

Jan Pospisil is Senior Fellow at the oiip and Lecturer at the University of Vienna. His research focus is on the development-security-nexus, with a particular interest in state fragility, new concepts of security like resilience, and Whole-of-Government-approaches in security policy.

Ufuk Sahin is a PhD candidate at the University of Vienna. His research focus: Turkish Geopolitics, Foreign and Energy Policy of the European Union, Turkey-EU relations, Turkey-Iraq relations.

Lisa Sigl is a member of the oiip since June 2012 and heads the international science and technology policy group. Her scientific background is in the natural sciences, sociology and science and technology studies (STS). Her research interest lies in the comparative study of research cultures and the global development of knowledge societies and economies.

Aktuelle Publikationen / Recent Publications

oiip

Buchpublikationen / Monographies

Alexander Klimburg/Jan Pospisil (Hrsg.), *Mediating Security. Comprehensive Approaches to an Ambiguous Subject. Festschrift für Otmar Höll.* Peter Lang Edition, Frankfurt a. Main, 2013.

Hakan Akbulut, *Zur Normalisierung in den zivil-militärischen Beziehungen in der Türkei.* In: Olaf Leiße (Hrsg.), *Die Türkei im Wandel. Innen- und außenpolitische Dynamiken* (= Jenaer Beträge zur Politikwissenschaft, 16, S. 199-221, Nomos, Baden-Baden, 2013.

ADD-ON 2012. Jahrbuch oiip. Wiener Beiträge zur Internationalen Politik Yearbook oiip. Viennese Contributions to International Affairs. Hrsg. v. Cengiz Günay und Jan Pospisil. Facultas.wuv, Wien 2013.

Alexander Klimburg (Hrsg.), *National Cyber Security Framework Manual.* NATO CCD COE Publications, Tallin 2012.

Heinz Gärtner (Hrsg.), *Der amerikanische Präsident und die neue Welt.* Reihe Politik Aktuell, Band 13. LIT Verlag, Wien 2012.

Cengiz Günay (Hrsg.), *Geschichte der Türkei: Von den Anfängen der Moderne bis heute.* Böhlau Verlag, Wien 2012.

Asia in the Eyes of Europe. Edited by Sebastian Bersick, Michael Bruter, Natalia Chaban, Sol Iglesias, Martin Holland und Ronan Lenihan. NOMOS, Baden-Baden 2012.

John Bunzl, *Der Feind meines Feindes ist mein Freund? Islamophober Populismus und Israel.* In: Farid Hafez (Hrsg*.), Jahrbuch für Islamophobieforschung 2012*, S.17-33, new academic press, Wien 2012.

Jan Pospisil*, Internationales Strafrecht und die Anklage von „Genozid": Der IStGH und sein Fall Bashir.* In: Arno Pilgram, Lorenz Böllinger, Michael Jasch, Susanne Krasmann, Cornelius Prittwitz, Herbert Reinke, Dorothea Rzepka (Hrsg.), *Einheitliches Recht für die Vielfalt der Kulturen? Strafrecht und Kriminologie in Zeiten transkultureller Gesellschaften und transnationalen Rechts*, Reihe: Schriften zur Rechts- und Kriminalsoziologie, Bd. 4, S. 81-95, LIT Verlag, Münster 2012.

ADD-ON 2011. Jahrbuch oiip. Wiener Beiträge zur Internationalen Politik Yearbook oiip. Viennese Contributions to International Affairs. Hrsg. v. Katrin Alas, Cengiz Günay und Jan Pospisil. Facultas.wuv, Wien 2012.

Heinz Gärtner, *National Arms Export Control: Between Realism and Institutionalism.* In: Quentin Michel (eds.), *Sensitive Trade. The Perspectives of European States.* Peter Lang Verlag, Brüssel 2011.

Obama and the Bomb. The Vision of a World Free of Nuclear Weapons. Ed. by Heinz Gärtner, Reihe Internationale Sicherheit, Peter Lang - Internationaler Verlag der Wissenschaften, 2011.

Heinz Gärtner, *USA - Weltmacht auf neuen Wegen.* LIT-Verlag Wien – Zürich 2010.

Nico Prucha, *Die Stimme des Dschihad. "Sawt al-gihad": al-Qaidas erstes Online-Magazin.* Verlag Kovac, Juni 2010.

Arbeitspapiere / Working Papers

AP 72   Heinz Gärtner, *North Korea, Deterrence and Engagement*, October 2013

AP 71   Vedran Dzihic, *Bilanz und Zukunft des Westbalkans: Ungelöste Grenz- und Minoritätsfragen im Kontext der EU-Beitrittsbemühungen,* September 2013

AP 70   Hakan Akbulut, *Die zypriotische Hürde: Stand und Perspektiven des Zypernkonflikts und die Implikationen für den EU-Beitrittsprozess der Türkei,* Juli 2013

AP 69   Heinz Gärtner, *Where is Europe?,* June 2013

AP 68   Heinz Gärtner, *Deterrence, Disarmament and Arms Control,* May 2013

AP 67   Hakan Akbulut, *The G8 Global Partnership: From Kananaskis to Deauville and Beyond,* March 2013.

AP 66   Jan Pospisil, *Schneller, höher, stärker ... im globalen Vergleich: Eine empirische Analyse der Olympischen Spiele 2010/2012*, September 2012.

AP 65   Alexander Klimburg/Philipp Mirtl, *„Cyberspace and Governance— A Primer"*, September 2012.

AP 64   Hakan Akbulut, Heinz Gärtner, Daphne Warlamis u.a., *„Nuklear-radiologische Proliferation: Gefährdungspotential und Präventionsmöglichkeiten für Österreich."* Dezember 2011.

AP 63   Paul Luif, „*Challenges for Integrated Peacekeeping Operations.*" Dezember 2010.

AP 62   Stefan Khittel und Jan Pospisil, „*Früherkennung von bewaffneten Konflikten? Ein Vergleich standardisierter Konfliktanalyseverfahren*", April 2010.

AP 61   Paul Luif, „*Strategien kleinerer europäischer Staaten in der Technologiepolitik als Antwort auf die Herausforderung durch China und Indien: Die Entwicklung von Strategien in Finnland, Schweden, der Schweiz und den Niederlanden, mit einem Anhang zur F & E – Politik der Europäischen Union*", September 2009.

AP 60   Hakan Akbulut, „*Die zivil-militärischen Beziehungen in der Türkei: zwischen Putschbestrebungen und Demokratisierungsbemühungen*", September 2009.

Kurzanalysen / Policy Papers

Jan Pospisil, *Auf dem Weg zu einem europäischen Ansatz in der internationalen Krisenbearbeitung? Anmerkungen zum „Action Plan for Resilience in Crisis Prone Countries, 2013-2020".* Policy Paper, August 13/2013.

Vedran Dzihic und Astrid Reinprecht, *Kroatiens Beitritt zur EU: Erwartungen, Euroskeptizismus und regionale Implikationen.* Policy Paper, Juli 12/2013.

Vedran Dzihic, *Ein Plädoyer für die EU-Erweiterung: Warum es zum europäischen Erweiterungsprojekt am Westbalkan keine Alternative* gibt. Policy Paper, Dezember 11/2012.

Ruth Müller, *Wissen und Forschen in einer globalisierten Welt.* Policy Paper, Oktober 10/2012.

Cengiz Günay, *Interdependenzen: Wie die Dynamiken des Syrienkonfliktes den Demokratisierungsprozess in der Türkei gefährden.* Policy Paper, September 9/2012.

Hakan Akbulut, *Die Obama-Jahre: „A Season for Nuclear Disarmament"?*, Policy Paper, September 8/2012.

Heinz Gärtner, *Die NATO nach dem Gipfel in Chicago 2012*, Kurzanalyse, Juni 7/2012.

Vedran Dzihic, *Serbien nach den Wahlen – Neue Konstellation, gleiche Problemlagen*, Kurzanalyse, Juni 6/2012.

Hakan Akbulut, *Von der Vormundschaft zur Normalisierung in den zivil-militärischen Beziehungen in der Türkei*, Kurzanalyse, Mai 5/2012.

Gerhard Mangott, *Putin 2.012*, Kurzanalyse, März 4/2012.

Cengiz Günay, *Ägypten – von der Revolution zur islamischen Demokratie?*, Kurzanalyse, März 3/2012.

Heinz Gärtner, *Deterrence and Disarmament*, Kurzanalyse, März 2/2012.

Jan Pospisil, *Eiskalte Interdependenzen: Der Südsudan radikalisiert seine politische Neuorientierung an der Erdölfront*, Kurzanalyse, Februar 1/2012.

Gerhard Mangott, *Ämtertausch und kontrollierte Wahlniederlage. Russland an der Schwelle zu neuer Instabilität*, Policy Paper, Dezember 2011.

Tobias Lang und Cengiz Günay, *Regionale Auswirkungen der Entwicklungen in Syrien am Beispiel des Libanon*, Kurzanalyse, November 2011.

Bernardo Mariani, *Starting to Build? China's Role in UN Peacekeeping Operations*, Policy Paper, November 2011.

Melanie Pichler, *Sustainable Palm-Based Agrofuels? Current Strategies and Problems to Guarantee Sustainability for Agrofuels within the EU*, Policy Paper, November 2011.

Hakan Akbulut, *Der Zypernkonflikt und seine Auswirkungen auf die EU-Ambitionen der Türkei*, Kurzanalyse, Oktober 2011.

Heinz Gärtner, *Die österreichische Sicherheitsstrategie (ÖSS) im globalen Kontext*, Kurzanalyse, Oktober 2011.

Daniela Härtl, *Kolumbien zwischen Gewalt und Hoffnung. Analytische Betrachtungen und Eindrücke vor Ort*. Report, September 2011.

Cengiz Günay and Maria Janik, *Egypt in Transition – Ready for Democracy?*, Current Analysis, September 2011.

Alexander Klimburg and Philipp Mirtl, *Cyberspace and Governance - A primer*, Special Issue, September 2011.

Heinz Gärtner, *The Responsibility to Protect (R2P) and Libya*, Kurzanalyse, Juli 2011.

Gerhard Mangott, *Putin 2.0. Russland vor den Präsidentenwahlen 2012*. Kurzanalyse, Juli 2011.

John Bunzl, *Die Umwälzungen in der arabischen Welt und der Palästinakonflikt*, Kurzanalyse, Juni 2011.

Heinz Gärtner, *A Nuclear-Weapon-Free Zone in the Middle East*, Kurzanalyse, April 2011.

Nico Prucha, *Eyeballing Libya – al-Qa'ida's New Foothold?*, Policy Paper, April 2011.

Henriette Riegler, *Kroatien: Demonstrationen mit ungewissen Folgen*, Kurzanalyse, April 2011.

Gerhard Mangott, *Nordafrika und die Rohölversorgung der Europäischen Union*, Kurzanalyse, März 2011.

Cengiz Günay, *Transformationen in der arabischen Welt Kontinuität versus Wandel und Folgen für die Region*, Kurzanalyse, März 2011.

Cengiz Günay, *This was Mubarak's Egypt*, Hintergrundinformationen, Februar 2011.

Cengiz Günay, *Ägypten – Der Zweite Dominostein?* Kurzanalyse, Januar 2011.

Jan Pospisil, *Visionen, Realitäten und Risken eines unabhängigen Südsudan: Implikationen des Referendums vom Jänner 2011.* Kurzanalyse, Januar 2011.

Paul Luif, *Die „neue" Gemeinsame Außen- und Sicherheitspolitik der Europäischen Union: Was hat Lissabon gebracht?* Kurzanalyse, Dezember 2010.

Heinz Gärtner, *IAEA: Y. Amano's first year as Director General.* Kurzanalyse, November 2010.

Otmar Höll, *Sudan – Mögliche österreichische Beiträge zur gesellschaftlichen Entwicklung.* Policy Paper, September 2010.

Heinz Gärtner, *NATO zwischen Tradition und Modernisierung. Stellungnahme zum Bericht „NATO 2020: Assured Security; Dynamic Engagement. Analysis and recommendations of the group of experts on a new strategic concept for NATO," 17 May 2010.* Kurzanalyse, Oktober 2010.

John Bunzl, *Frieden oder Friedensprozess? Zum Treffen von Netanyahu, Abbas und Obama in Washington.* Kurzanalyse, September 2010.

Heinz Gärtner, *Die Bedeutung von internationalem Engagement der österreichischen Sicherheitskräfte für Österreich.* Kurzanalyse, Juli 2010.

Markus Schwarz-Herda, *Die Präsidentschaftswahlen in Kolumbien.* Kurzanalyse, Juli 2010.

Henriette Riegler, *Kroatien: Ivo Josipović' erste hundert Tage. Ein Präsident zeigt sein Profil.* Kurzanalyse, Juni 2010.

Heinz Gärtner, *Kann sich Österreich im Mittleren Osten erneut engagieren? Zur Schaffung einer nuklearfreien Zone in dieser Region.* Kurzanalyse, Juni 2010.

Heinz Gärtner, *Amerika und Europa: transatlantische Beziehungen oder globale Verantwortung?* Policy Paper, April 2010.

Heinz Gärtner, *Disarmament – Non-Proliferation – Deterrence.* Policy Paper, März 2010.